SEARCHING FOR PEARLS

Benjamin Simon O'Neill

Published by:
Benjamin O'Neill
PO Box 414
South Fremantle 6162
Western Australia
Australia
Email: benjaminsoneill@protonmail.com
ABN: 36067346303

Copyright © Benjamin O'Neill 2022
The moral right of the author has been asserted.

All rights reserved. No part of this book may be reproduced or transmitted in any form or by any means, electronic or mechanical, including photocopying, recording, or by any information storage and retrieval system, without permission in writing from the publisher.

Edited by Sarah Pye
Designed by Gram Telen
Maps by Shar Dean
Cover photograph: Benjamin O'Neill
Photos: Benjamin O'Neill, Wayne Lawler, Andrew Pickard

National Library of Australia Cataloguing-in-Publication Data

O'Neill, Benjamin Simon
Searching for Pearls

ISBN 978-0-6454162-3-7 (pbk.)
ISBN 978-0-6454162-4-4 (hc.)
ISBN 978-0–6454162–2–0 (ebook.)

Benjamin O'Neill lives in Australia. After leaving the pearling industry in 2011, he travelled extensively, became an aeroplane pilot, and sailed around the world. In 2017, Ben found himself concerned about our throwaway society, so he started a bicycle recycling business. The people he met through this new endeavour inspired him to cycle around Australia giving away copies of his book to disadvantaged and at-risk youth, in the hope that he can help change someone's life for the better.

CONTENTS

1. The Pearl 10
2. Mike 15
3. Australia 22
4. Into the Interior 28
5. Walhallow 34
6. Stockcamp 43
7. Red Dirt and Blue Sky 50
8. I Don't Think You Should Go 57
9. Survival 65
10. The Breaking and the Making 74
11. Are You Coming Back? 80
12. Back to the Sunshine Coast 89
13. Year of the Outback 94
14. Realisation 105
15. Coolum Beach 124
16. Setting Out 133
17. Carnarvon Gorge 139
18. Battleship Spur 146
19. Wilderness Guide 155
20. The Weavings of Nature 160
21. Sacred Journeys 172
22. A Tapestry is Formed 188
23. Nature's Teachings 197
24. Who are You? 203
25. Speaking with an Elder 210
26. Awakening 215
27. Maryborough to Bendigo 242
28. Solitude 246
29. Darwin 252
30. The Osborn Islands 257
31. The Harvest 265
32. Kimberley Dreaming 276
33. A Turn of Tides 284

34	Kuri Bay	292
35	The Port of Pearls	303
36	The Fishing Season Begins	308
37	A Dive to Remember	315
38	Eighty Mile Beach	320
39	Turning	325
40	Loose Ends and New Beginnings	334
41	The Pearl	341
42	The Journey Back	357

PART ONE

CHAPTER ONE

THE PEARL

'If the doors of perception were cleansed everything would appear to man as it is, infinite.'
—*William Blake*

Fatigue penetrated my bones. A long fishing trip at sea in miserable conditions had beaten the lust for pearl shell from each of us. Grudging remarks about the lack of shell and complaints about the cold eddied around my feet in the foaming waves that splashed through the diver's ladder ports where six of us stood on the exposed aft deck of the *Pearl,* shivering in our wetsuits. I was quiet as I focused my last will of strength to get back into the water. It was the last dive of the day. It was the end of the fishing season.

Three months of physical and psychological endurance had sapped the strength from my body. I was as thin as a rake, shredded and sinewy, and the cold gnawed at me. The *Pearl* began a lazy turn to starboard, lurching over the waves like a giant tub and dipping a boom end into the water before lining up the last drift for the day. Waves slapped against her hull and sent a shuddering roll of acoustics through the fibreglass like she would break in half. She was showing her age. I steadied myself as a fresh gust sent spindrift over the bulwark.

'Can we just get this over with already?' Brad swore at the wretched cold.

His stinger guard muffled his voice, but I could see haggard tension in his bloodshot eyes as I watched his weary figure through the wet glass of my mask; the frustration of a man who wants to be done with diving after being wet and cold for twelve hours a day, eleven days straight. But this was the price of pearling. He knew it as well as any of us. The thought of home, somewhere warm and dry rather than the cold fibreglass, timber and steel that creaked and groaned beneath our feet, was an inviting thought. Our yellow dive hoses streamed away behind us, wriggling and curling over the waves like giant sea snakes before straightening again as the *Pearl* finished her turn.

Fins slapped excitedly on deck and regulators hissed. Hoffy, our restless old skipper, sounded one short blast of the *Pearl's* horn from the wheelhouse.

'Righto, in ya get!' Mick shouted.

Mick was the *Pearl's* head diver, and he always had the energy to push the men to the last. I guess he needed to, and I respected him for it. But he was nothing like the head stockman, Daisy, from Walhallow Station, who I had learnt so much from under the burning sun all those years before. Mick commanded respect from all the divers, but he was also one of the boys. He knew how to make friends, and he always had time for his crew at, and outside of, work. I admired him for that. He was a friend, not a tyrant. That was one of the reasons I wanted to work on the *Pearl*.

'Last chance for a cribby, Benny.' Sam waved me a *hang loose*, then disappeared down the port ladder.

I returned the gesture, extending my thumb and little finger from a fist. Sam liked that. Sam was also a good friend, perhaps my first real friend in those early years of pearling. I was always on the lookout for *Cribrarula cribrarias*. We all were. Those pigeon-egg-sized, maroon-coloured cowrie shells with the creamy yellow spots were a prized treasure to any pearl diver and brought a tidy sum from collectors.

I followed Sean's lanky six-foot, four-inch frame over the side, and we made our descent to the seabed with Mick following closely behind. Conditions were more pleasant underwater—they usually were—and visibility was good. The cold easterly winds that blew off the desert were wretched to deal with up top, but, down below, they cleared up the water nicely. The hiss and gurgle of air through my regulator followed me to the bottom with athletic enthusiasm as the pressure of the water steadily increased. I felt my wetsuit compress the thin layer of cold water against my skin that had seeped in on entry. It began to warm. All else was quiet but for the dim metallic whine of the *Pearl's* propeller spinning relentlessly through the water above us. I caught hold of my work line and felt her tug. I glanced to my right, then left to catch a glimpse of the silvery trails of bubbles that followed Sean and Mick before they vanished into the watery, deep blue nebulous of the Eighty Mile pearling grounds. They were on the hunt and, by the looks of things, busy collecting shell already.

I scanned the alien-looking seabed. Within moments, the illusive oysters materialised. Shell by shell, I started filling my neck bag. It was all I had been thinking about for months, holding the image of those prized shells in my head and dreaming about them at night. It was the only way to get good at the job—to dream of pearl shells and to pay attention to what Mick taught me. But my mind drifted often to the warmth of Broome town with all its comforts and the throng of unusual characters I had come to know there over the past year and a half. To many of those people, and to the countless travellers I met who passed that way, us divers were part of the legend that had woven more than a century of history into the town's romantic and tragic pearling odyssey. When I was cold, tired and soaked to the bone, when my work line slipped through my defeated hands because my arms were so fatigued that I could barely hang on any longer, I dreamed of that home.

I finished gathering a patch of several good oysters when a particularly large specimen caught my eye. It was partially hidden under a clump of waving weed. For some reason, I picked it up. The shell was old, and likely worthless. It wasn't customary to pick up such large old shells because they were no good for culturing pearls. Young, healthy specimens were what we were searching for. I shoved it in my neck bag anyway. When a quiet moment came during the drift, I locked my fins fast in my work line to free my hands (the way Mick had taught me), then pulled my knife from its sheath in my neck bag and opened the old shell to satisfy my curiosity.

With a quick, firm slice, the oyster gaped open. I gingerly poked at its slimy innards, not really expecting to find anything. A hard lump caught my attention. I squeezed the membrane surrounding it. Slowly, the tissue peeled back to reveal a large gleaming pearl. I was astonished. My heart pounded the walls of my chest as I extracted the pearl from the oyster. Being careful not to fumble and lose it on the seabed, I pushed it just under my wetsuit sleeve, above my wrist. I checked the oyster to make sure I hadn't missed anything, then dropped the bivalve to the sea floor and looked around. Neither Mick nor Sean was in sight. I tried to refocus my attention on the job at hand, finding more pearl shell, but I couldn't. I pushed my hand against my wrist to make sure the pearl was still there and anxiously looked at my dive watch. Ten minutes to go.

Some moments we never forget. The morning the pearling fleet steamed back into Roebuck Bay for the final time that fishing season was one of those moments. A saffron sunrise streaked the sky over the Port of Pearls, welcoming us divers home. After the usual morning clean up and wash down, we disembarked from the *Pearl*. Some divers had girlfriends waiting ashore, and some couldn't wait to get down to the local watering holes—Divers Tavern and Roebuck Bay Hotel. They would be three sheets to the wind by sundown. Each had a story or two to share from the sea, and a few brought home with them a treasure or two.

I collected my bicycle from Mick's place and cycled home—past the high golden dunes of Cable Beach, towards the outskirts of town and my bungalow in the leafy suburb of Hidden Valley.

In the privacy of my residence, I riffled through my bag for the object that had seduced my thoughts from the moment I found it. I carefully unfolded the small piece of cloth. My heart quickened as the pearl appeared, and I smiled to myself. It was a beautiful, large and lustrous button shaped gem. I held it in my gaze for a long moment, entranced by its lustre. In the pearl's sheen, the culmination of a long and arduous journey softly reflected back at me. I sat on the end of my bed and gazed around the bungalow. The photographs that lined the rafters were markers on the road I had travelled to get here. Colourful, ornate looking shells lined the windowsills from my days spent diving the Eighty Mile. Pearls of memories; pearls of wisdom.

I thought back to when it had all started. One man's adventure. A quest, an odyssey, a pilgrimage of sorts. I had been at it for so many years, and now was the moment of truth. I faced the decision that would bring this story full circle. I had one thing left to do—return home. My mind raced back to another time and place—to my unlikely friend and mentor who had inspired the journey.

CHAPTER TWO

MIKE

'We know what we are, but know not what we may be.'
—*William Shakespeare*

Ink covered nearly every inch of Mike O'Sullivan's body. Piercings of silver ran up his ears and studded his hawk-like nose. Rings stood out like knuckle dusters on his fingers. His hair, close cropped, had silvered.

'Turn that heater up, will you? It's freezing today,' Mike said, as he prepared his tattoo guns for his next appointment.

He loaded the needles and secured them, then tested the guns and fine-tuned their settings before lining them up on his workbench. He squeezed an exact amount of each prime and secondary ink into its own miniature cup and sat them in the palette.

I turned the dial up to full, then walked over to the shop entrance. For a moment I just stood there, staring at the miserable scene outside: men and women, rugged up in heavy jackets with their heads down, shoulders hunched, and hands buried deep in their pockets, scurried past with glum faces. Cars passed with fogged windows and blurred occupants, splashing through puddles and spraying water over the pavement. The industrial paradigm; was this life? I had pulled myself from the depths of suicidal depression to mere clinical depression, but now the long winter months had settled in. I needed to escape it before it killed me. Instead, I walked back to the counter and helped Mike finish setting up.

The doorbell rang and a dark-haired girl with gothic eyes and several piercings in her ears and nose came through the door in a swirl of cold air.

'Just down the back here, love,' Mike called out.

The girl pursed her lips in a wintery smile as she walked past me and took her seat in 'The Chair of Change', as Mike liked to call it.

'Okay, are you ready?' he asked.

'I think so.' Her voice shook—either from the cold or a healthy disposition about going under the needle.

'Don't worry, you'll be fine. I can't stand needles.' Mike warmed her with a few soft words. I pulled the hessian privacy curtain, then walked back over to the door to gaze through the window. I was soon lost in thoughts about travelling.

The high pitch rattle of the tattoo gun in the background brought me back. People came in here to change themselves, if not on the inside, then on the outside. Change. Interesting concept: requires a dash of pain and a sprinkling of courage. Like getting a tattoo. I gazed a moment longer at the insentient faces in the street and asked myself, 'Where to from here?'

Mike, happy with his work, pulled back the curtain and lined up a bare shoulder through the camera lens to capture the new piece for his portfolio. Taping a gauze patch over the tattoo, he explained the care instructions that were written on the back of his business card, then thanked the girl for her custom. Happy with her new bright splash of body art, she handed him the money, thanked him with a surprisingly warm smile and walked out of the door, disappearing into the cold a changed person.

People from all walks of life came into the Tattoo Company. Some came in from the suburbs. Others had come from the other side of the world. A few months earlier, I had quit my job as a hotel porter and come to work for Mike in anticipation of exploring that world. I had thought little about where I would go or what I would do; I just knew I had to get out of Christchurch.

'Well, I think that'll do us for the day, man,' Mike said. 'We'll shut up shop.'

'Okay.' I was looking forward to our usual evening discourse about life.

I first met Mike two years earlier, outside his shop on Colombo Street. I was 16, and I had just been kicked out of home for the second and last time. Together we stood on the pavement inspecting the damage to my

Kermit-green Mark IV Ford Cortina station wagon—the aftermath of my final confrontation with my stepfather. I didn't know it then, but that day was the beginning of a friendship that would change my life.

From a life on the high seas from the age of 17, to a life on the high roads as a gang member, Mike revealed a world that was so foreign and engrossing to me that I quickly allowed myself to admire and trust him. He recounted the camaraderie his fellow seafarers had offered: the kinds of lives they had lived, the places they had been, the things they had seen and the characters they were. He spoke gravely about the brotherhood of gang life and the strict rules that were observed amongst its affiliates; how it offered him a family after suffering a severely abusive childhood. He confided in me the things he had done to survive that life. I could see the steel in his eyes and iron in his fists. He had stared death in the face and lived to tell the tale. From the spark of excitement in his voice to the flicker in his eyes, I craved a life I could one day look back on and speak about with as much passion.

After several months of watching me struggle to improve my situation, Mike stepped in. At first, he entrusted me with small jobs, then important errands. Eventually, once he decided I was worthy of his time and teaching, he offered me a part-time job at the Tattoo Company.

Our conversations had explored an array of topics about life. But, like a boomerang, those conversations had a habit of returning to the same subject: going on a journey and becoming a man. Although I didn't really understand what that would entail, I was intrigued by the idea. Mike had painted a picture of what life could be outside of my limited notions. In the process, he had planted a seed—an idea that, in later years, would encompass the globe.

I finished vacuuming the polished wooden floors, then wiped down the glass cabinets with their odd paraphernalia: poisonous insects in sealed glass domes, assorted lighters, and various smoking apparatuses. After emptying the rubbish bins, I sat down on the green chequered couch that every customer anxiously sat on before they went under the needle. A few months earlier, I too had sat there waiting my turn.

Mike swung around in his chair. 'What if I were to tell you that anything you can imagine is possible?'

'And when will anything I can imagine be possible?' I said it dubiously.

'Now man, anything is possible now.' He chuckled to himself, spun back around in his chair, and continued cleaning his tattoo guns.

He meticulously washed and inspected the needles, then sterilised them in the autoclave while I struggled to comprehend his meaning. Washing the palette and wiping down his work desk, he sighed. Business had been quiet: the cold weather kept people away. The cold also bothered his health.

'I like the idea that anything I can imagine is possible,' I finally said.

Mike lowered his head and peered over the top of his spectacles, fixing me with an intense gaze that focused all his attention and energy into a single point. He raised his right eyebrow. 'You're a smart guy, Ben. Don't let your past hold you back.'

Mike laid his spectacles on the counter, walked to the shop door, opened it, and took a step outside. He folded his arms across his chest and gazed up and down the street, as if to scrutinise the scene. He was wearing his usual work clothes: tartan trousers, a black Harley Davidson shirt and Dr Martens boots. His strong athletic frame stood confidently at six foot two inches. He was an impressive sight, and I noticed that most people only glanced at him before averting their gaze. That grudging respect was something he was accustomed to, although now it was slipping from him, in the claws of his deteriorating health.

Mike stepped back inside and locked the door. He turned out the lights, and we went upstairs.

'Do you want a cup of tea, Ben? I'm just about to put the kettle on.'

'Sure.'

I took my seat in his lounge overlooking Colombo Street. The room was minimalistic: a small bookshelf full of old books, a CD rack containing an assortment of rock and heavy metal CDs, and a small, wooden, single draw drum table. The titles on the bookshelf illustrated Mike's interest in anthropology, in particular the Neanderthals, Celts, and medieval Ireland. As if to pay homage to the warriors, clans and tribesmen of those ancient times, three medieval swords stood, one in each available corner of the room. Like the old peoples, he held firm beliefs that certain possessions held special powers. On the opposite side from where I sat, an unused home gym stood beside an old television set and two neatly trimmed pot plants.

In a way, Mike had filled the hole my father had left. Night after night, Mike would sit in his big, grey La-Z-Boy while I would settle on a stately old wooden chair with red felt on the backrest and seat, which over the years had moulded to the shape of a backside. It was Mike's curious mix of intelligence, fierceness and strength that demanded my respect and attention. But it was his integrity and high expectations of others that I aligned myself with. When he took an interest in something, or someone, he gave that thing or individual all his attention.

Mike came back into the room with two hot cups of tea and handed me one. Then plonked himself in his La-Z-Boy.

'Do you want a smoke man?' he asked, retrieving his pipe and a small tin of cannabis from the drawer in the drum table. He ceremoniously cleaned and inspected the pipe before packing the cone, which resembled a skull carved from wood. The pipe had a whalebone mouthpiece.

'No thanks.'

The weed sparked and hissed while he drew a long, deep toke from the pipe. He held his breath for a few seconds before coughing a pungent, sweet smoke cloud into the room. I didn't understand why he still smoked after suffering from a collapsed lung, but he said it helped subdue the chronic pain.

'So, what have you decided to do?' Mike asked, after recovering his breath.

'I'm going to travel,' I said, trying to sound decisive even though I lacked confidence.

He raised an eyebrow and nodded thoughtfully. 'It'll do you good to get away from this place. And besides, all this will be waiting here for you when you get back. That's if you come back. Are you still thinking of going to Australia?'

'Yes, Australia to start. I'll find a job there and save up some money, then carry on overseas.'

'Well, anything is possible once you get out there and start seeing life. Even your wildest dreams. That reminds me of a quote from Shakespeare.'

'Shakespeare?' I wondered what a late medieval writer had to do with me travelling.

'There are more things in Heaven and Earth, Horatio,' Mike announced with the passion of a poet, 'than are dreamt of in your philosophy.'

I looked at him, puzzled.

'That just means there's more out there in the world for you to see and do than in all your wildest dreams, young man.' He waved his index finger at me to emphasise the point.

'I hope so.' My mind was clouded with doubt.

'The most important thing is not to return the gift unwrapped, the gift of life, that is. Understand this above all: you can do nothing to change the past, and the future will never come exactly as you expect or hope for. Your sorrow, your fear and anger, regret and guilt, your envy and plans and cravings live only in the past, or in the future. Take hold of the present, Ben. All the possibilities of your life are contained within it. This moment is all you have ever had, and it's all you will ever have. When you realise that, you will be free. There's nothing left here for you. Your family has left. You've grown out of this place. You need to make a journey of your own now; learn to become a man and form your own ideas and views about life and the world. You won't do that here worrying about what everyone else is doing.'

I nodded pensively, wondering about that better life and how I would manage to find it alone.

Mike broke the silence and my introspection. 'So, when are you going to leave?'

'I was thinking around the end of July.'

'That's not too far away.' He took another toke from his pipe. 'I think you're making the right decision. And don't doubt yourself, doubting will get you nowhere.' The words hung in smoky syllables. He was right. It was time to take hold of the reins of my life.

As Christchurch slipped further under winter's cold grasp, I thought more often about the journey that Mike spoke of. The cold was all the prompting I needed to book my ticket to Australia. I was to leave on the 27th July 2002. I was 19 years old.

CHAPTER THREE

AUSTRALIA

'Let go of the past, let go of the future, let go of the present, and cross over to the farther shore of existence.'

—*Buddha*

'I don't think you should go, Ben.'

Before she left for Otago University, in Dunedin, Stephanie had been the most important person in my life, but our relationship had ended when she left Christchurch. Her leaving for university, and the space she wanted to pursue that life, had left a deep wound in my heart, deeper than I wanted to admit.

I gazed out the windows of the airport, watching planes taxi, take off and land. I was heading off to Australia with no real plan and only a few hundred dollars to my name. And why was she saying this now? I didn't know why she didn't want me to go all of a sudden.

'I need to go.' I turned to face her. 'Perhaps you can come and visit?'

The ocean-blue of her eyes caught my disengaging gaze, and she shifted her attention to the aircraft that waited at the end of the passenger boarding bridge. I knew she was hurt.

'He put these ideas in your head, didn't he?'

'Mike?'

'Yes, Mike.' Her conspicuous dislike of him had evolved as she realised he had changed many of my ideas about myself and life—ideas that no longer fit her world.

'It's my choice to go.'

She turned to face me, then averted her eyes. 'I'm sorry, Ben. I'm sorry that things didn't work out the way we thought they would.' She slipped her hand into mine, then looked up to face me. With magnetic attraction, she lent in and gently pressed her lips against mine slowly and deliberately. I wondered if it would be the last time. 'Oh, I almost forgot,' she said, breaking the knot of our hands and frantically digging through her bag. 'I have a present for you, but don't open it until you're on the plane.' She handed me a small flat parcel and smiled with wet eyes. I forced back a sad smile, feeling like a change was taking place that I wasn't sure I was ready for.

'Good luck, Ben.' She turned and walked from my life.

I boarded the aircraft and took my window seat. Soon, the plane was hurtling down the runway. I watched the frosty blanket that shrouded Christchurch disappear below. The plane crossed the snow-white backbone of the South Island—the Southern Alps—and the west coast of New Zealand slid from sight.

I pulled my carry-on luggage from under the seat in front of me as the plane headed out over the Tasman Sea. With undivided attention, I retrieved the small parcel Stephanie had given me. I peeled back the tape and unfolded the careful wrapping that she had lovingly folded around the gift. She was always particular about things like that.

Inside was a beautiful diary in which she had inserted photos of us, along with pictures of New Zealand and little phrases like: *Don't forget beautiful New Zealand.* The words sprung off the pages and lassoed me. A part of me wanted to hijack the cockpit, turn the plane around and fly right back into her arms.

Three hours later, an eruption of eucalyptus-green appeared as the coast of Australia came into sight; a thin white strip of beach declared the beginning of the continent in opposing contrast to the heaving aquamarine of the Coral Sea. Beyond lay a sprawling metropolis.

The plane banked low over the urban jungle, its wheels touching Australian soil at Brisbane International Airport at exactly 9:00 am. After collecting my backpack and navigating my way through customs, I took the train into the city.

The warmth of the winter morning was the first thing that struck me, then the people. The streets were filled with men and women dressed in shirts, shorts and t-shirts, dresses and skirts. They moved with animated purpose. A blue sky harboured lazy clouds. The air was a bouquet of subtropical aromas blended with the pinch of western city flavours. Cars hurtled past with number plates reading: QUEENSLAND—BEAUTIFUL ONE DAY; PERFECT THE NEXT. So, this was the beginning of possibility.

I pulled an old, crumpled piece of paper out of my backpack and unfolded it. The contact details were barely legible and the personal connection flimsy. Biruta was an old friend of my grandparents. Her husband and my grandfather's friendship began on a Swedish ship when my grandfather was 22. She lived in a small town called Caloundra, on the Sunshine Coast, about an hour's drive north of Brisbane. I gathered my courage, picked up the payphone, explained who I was and asked if I could stay with her while I looked for work. After explaining my situation, she readily agreed to give me a bed for a few nights. I boarded the next bus to the Sunshine Coast.

It was nearing sunset when I arrived in a sleepy little seaside town. A small woman with shoulder-length, dark brown hair and a stern face that gave away her Latvian heritage, was waiting for me at the bus station in an old, yellow Volvo station wagon. I dropped my backpack in the back and we motored off in a series of brisk, jerky movements.

'So, how are you, Ben?' Biruta asked.

'Better now I'm out of the city and have somewhere to stay, thanks,' I replied. I felt awkward. A scene of Norfolk pines, hibiscus and frangipani crowded the coastline in vivid green, splashes of cream and lemon, and blushes of pink. I wound down the window and a humid plethora of new evening aromas hit me. I was instantly in love with the place.

'Okay, well, that's good. So, what are you going to do now you're here?' The implication of her question jolted me back to reality.

I deliberated over my answer. I had thought of heading straight up the coast to pick tomatoes in Bundaberg but was dissuaded by the rapidly climbing temperatures. I was further put off by the ticketing lady at the bus station in Brisbane, who said it was tough, menial work for poor pay.

'Well, I'm going to look for work. When I have enough money, I'd like to travel.'

'Okay then, well, that's good. It shouldn't be too hard to find work. I might be able to help you.'

'That would be great.'

We followed the glistening coastline south to Golden Beach and pulled up the driveway of a small brick home nestled amongst a riot of subtropical flora.

'I'm not sure where you're going to stay, but you can sleep on the fold-out in the lounge until we work something out. Just me and Janis live here. He's my father, and he's 92 years old. We don't do much, so it might be a bit boring for you,' Biruta explained.

An ancient-looking face peered at me through the glass sliding door entrance. He looked surprised, and confused, as I walked towards him. Perhaps I could pass as a long-lost relative?

Biruta introduced me to Janis in very loud Latvian, her native tongue, and explained I would stay for a while. Janis gave a nod. 'Hello,' he said in a shaky, friendly voice. I reached out to shake his shrivelled hand when suddenly, his false teeth flew out of his mouth and onto the ground in front of me. I stood back, shocked. Janis looked at his teeth as if to say, 'How the hell did they end up down there?' Biruta quickly bent down, picked them up, and started brushing them off. She ushered Janis inside. 'Just make yourself at home, Ben.'

After unpacking, I walked down to the beach. The sky morphed through salmon pink into blood orange as the sun dipped below the tooth-like, jungle-clad points of the Glasshouse Mountains. I was filled with uncertainty about finding work and the importance of the coming days.

During the next two weeks, I applied for dozens of jobs through employment agencies, newspapers and even walking the street. But I had little success and my funds quickly depleted. The thought of going back to New Zealand with nothing clouded my thoughts. Finally, thanks to Biruta, I picked up some work as a labourer on commercial construction sites. The work was irregular but paid well. A few days' work enabled me to live for a week.

While I moved wheelbarrow loads of rubble and building waste, I watched sulphur-crested cockatoos fly overhead and screech and squawk from waving gum trees. Every day was sunny and hot. The work was a socio-linguistic lesson too. Those big, smiling, tanned, bearded construction workers taught me the lingo: 'G'day mate', 'No worries', 'Too easy', 'Fair dinkum', 'How ya goin'?' It didn't take me long to feel at home.

Biruta was like a caring grandmother. She made me packed lunches and dropped me off at the construction sites in the mornings. Then one day she told me I could stay as long as I wanted and offered to turn half of her double garage into a room for me. Her selfless display of warmth and tenderness thawed the ice of neglect and abandonment that imprisoned my heart. I went to work transforming half of Biruta's garage into a sleep-out. As a way of showing my gratitude, I maintained her garden and tended the fruit on her tantalising pawpaw trees.

The Esplanade was a short walk from Biruta's place through a narrow alley. I strolled along the white, sandy shores and swam in the warm turquoise waters of the Pumicestone Passage between Golden Beach and Bribie Island. Most evenings I watched a fracas of rainbow lorikeets darting like missiles between the Norfolk pines. I contemplated my future and my past, thinking deeply about what was in my head and what was in my heart. Mostly, I felt content in those moments, happy with the way things were in my new home, but the idea of going on a journey niggled at my conscience.

A huge map of Queensland hung on Biruta's dining room wall and the odd-sounding places—Pimpinbudgie, Wonglepong, Burpengary, Humpybong and Yorkeys Knob—along with the national parks: Sundown, Expedition, Whitsunday Islands and the Daintree—seemed to embody that idea. Maybe I would find what I was looking for in one of these remote locations? Then a travel television show called *Getaway* featured a cattle station in the Kimberley, way out in Western Australia. Dusty, whip-cracking cowboys rounded up cattle and rode into the sunset. I knew straight away what I wanted to do.

I told Biruta. To my surprise, she knew a man named Chris who worked on a cattle station as a mechanic in the Northern Territory. Close enough, I thought.

'I'll give Chris a call if you like. They might not have any work going, but we can try. Are you sure you want to go out there? It's very hard work and stinking hot in the desert.'

I felt her motherly concern for my wellbeing. A twinge of uncertainty lingered for a moment, but it dissipated. I wanted it—to be in the middle of a continent as vast and wild as Australia.

'Okay. Can we give this Chris a call?' I asked.

Before long, I was talking to Cameron, the manager of Walhallow Station. His voice was sharp and to the point; not unfriendly but matter-of-fact. I tried to imagine his face, rugged and lined with the life of the tough Australian outback. He gave me the full run-down of the job: working cattle, riding horses, long days and damn hot this time of year. He stressed the *hot* part. I asked him to repeat the size of the property. 'Two and a half million acres,' he said. My jaw dropped. I knew the man had heard all my questions before by the tone of his short responses to my naïve enthusiasm and inexperience. 'Okay, well, we'll give you a go. But you'll need to get all your gear together before you arrive.'

Over the next week I acquired the trappings I needed for the outback: riding boots, jeans, shirts, an Old Timer knife and stockman's belt with knife pouch, an Akubra hat and a bus ticket to a place called Barkly Homestead somewhere in the middle of the Northern Territory. I had a few dollars left of my savings from the construction sites for the journey there.

I was packing my bag when the manager of the Hyatt Regency Mt Coolum phoned. They had a job for me as a concierge. When could I start? A wave of uncertainty crashed into my resolve to head west. All I had to do was say yes. What was I thinking, throwing away my comfortable new life on the Sunshine Coast to head off into the middle of the continent in search of something I wasn't even sure existed? '*Remember the journey.*' Mike's words waved a distant signal flag. Perhaps opportunities like Walhallow didn't come around so often. I declined and explained I'd found another job.

CHAPTER FOUR

INTO THE INTERIOR

'The whole secret of existence is to have no fear. Never fear what will become of you, depend on no one. Only the moment you reject all help are you freed.'
—Swami Vivekananda

Biruta hugged me goodbye before I got on the bus to Brisbane. 'Now you take care of yourself out there, Ben. If there's anything I can get you, just let me know and I'll post it to you.'

I had grown fond of Biruta over the past two months. Her strength and determination, drawn from being a child refugee from her home country, being married to a merchant captain, and bringing up three boys, inspired me to be strong to get what I wanted from life.

Biruta got back in her old Volvo, tooted the horn as she waved goodbye and drove off. I was leaving home for the second time in two months.

In Brisbane, I loaded my backpack into the undercarriage and boarded the 6pm Greyhound coach to the Northern Territory. It was a Monday the 14 October 2002. I took one last look at so-called civilisation. It struck me that something was missing from society in an advanced stage of social development and organisation. I wasn't sure when I'd be back, or how long it would take me to find what society had failed to offer me.

The bus from Brisbane took 31 hours to reach Barkly Homestead in the Northern Territory. Through the window, kilometre upon endless kilometre of mulga, desert oak and saltbush passed by. The bus made a few stops to pick up passengers, mostly stockmen, miners and Aboriginals from places like Longreach, Cloncurry, Mount Isa and Camooweal. I spent the hours listening to my Discman, sleeping and staring at the barren landscape. I had no idea how empty Australia was.

The road was a single lane in places. Kangaroos and cattle roamed beside it and across it. At night, several large kangaroos collided with the bus's bulbar with a sickening thump. We didn't stop. The arid daylight hours burned and shimmered under a vast, cloudless, azure sky that rippled into a white mirage of haze on the highway ahead. Flocks of pink and grey galahs scattered at our approach. The sun burned every ounce of moisture out of the atmosphere. The land was cracked and hard as iron. We passed rusted Southern Cross windmills pumping bore water up into troughs by the road. Survival out here without water would be short lived.

Looking out the window, the landscape filled me with loneliness. I didn't know what to expect going to work on a cattle station in the far reaches of the outback. I sensed it might hold some answers to some questions I had.

Barkly Homestead was what was known in Australia as a *roadhouse*. It sold fuel, food, and alcohol. And like many roadhouses in the remotest parts of Australia, it had basic accommodation.

The bus slowed, having traversed just over 2250 kilometres, and Barkly Homestead loomed out of the darkness. It was 1:00 am. I hadn't looked at a map to see where I was going before I left Caloundra, but I knew I was now somewhere near the centre of Australia. Stiffly, I got off the bus, collected my bag from the undercarriage and then watched my transport vanish into the black abyss of night. For a moment, I just stood there in the heat and the silence. I gazed at the night sky in utter amazement. Millions of stars reached down to the dark mass of the horizon in a brilliant, glittering blanket. Perhaps this was what the Aboriginal people meant by the Dreamtime? I realised I was now in a place where human time did not exist. Not out here.

Slowly, I became aware of the high-pitched chirp of excited insects and the low growl of a nearby generator. Several lights around the roadhouse were pulsating with a dull glow.

What God-forsaken outpost was this? Just then, I spotted a lean, dark-haired man walking around the roadhouse. He appeared to be doing his last rounds for the night. The man looked in my direction but seemed to see straight through me. In case he hadn't seen me, I walked towards him and into the light.

He looked up with a start. 'Gees, ya scared me half to death there, cobber. Shouldn't sneak up on a bloke like that.' The bloke's name was Kris. 'With a K,' he said. 'What can I do ya for?' Kris asked me in a casual sort of way.

I'm not sure what he thought I was doing standing in the middle of nowhere, in the middle of the night, with nothing but a backpack.

'I was just wondering if there is anywhere I can stay for the night?'

After I had explained my plight, he nodded and stared at me for what felt like an eternity. Finally, his answer came. 'Okay, you can bunk down in that girl's cabin that just left.'

'How much?' I asked, knowing full well I couldn't afford to pay for the room.

'Don't worry about it, mate. She already paid me.'

My single word of 'thanks' was said with heartfelt gratitude.

The searing light of day revealed desolation. I grabbed my pack and made for the roadhouse with a cloud of flies engulfing me. I came through the door cursing.

'Everything okay?' Kris asked with a smirk when he saw me.

'Fine, thanks. Have you got anything cheap for breakfast?'

'Milk and cereal,' Kris replied drily.

Kris shoved a small box of cereal in front of me with a bottle of milk. 'There ya go. So ya goin' out to work on one of the stations, are ya?'

'Walhallow.'

'Ahh yeah,' Kris replied discouragingly, his eyes drawn, distant and as empty as the desert.

The oscillating hum of a plane circling for landing caught Kris' attention. 'You getting picked up by plane?'

'Yep.'

'Well, that sounds like him now.' Kris flicked his bar cloth over his shoulder, turned and went back to work. I shovelled down my cereal then gathered my gear. I heard the plane touchdown and the staccato purr of the engine cease.

A stocky, clean-cut, dark-haired young man burst through the doors of the roadhouse. I was the only customer in the bar. He had a hard look in my direction then strode towards me, thrusting out his arm. 'You must be Ben? I'm Ozzie, is that all your gear?'

'Yep,' I said, shaking his hand.

'Okay, good. I just need to know how much weight I'm taking in the plane, it effects the take-off and landing. So how much do you weigh?'

'About 70kg.'

'That's fine, we'll get off the ground. I'm just going to get something to eat then we'll go.'

Ozzie went to the bar and bought a packet of chips and a soft drink. He and Kris chatted for a few minutes, the two men glancing in my direction a couple of times, and then Ozzie came back to me. 'You ready?'

'Yep.' I took a deep breath, swung my pack over my shoulder and shouted my thanks to Kris. We strolled from the air-conditioned bar into the sauna outside.

A blue and white Cessna 182 sat in the middle of the airstrip. I loaded my gear into the small plane, climbed aboard and buckled up. Ozzie handed me a headset. 'Here, put these on. It gets a bit noisy up there without them and we'll be able to talk.' He turned the Cessna's key, and the plane fired to life. 'You ever been in one of these before?'

'No.'

'Well, take-off can be a bit scary. It banks pretty quickly.'

'Okay.' I wondered how long it would take a search and rescue party to find us if we went down somewhere in the two hundred kilometres of nothingness between Barkly Homestead and Walhallow Homestead. Maybe we'd get lucky and survive the crash, only to die of thirst.

Ozzie gave me an encouraging smile, then pushed the throttle forward. The Cessna's engine howled with delight, and we started rolling down the red-dirt airstrip. Ozzie pulled back gently on the control yoke, and we left the runway. Soon Barkly Homestead became a speck in the great, empty wilderness that surrounded it.

The views from 3500ft gave me a fresh perspective of the remoteness of cattle stations in northern Australia. A huge, vast, dry expanse of land known as the outback opened up around us in all its glory. I soon forgot about falling out of the sky and started thinking about riding horses and chasing cattle through the wilderness that was expanding below.

Dry creek beds lined with gum trees snaked their way across the desert. Thin straight lines of dirt roads and tracks crisscrossed the landscape before disappearing into the hazy wilderness beyond. This was what Australians called *the bush*.

'Cattle pads!' Ozzie's voice scratched through the headset. They stretched out over the land like veins from small dams—the heart and lifeblood of each paddock. The dams were used to store bore water pumped up from deep underground. They were created by pushing up a circular dirt wall and known as turkeys' nests, named for the scrub turkey which mounds up dirt to build its nest and incubate its eggs. Each nest supplied water to several nearby troughs for the cattle to drink. In places nothing but dust surrounded them.

Ozzie set course for Walhallow. 'So, what brought you out here then?'

'I wanted to see the outback.'

Ozzie gave me a sidelong glance. 'So you decided to come and work on a cattle station?'

'I thought it looked like a good adventure.'

'Good adventure ay?' Ozzie looked at me and laughed. 'You're from New Zealand, aren't you? Now that's a good place for an adventure. This is just a desert and there's better ways to see it, like being a tourist. How old are you?

'Just turned 20.'

'I was chasing girls at your age, that's what you should be doing. Well, I suppose it's interesting to see. The people are a bit different out here, and stockcamp, that's the name for the guys you'll be working with, well that's something else altogether.'

'So why are you out here then?' I was thinking it couldn't be all bad if people came out to these parts for work, and besides the travel show had made it look so idyllic.

'I'm out here to get my flying hours up. It's too expensive otherwise. Once I've done 150 hours, I can go for my commercial licence. As soon as I've got enough, I'm out of here. I came over from Melbourne, Victoria, and was at university before this. I had a serious girlfriend, but all that changed. I like flying better.'

'Okay.' I realised then I wasn't the only person in the outback escaping an old life and in search of a new one.

'You want to have a go at flying?' Ozzie motioned to the controls.

'Sure.'

'Alright, grab hold of the control yoke then and get a feel for it.' Ozzie explained what the different controls and instruments did and how to read them, then he handed the responsibility of flying the plane over to me.

'Just don't tell anyone, promise?'

'Okay, I promise.' I gave Ozzie a reassuring nod, tested the ailerons, rudder and elevator, and checked our altitude and airspeed.

For those precious few minutes that I held us on course, I felt for the first time like I was in control of my destiny.

Ozzie informed me we were flying over Walhallow. He took back the controls. After swooping low over several turkeys' nests to check their water levels, we lined up a razor stroke of cleared land that had been neatly scraped from the tree-beard of surrounding bush. Beside the airstrip stood a long, corrugated iron shed, the name WALHALLOW emblazoned across its yellow roof in huge, black capitals.

Scattered around the shed, a small collection of buildings stood amid a patchwork of lawns and shady trees; an oasis in dramatic contrast and opposition to the burning desert around it. Several dusty roads trailed away into the haze of the tremendous wilderness beyond the homestead. This was home to nearly two dozen people: 15 workers, some with wives and children.

The Cessna yawed and rolled as if resisting Ozzie's commands to land. We scudded above the runway before the wheels bounced off the compacted uneven surface, temporarily sending the plane back into the air before bouncing again. Finally, our air speed backed off sufficiently, and we rolled down the airstrip to a gradual, spluttering stop.

Ozzie turned to me as he shut down the engine. 'Welcome to Walhallow, I don't know why anyone would want to come out here.' He shook his head as he stared out of the windows.

CHAPTER FIVE
WALHALLOW

'Be ready; now is the beginning of happenings.'
—Robert E. Howard

The only familiar object I beheld was a pair of gumboots at Cameron's doorstep. What the hell did he need gumboots out here for? Ozzie knocked on the door and a well-built man of average stature with a pronounced hawk-like nose, light brown hair and blazing blue eyes appeared. He wore blue jeans and a khaki shirt with Walhallow embroidered into the left chest. His face was lined from years of hard labour under the sun.

'G'day,' Cameron greeted us with a sharp Australian twang, his face stern. He placed his hands on his hips. Barely glancing at me, he asked Ozzie, 'How are the turkeys' nests looking?'

'They look okay Cameron. About three quarters full.' Ozzie paid his full attention to Cameron, like a soldier addressing a higher-ranking officer.

'Okay then. That's alright. Thanks for doing that. So how are you, Ben?' Cameron raised his eyebrows as he gave me a stern assessment; he didn't look too impressed.

'Good thanks.'

'Flight alright?'

'Yep, good.'

'That's good. So, you've got your work gear with you?' he asked.

I was a little taken aback. 'Yep.'

'Then, you better get changed. Ozzie will show you where your room is and then take you over to the kitchen so you can have some smoko. The other men should be over there somewhere but they'll be heading back down to the yards soon, so you'll have to be quick.'

'Okay.' The jarring impact of his words knocked the naïve enthusiasm right out of me; at the very least I thought I was going to have some kind of induction and get settled in.

Cameron turned back to Ozzie. 'I think Chris needs a hand in the shed if you want to help him after smoko. I'll come over and see you when I'm done here.'

Cameron turned and closed his door. I looked at Ozzie. 'Righto, let's get you ready then,' he said.

On our way over to the kitchen we passed three dusty lads lying on the grass under the scattered shade of a spindly gum tree, brushing flies away. Ozzie told me they were from stockcamp. I was briefly introduced to Alan, a short, chubby kid with bright blue eyes; Mark, a tall, heavy-set bloke who was squeezing pimples on his chin; and Andrew, a towering, scraggly guy with a badly sunburned face. I shook a trio of strong, rough hands and exchanged g'days. I studied their dirty red faces under broad-brimmed Akubras.

'So, you're the Kiwi ay?' Mark asked.

'That'd be me.' I was unsure if that was going to be a good or a bad thing.

'Where's Daisy?' Ozzie asked.

Andrew took a drag from his cigarette. 'He's over at his place checking on Yvette and Adrian.'

'Yeah righto. You guys can introduce Ben when you see him then, I've got other things to do after smoko.'

'Yeah, no worries. We can take care of that,' Andrew said.

'Who's Daisy, Yvette and Adrian?' I asked Ozzie as he showed me to the kitchen.

'Yvette is Daisy's partner and Adrian is his son. He's two years old. Daisy is the head stockman. His name is actually Craig. You'll meet him soon.'

'Here's the new jackaroo, Ronnie,' Ozzie called out as we walked inside.

A portly, elderly guy with a shock of white hair and big round glasses was sweating over a huge pot on the stove. He wore white sneakers, stubby shorts and a half-open shirt revealing a broad grey-haired chest. An off-white apron stained with hand smudges ended above his knobbly knees. The smell of beef filled the room. 'Oh yeah, g'day.' Ronnie acknowledged my presence with a glance and nod, before turning unconcernedly back to his work. I guessed he had seen one or two jackaroos come and go in his time. Ozzie looked at me as if to say, 'don't worry about that grumpy old fart' and we each grabbed a plateful of food and a beaker of water. We sat at one of four small, white, chipped Formica tables set around the kitchen. Even with the fans spinning overhead it was hot. I took a moment to look around as I ate. Old mustering photos featuring thousands of head of cattle adorned the walls, along with horses, motorbikes, helicopters and pictures of big floods on the Station. The wild scenes portrayed a sense of the real Australia—an untamed frontier where men toiled the land in extreme conditions. While we sat there, I asked after Chris and explained how I'd got the job. 'I promised Biruta I'd deliver the bag of gifts to them,' I said.

'I'll let Chris know you're here when I see him at the shed and introduce you later,' Ozzie said.

We left the kitchen and walked into a wall of hot air as the day continued to heat up. I was reminded of Cameron's words when I had spoken to him on the phone back on the Sunshine Coast: *'Damn hot this time of year'.* That was an understatement. It was a bloody furnace. Ozzie pointed me toward stockcamp. 'Good luck, I'll see you later.' I walked toward the main shed where stockcamp were filling up large, insulated plastic water bottles from a huge rainwater tank at the end of the shed.

His hat was pulled well down to protect him from the glare of the sun, his eyes fixed ahead, and a cigarette compressed between his lips. He studied my approach. 'You must be Ben. I'm Craig, the head stockman. This is stockcamp. You'll be working with us.' He was dry, but not unfriendly.

'Just call him Daisy,' Mark shouted cheerfully, as he dumped a full water bottle in the back of the Toyota Land Cruiser. The number plates on the cruiser read: NT OUTBACK AUSTRALIA.

'Shut up, Soapy, or I'll make you work the head for the rest of the day,' Daisy yelled back at him. 'Don't listen to him, Ben, he was as round as a watermelon when he turned up here, but we worked the surplus off him alright, now he thinks he can give me a bit of tongue and cheek. Righto, you sit up here with us.' Daisy pointed to the cab as the other men jumped on the back.

I climbed in the cab with Daisy and another young bloke. I noticed a rifle sitting on the dashboard. We headed out of the homestead and off down a wide, corrugated, red-dirt road. Both men stunk; what looked like blood and a ton of stale sweat stained their jeans and long-sleeved shirts. I looked at their boots, covered in cow shit and more blood. They were obviously used to the stench and didn't notice it. Both blokes wore well-worn, wide-brimmed, discoloured white hats, which were also stained with blood, sweat and dirt. A few days stubble canvased their weathered faces.

'So, you're a Kiwi, ay?' Daisy asked jestingly. He eyed me through his coke-bottle lensed spectacles, which magnified his eyes in a slightly unnerving way. 'Well, we won't hold that against you, will we Pud?' Daisy grinned at the bloke beside me. 'Do you know the haka?'

'Not really.' Rugby wasn't my thing, but everyone seems to think that if you're from New Zealand you must play rugby and know the haka.

'That's a shame, those Maoris always think it's smoko time. You know, *cup-a-tea, cup-a-tea*, isn't that how the haka goes?' Daisy laughed at his joke.

I had to admit, I hadn't heard that one before and it was kind of funny.

'We'll call you Kiwi, and this young fella here beside you is Damien. But you can call him Pud.'

'So, what did you want to come out here for then?' Pud asked.

'I wanted to see what it was like to work on a cattle station.' I guarded the reasons for my self-exile.

'Oh yeah? I could think of better things to do.'

'You ever worked with cattle before?' Daisy butted in.

'No.' The only livestock I'd spent any time around was deer. Both my father and my grandfather had farmed them.

'That's okay. You'll see what it's like to work on a station all right. We'll teach him, won't we Pud?'

'Yeah, I guess so.' Pud nodded with apparent disinterest.

We pulled up to a large set of yards known as the *House Yards* because they were nearest the homestead. The men jumped off the back of the cruiser with the water bottles and hurled themselves over the rusty iron railings into the dusty yard. I got out of the cab with Daisy and Pud, grabbed hold of the top rail with both hands and clambered after them. As I swung my legs over, I lost my grip in shock as the skin on my palms and fingers sizzled. I swore and landed heavily in the yard. For a moment, I stared at my hands in utter disbelief.

'Bit hot there, Kiwi?' Daisy asked. The other men stared with blank faces.

I walked over to join them, and we got straight into the job which, today, was weaner branding. Weaners are young cattle not yet fully grown. Andrew threw his scraggly frame into a small pen that led to a narrow race and began yelling, prodding, nudging and generally encouraging them with a length of poly pipe.

'Don't worry they hardly feel it,' he said, when he noticed my cringing disgust. His face scrunched into manic laughter, and he carried on whacking them.

I thought he was being overly aggressive, but what did I know about dealing with cattle in the outback?

Now and then one of the other men jumped into the pen and helped Andrew. Alan, who was better known as Chunky, appeared to be fairly adept at throwing himself into the midst of the chest-high beasts. He pushed his short, chubby kid body to the full extent of its ability without complaint. Together, the two men forced the weaners up the race like rugby players in a scrum. I was hoping I wouldn't have to join them when Daisy handed me a knife.

'I'll show you how to bang tail,' Daisy said.

'Bang what?'

'Bang tail.' Daisy caught hold of a weaner tail, wrapped the tassel around the blade and sliced it off in one neat movement. I asked him to slow down so I could see what he was doing before I had a go.

'That's called the poo stick,' Chunky yelled.

I grasped my first tail, doing a miserable job on the tassel. I looked at my hands, covered in shit. I could see why.

'Just watch your hands and arms, Kiwi,' Daisy said, 'we don't want you getting them crushed or broken on your first day.'

'And watch their flaming hooves too, they've got a nasty kick,' Soapy added.

I cut the corner off my thumb on my second attempt.

'You alright?' Daisy asked, when he saw me shaking blood off my hand. He grabbed hold of my hand for a look. 'Just took a bit of bark off. You'll be alright, it'll grow back. Watch the fingers, the knife's sharp.' We got straight back into it.

Bang tailing, I learnt, was performed to show that the cattle had been through the yards. Any cattle roaming around paddocks with long tassels had escaped the yards and were not accounted for. Later, I learnt how to inject botulism shots into the cattle's necks with a quick, hard, stabbing motion. The cattle flinched at the needle and often leapt forward, taking my hand and the syringe with them until I got faster at it. Botulism is a paralysing disease caused by a toxin produced by a bacterium called *Clostridium botulinum*, which is common in pastoral areas where soils are phosphorus deficient. Australia has a plentiful supply of such areas.

From the race, each beast was let out in turn through a small sliding gate and sprung forward into the teeth of a large metal contraption called a cradle. Here they were captured and locked in place before they had a chance to escape. The cradle was hinged to a large concrete slab and once the beast was securely in place it was slammed down onto a truck tyre on the ground so that the beast was on its side. One man then grabbed hold of the up-side back leg and pulled it back out of the way to give Daisy a clear shot at castration. Although the beast kicked and mooed in a hopeless bid to escape, it inevitably became a steer.

After that, hot branding irons were pulled from a gas flame and applied to the animal's hide so that it could be identified as one of the Station's cattle.

'Strike while the iron's hot!' Daisy yelled, when he saw me holding back as the smell of burnt hide assailed my nostrils and I dodged the flying testicles he was deftly removing. He had a good point.

Meanwhile, Soapy was busy on the head of the beast. I watched as he de-horned, ear tagged, and inserted hormone pellets under the ear skin of the castrated males. It was a bloody and merciless job that involved a barbarous use of knife and loppers. Once removed the horns would never grow back. Blood spurted a metre into the air from the fresh gaping wounds. It covered the beast's head and neck, Soapy's whole body, and anyone else nearby. The exertion and self-discipline it required contorted his face into a mix of anguish and savage ability. Defiance, a type of antiseptic dressing, was then splashed over the gaping wounds to protect the cattle from flystrike and infection before the cradle was flung open and the beast scrambled free. If it didn't get up, it got a kick or a yank on its tail. This whole process took less than a minute to perform.

We worked manically under a primitive shelter that offered little shade from the fierce sun. Sweat poured from our bodies and adhered our shirts to our backs as bloody hands and dirty lips fumbled water bottles to relieve dry mouths. Stockcamp seemed a well-oiled beef-processing machine. I felt like a timid city slicker.

Daisy suddenly called to me. 'Come here, Kiwi. I'll show you how to castrate.'

I walked towards him, unsure about cutting an animal's nuts off on my first day at work. 'Are you right or left handed?'

'Right.'

Daisy clasped my right hand against the knife's handle with the strength of an Olympic wrestler. I thought he was going to crush the bones in my fingers. I was lean but athletic, average in height and not weak by any means, but the sheer size and strength of his hands made mine feel soft and fragile. I wondered if all the men were this tough.

'Now make sure you hold the knife tight, so it doesn't slip. Have you got it?'

'Yep.' I tried not to wince as his vice-like grip tightened.

He guided my left hand over the soft hide around the scrotum of the beast, feeling for the testicles, explaining what we were doing and why. Then, moving a testicle up and out to the surface before pinching the hide tightly beneath it so it didn't slip away, he moved the knife in a quick, steady, slicing motion. I feared for my fingers as the blade slid just millimetres past them. Out popped a warm slimy testicle. He grabbed it and gave it a tug to pull it clear before, with two more quick slices, cutting the cords that connected it to the poor beast. He threw the testicle to the ground for the meat ants to drag away. We went for the second testicle and after a few more rapid slashes it was all over. I was surprised at how quick the operation had been.

'Congratulations, Kiwi, you just did your first castration. Now remember, you only get one shot at it, and you have to be quick otherwise that weaner will suck those testicles up and you won't be able to find them. Got it?'

'Yep, sure.' I wasn't sure at all.

From time to time the disgruntled beasts we had finished with charged at us. I started getting jumpy as the men yelled, 'Watch 'em! Watch 'em!' whenever another beast came snorting and charging in from behind.

Dust, flies, sweat, blood and shit. We were covered in it. Was I this kind of man? I wasn't sure right then, but I was going to find out.

I retired to the jackaroo's quarters—a temporary transportable building known as a *donga*. There were six rooms, one per man, and shared amenities comprising two showers and a couple of basins heavily stained by the minerals in the bore water. The men's rooms were austere; simply furnished with an old stretcher bed, chair and wardrobe. There was a communal refrigerator and washing machine. I peeled off my clothes and turned on the cold shower tap, only to discover there was no such thing as cold water in the outback. The green tree frog that climbed out of the drain hole didn't seem to mind the temperature of the water or my company. I was nursing a pounding headache from the severe heat and slight dehydration. It had been a long day.

Over dinner, crass conversation flowed about the day's work. I was quietly exhausted as I chewed on a tough piece of steak. Ozzie asked me how I got on for the day.

Andrew, who was looking over at me and listening, chuckled. 'Whada-ya think, Kiwi?'

'It's hot work.' I wasn't much of a conversationalist.

'Yeah, and it's gonna get hotter. So ya don't mind gettin' covered in all the blood and shit then?'

'Nup.' I lied.

'Well, we'll just wait and see how ya go in them yards with some of them mad bulls then.' A sardonic grin stretched the sunburned, bony features of his pinched face. His eyes looked both empty and angry at the same time.

'Don't worry about Brains,' Soapy piped up, 'he just thinks he's a big shot. Don't ya Brains? And he's not called that for his level of intelligence either.'

'Yeah, bigger than you, Soapy,' Brains snarled.

Pud looked at them, then at me and shook his head. Changed out of his work clothes into shorts and t-shirt, he appeared almost timid and boyish. His thick brown hair framed a roundish face with a small nose and brown eyes that held a sort of mischievous innocence in them that defied his life in the bush.

'Would you listen to the shit I gotta put up with,' Soapy moaned like a big, domesticated bear.

Chunky, shuffling the food around his plate, murmured, 'Welcome to stockcamp.'

CHAPTER SIX

STOCKCAMP

'I know of no more encouraging fact than the unquestionable ability of man to elevate his life by conscious endeavour.'

—*Henry David Thoreau*

The weeks that followed were some of the most trying of my young life as I learnt the way of the Australian stockman: riding horses, mustering, and yard work. The latter was a dangerous, onerous and monotonous task of pushing cattle through the yards, drafting and branding that never seemed to end. I was often charged at, stood on and kicked, and nearly crushed to death in herd compressions. I learnt to calf scruff—a tough, and these days controversial, sport that pits pairs against each other, the goal being to bring a calf to the ground as quickly as possible for branding. It required using my strength with as little possible remorse, and an effort that, in the heat, would surely kill a man if he pushed himself too hard.

I learnt how to get a *killer* which involved going out and selecting a beast for slaughter to feed the entire homestead. I'd killed birds and rabbits when I was growing up on the orchard in New Zealand, but I'd done nothing like this. The scene was one I would never forget. Hundreds of flies crowded around the freshly killed beast as bloodied hands grasped at huge, sagging, twitching chunks of flesh. The stench had me by the throat as I watched the men hack and slash different cuts from the beast like a pack of starving hyenas in the Serengeti. Within minutes the carcass lay bare. The men splashed water over their hands and steel teeth then wiped them both on their jeans. The ritual of slaughter brought me closer to the land and fuelled an understanding of life within the context of nature. Survival. The beast died so we could go on living. Its flesh became our own. I felt a primal, wild man spirit inside me awaken.

From dawn till dusk, stockcamp toiled the land; cursing at nature in defiance of its pitiless heat, suffocating on clouds of dust in the yards while armies of thirsty flies feasted on the sweat of our shirt backs. Dehydration, heat exhaustion, the tyranny of isolation were adversaries many men couldn't tolerate. I thought of the cattle station I had seen on the travel show before I left. This wasn't that. This was bloody hard work.

I admired the strength and resilience in the men. Their work ethic, skill and agility in dealing with large, aggressive animals was astounding. Their capacity to endure long hours in the harsh climate without complaint, coping with the many dangers that plagued their day and the injuries they sustained, showed that they were what Frederic Remington called *Men with the bark on*. They were indifferent to hardship, neither callous nor ascetic. They exuded a calm acceptance of everything that came, perhaps from a source of inner quiet and security that I did not yet know or understand. Through all of it, they maintained a sense of humour, crass as it was. These were tough men, moulded from tough country. To survive, I had to learn how to be tough with them.

Camp was situated near a turkey's nest, known as No. 12. It was out on the *flat*, as the blokes called it, in the north-eastern corner of Larry's Paddock, an 857 square kilometre paddock in the western reaches of the Station situated below the 256-kilometre Calvert Road. A sign at its turnoff from the Tablelands Highway reads in large, white lettering on a red background: NO FUEL NEXT 320 km. As the crow flies, camp was over 70 kilometres from the Homestead.

We arrived there mid-morning and pulled up to a hot, dusty, apparently abandoned campsite situated several hundred metres off the Calvert Road. A small, corrugated iron shed stood in one corner of the camp and provided storage for old metal stretchers and dry stores. Portable yard panels surrounded the site to keep cattle out. A few trees provided sparse shade. After unloading our camping gear and food supplies, we headed to the yards.

Our first day out saw us working the yards at No. 12. Stockcamp sat on the high rails of a small yard in which a red-eyed cow kicked up the dust. I wasn't thinking much about the situation when Cameron turned his gaze on me. 'Come on Gumboot Man, get in there and push that cow up. Come on get in there. It's *your* job!'

I was stunned, and where did this *Gumboot Man* come from? Why was he picking on me? He was the one with the gumboots. I looked at Cameron and then at Daisy. 'Come on Kiwi. Do what Cameron tells you.' Both men were blank serious. I looked at the cow and then at the other men on the rails, hoping one of them would offer to take the challenge.

'Yeah, come on Kiwi!' they yelled. 'Show us how the Kiwis do it!'

I had no idea how the Kiwis did it as I racked my brain for an excuse to avoid being mauled by the mad beast. 'Nah,' was all I could manage with a shake of my head.

Everyone was quiet while they waited for Cameron's reply to my obstinance. I looked at the mad cow and thought some more. Getting in that yard seemed like suicide. Quick wit saved me. 'Show me how to do it first, then I'll have a go.'

Cameron and Daisy looked at each other, stumped. Neither of them was game to get in there. Cameron turned to Brains. 'Come on Brains, you get in the yard and show Gumboot Man how it's done.'

'Ha-ha, nah, I'm not getting in there with that mad thing,' Brains said.

'Come on Brains, or you won't get paid!' Cameron taunted.

A serious look appeared on Brains' face as he thought about missing a pay cheque. Then a string of obscenities issued from his mouth as he began lowering himself down the rails into the yard, slowly, one rail at a time. Suddenly, the beast charged, kicking up a cloud of dust as it accelerated into top gear and crunched into the rails just below Brains' heels with a ringing thump. Brains barely scrambled to safety. 'Nah, I'm not doing it. That thing 'ill kill me!' he shouted, clearly shaken from the near miss.

'C'mon Brains, you'll be right,' Cameron tried to sound encouraging as his most fearless man backed away from the challenge. 'Come on you men, give him some support.'

The support took the shape of yelling at Brains. 'Come on Brains! Yeah, come on Brains ya big girl's blouse! Get in there and show us how it's done, like you're always telling us!'

'Nah, you's can all get fucked.' Brains' sunburned face turned a vivid carmine as the defeat and shame of his cowardice mocked his boasting over the dinner tables back at the homestead.

That was the last time I ever heard the name *Gumboot Man*, and I was glad for it.

Cameron left the beast in there for a couple of days to 'dry out' and 'give it something to think about'.

That night, back at camp, I learnt how the men lived out on the flat. Our first chore was to gather firewood and build a fire under an old cast iron boiler which heated water that was supplied from a nearby turkey's nest for our showers. Once the water had heated, we jumped one by one into a small tin cubical for a quick shower or *bogey*, as the men called it.

While the men took turns showering, Soapy prepared our evening meal and busied himself cooking it on the campfire. The flames served as our only source of light and created a lot of unnecessary warmth. Camp dinners, which we took turns to cook, consisted of fresh beef, potatoes, onions and tinned vegetables with tinned fruit for dessert. Breakfasts comprised of bread, eggs, more onions, bacon and steak, and lunches were corned beef and chutney sandwiches, sometimes with cheese if we were lucky. It was bland and basic, but this bush tucker kept us well. A fridge, borrowed from stockcamp's quarters, kept the meat and the few other perishable food stores cold. This was powered by a small generator which we left running during the day, when the heat was at its zenith, but switched off at night when the silence of the outback was absolute.

I plonked myself on one of the chairs by the fire, refreshed from showering and looking forward to Soapy's camping cuisine. The savage heat of the day had abated into the more reasonable stifling warmth of the night. Glowing embers rose from the fire into the cosmos. I was exhausted. My stomach was churning and cramping from the salty drinking water we had at camp.

'So, how are you finding all this work, Kiwi?' Daisy asked. He sensed I was struggling.

'It's hard work.' I didn't let on just how hard I was finding it. I was too proud. The way I figured it, if the other men could cope with it then so could I.

'I think he's a bit soft,' Brains said, offering me a hostile glare from the other side of the fire.

I studied his sunburned face and bony features, looking for signs of a challenge and contemplating my ability to meet it. His head looked like a skull from the pits of hell with flames dancing around it. It looked like it would break my fist. His ape-like hands would hit like sledgehammers. I knew there and then I probably didn't stand a chance against him. He was a full head taller than me and, although he was lean, I knew he was strong. I was softer than these blokes, there was no doubting that right then, but I also knew Brains was sullen after the mad cow incident earlier that day and was looking to take it out on someone.

'Leave him alone, Brains. You don't exactly do a lot around here,' Pud said.

'It's all you guys can come up with, isn't it?' Brains snarled. 'Brains is off riding the motorbike all day. What does he know about work? Well, if any of you guys were any good at riding them motorbikes then you'd be doing it too wouldn't you? But ya can't ride em bikes like me.'

Pud looked at me and shook his head. 'Can you believe this bloke?'

I liked Pud. He was quiet, but I could relate to him. He was from a town called Rockhampton, on the central Queensland coast. After Daisy, he was the most experienced stockman in camp.

'Oh, here we go,' Soapy piped up, 'Brains is on his big *I'm better than you* rant again.' Soapy was from Adelaide, the opposite end of the country to Brains.

'Shut ya cake hole Soapy.' Brains growled.

'Ahh, getting narky now, are we?' Soapy said, winding up Brains.

Brains jumped up out of his chair, thrusting his finger like a spear at Soapy. 'You wanna shut ya cake hole Soapy or I'll…'

'Sid-down Brains! And stop winding him up Soapy,' Daisy yelled at the men.

'Just telling it how it is,' Soapy muttered.

'I'm warning you. The both of you can shut-up.' Daisy's word was final.

'Geez, can't we just have dinner in peace?' Chunky murmured.

Brains sat down muttering to himself and started rolling a cigarette. I felt responsible for the whole argument.

'So, you finding it a bit tough are you Kiwi?' Daisy continued. 'Well, don't worry about that. We'll toughen you up.'

I wasn't sure whether to take his words as encouragement or an ultimatum. 'It's that water that we're drinking out here, I can't stomach it.'

'Bore water,' Pud said.

'It shouldn't be bore water. Chris said he filled it up with rain water,' Daisy said.

'Nup, it's gotta be bore water. It tastes disgusting,' Pud asserted.

The men started complaining that they shouldn't have to drink bore water. I put my head down and concentrated on the tough piece of steak on my plate while the unbiased silence of the wilderness enveloped our campfire light with indifference.

As everyone helped clean up, Daisy pulled me aside. 'Don't let Brains get to you Kiwi, he's just sizing you up. Station life didn't come easy for him either. One night two men in stockcamp who were sick of his antics came into his room while he was sleeping and beat him up good. The cowards were fired, but it affected him, and he hasn't forgotten about it.'

I didn't know what to say, part of me hated Brains and now a part of me felt some compassion for him.

'He's just a bit lost and messed up, Kiwi. It was juvenile prison up in Darwin or the Station for him.'

'Juvenile?' I was surprised.

'He's only 17. I know you wouldn't think that to look at him, you'd think he was 25.'

It took me a few moments to wrap my head around it.

The men retired to their swags. The Australian swag is a foam mattress rolled up with bedding inside a sheet of green canvas that either zips or buttons up to form a large, green cocoon-like bed. Some even have fly nets and pitch up like small tents. Soapy had one like that. Once inside it was actually quite comfortable and weathered the elements reasonably well. I was fairly confident that it was secure until Daisy recollected a story about a snake joining a bloke in his swag one night for the warmth.

I didn't own a swag, so I was loaned a young Aboriginal man's swag that had been left at the Station. They said the man's name was Elvis. I wasn't sure if they were having me on or not. I thought they'd be telling me that Johnny Cash left his boots here next. Elvis wasn't on the Station when I arrived. Apparently, he would float in and out when it suited him.

'He's gone walkabout,' Daisy said, with disinterest.

'What does that mean?' I asked.

'Those Aboriginal blokes just walk off into the bush sometimes. Sometimes they're gone a few days, sometimes weeks, or even months. Can't stop 'em, it's in their blood. Sometimes you never see them again. They usually gravitate back to the Aboriginal camps they're from. Elvis comes from one called Corella Creek. It's just south of here, off the Tablelands Highway.'

I was dumbfounded. How on earth could a man just wander off into the bush out here and survive? Obviously if you were Indigenous, you could.

'It's annoying,' Daisy continued, 'you never know how long they're going to stick around for, or if you'll see them again. But they always promise they'll stay. Shame too because Elvis is a good stockman. But it makes it hard to run a stockcamp when you can't rely on men.'

It was an odd feeling, lying in an Indigenous man's well-used bedding in the middle of a continent I knew very little about. I'd never even met an Aborigine. I started wondering what this mysterious Elvis looked like and if he might just walk out of the bush and into camp and ask for his swag back. I made the mistake of asking the other men.

'Yeah, he's a big mad fella, Kiwi, and he doesn't like anyone using his swag,' Soapy mocked, as he lay in his mansion beside me.

'And he hates Kiwis,' Chunky bellowed from across the camp.

'Great, thanks guys.'

'Anything we can do to help, Kiwi,' Chunky said, with enthusiastic sarcasm.

I lay there thinking about the strangeness of the evening, falling into the immense arching night sky of the outback, getting lost in a moment that was the beginning of a journey I never would have dreamed of.

CHAPTER SEVEN

RED DIRT AND BLUE SKY

'He knows not his own strength that hath not met adversity.'
—*Ben Jonson*

If I had a win that first day in the yards at No. 12, it was to be the last for a very long time.

We were drafting cattle at a set of yards somewhere in the remote wilderness when I faltered in the heat. It's not a normal heat in the outback. It resembles something closer to turning on an oven and climbing inside when it's hot enough to slow cook a roast. The sun is ruthless and debilitating if you are not used to it and the baking red dirt that is witness to its torture radiates its intolerable heat back at you, trapping you in that furnace. You become acutely aware of a voice in your head that is telling you that if you do not get yourself out from under that fierce sun and into the shade, it will cook your brains and you will die.

No one said anything about my diminished activity. They knew I was struggling, and perhaps they were too. I knew I had to get to the shade of the turkey's nest, or I was going to end up a statistic. Yet the thought of asking Daisy if I could take a break while I watched the other men slog it out kept me in the yard. Brains was off mustering on the motorbike with Clem, the Station's helicopter pilot. The extra pressure to get the cattle through the yards with one less man in the camp was sorely felt. Daisy complained often that he didn't have enough men in stockcamp but no extra station hands were hired.

Cameron pulled up in his cruiser and marched over; perhaps the muster hadn't been going so well. He looked like a man who had just watched a thousand head bolt through the fence line into the neighbour's paddock.

'What's taking so long? You men should've had these cattle through the yards by now,' Cameron growled at us.

'We're getting them through as fast as we can Cameron,' Daisy said.

Daisy's reply seemed to inflame the situation. The men had words. Daisy must have told Cameron I wasn't feeling well. Cameron looked in my direction, disdain rippling across his face. He strode towards me.

'What's wrong with you?'

'I'm not feeling good. It's the heat,' I confessed, my mouth as dry as bulldust. Prickly heat was torturing me in waves of needles across my back. My head felt like it was on fire.

I didn't know what else to say, I wasn't sure what the signs or symptoms of heat exhaustion, or heatstroke, were but I was beginning to feel sick.

'Go and sit under the trees by the turkey's nest then if you're not feeling well,' Cameron growled. 'Go on!'

I could feel the piercing eyes of the men as I climbed over the rails and left them in the yard. I'd never felt so shamefaced as I walked over to the nest. The trembling silence that followed me was broken only by Cameron's yelling at the men to get back to work and his harsh criticism of their work ethic. 'You call yourselves men! You're not men at all!' The air boiled with rage.

While I sat on the bank of the turkey's nest I began to dry-retch. I crawled down to the water's edge, my head pounding to the rhythm of my heartbeat. I wondered at what temperature human body fluids begin to boil. I wasn't sure what to do, so I just started filing my hat with water from the nest and tipping it over myself.

When the drafting was finished, Cameron left and stockcamp came and joined me in the nest for lunch.

'Sorry about not staying in the yard but I couldn't do it,' I said to Daisy. I resented that, despite my resolve, the work and the climate had got the better of me.

'Don't worry about it, Kiwi. The heat will take a bit of getting used to. You've picked the wrong time of year to come out here, second round is the hardest time of the year on the cattle stations in northern Australia.

It can break the best of men. Better to start at the beginning of the year when the work is easier, like all these fellas did.'

I looked at the other men. Their red, dusty faces were lined with tributaries of sweat. Their bloodshot eyes gave away what they wouldn't openly admit.

'It's still hot,' Daisy continued, his magnified eyes revealing something that I thought resembled understanding, 'but the place is nice and green after the wet season, and first round will get you used to the work, and we do other jobs too, like fencing, and there's even time to go to rodeos. You'd like it then. And don't worry about Cameron. He gets impatient sometimes. You just have to earn his respect.'

I had no idea how I was going to earn Cameron's respect.

That afternoon, one of the Station's borerunners dropped by camp and had a word with Daisy. He looked about 60, had a sprinkling of short-cropped whitish-grey hair, a trimmed beard of the same length and colour and was sunburned to a cinder. After a minute, Daisy came over to me. 'Grab your gear Kiwi, you're going with Denis. We'll be back tomorrow. Just stay out of Cameron's way.'

'I'll be okay. I'll stay here with you guys,' I insisted, I couldn't stand the humiliation.

'No, don't worry about it. It's all organised.'

I gathered my gear and walked over to the cruiser that was waiting for me. I threw my bag and swag on the back and jumped in the cab.

'You Ben, are you?' asked the old borerunner.

'Yep.'

'Yeah, yeah, I'm Denis. So, I hear everyone calls you Kiwi?' We shook hands and got going.

'So, you from New Zealand, are you?'

'Yep.'

'Yeah, yeah, you're not one of those sheep-shaggers, are you?'

'Not last time I checked.' It's amazing what you find out your culture is recognised for once you leave your own shores.

'Yeah, yeah, are you sure?' Denis looked at me suspiciously.

'I'm sure.'

'Oh, that's good, I hear there's a few over there, though. But it's a beautiful country, and the Kiwis are pretty good too. Play a good game of rugby. So that heat getting to you a bit, is it?'

'Yeah, it's bloody hot.'

Denis paused, looked across knowingly, and drilled his warning into me. 'Yeah, yeah, well, you want to be careful out here in this heat. It can kill you. Your fate really is in your own hands out here. Take care of yourself, no one else will.'

I nodded. I knew.

I watched gum trees fly past the windows of the cruiser in a virescent blur, tumbling into ochre reds and yellows of the desert country. I felt lonely; felt like I might have made a mistake in coming out here.

'Cameron give you a bit of a hard time in the yards, did he?'

'I don't think I'm meeting his expectations.'

'It's not you. He doesn't know how to treat most people and he should know you're going to find it hard coming from New Zealand. Just call him sardine next time you see him. Tell him I said so.'

'Sardine?'

'Yeah, yeah you know, like them racing sardines in South Africa. He's got the long, pointed nose and the sharp face.'

'I think he'd kill me if I called him sardine.'

'Yeah, yeah, good point. You don't want to get yourself in any more strife, maybe hold off on the sardine then.'

We pulled up at the homestead and I grabbed my gear from the back of the cruiser. Denis called out his window, 'Get yourself a Powerade from the rec club when it opens, it'll help you rehydrate. Don't worry about what anyone says. You get that Powerade. Just say I told you to. And make sure you drink as much water as you can every night.' He drove off.

I walked over to the quarters and dumped my gear in my room, then stripped off my clothes and stood under the shower. I had little remaining enthusiasm for experiencing life on a cattle station or the adventure I thought it would be.

When the rec club opened at 6:00 pm, I reluctantly went to get my Powerade. I was reluctant because I didn't want to see Cameron. But he was there. The disdainful look returned to his face when he saw me enter. I considered turning around, but it was too late.

'What do you want?' Cameron asked.

I shrunk under his glare. 'Can I get a Powerade, please?'

'What do you want a Powerade for? I thought you were sick?'

'Denis said I should get one to help me rehydrate.'

'Whoa, go and drink some water then. You should be out helping the other men. You've gotta work to earn a drink here.' He shot me down in front of Clem and Chris who were sitting at the bar.

'You struggling a bit are you, Kiwi?' Chris asked in a grating voice.

The skin around his beady, grey-blue eyes was deeply lined from the sun but the huge silver-streaked beard that reached to his chest hid most of what would otherwise have been a rather soft and unremarkable face. He wore the typical uniform of the outback for his generation: a faded navy-blue singlet, khaki KingGee stubby shorts and Blundstone boots.

'Yeah, a bit.' I didn't know where to look.

'Yeah, well, I told you it would be hot out here,' Chris scoffed, and laughed at my naïvety. He turned to face Cameron and lifted his eyebrows. 'Ahh well.'

An awkward moment followed in which I didn't know what to do with myself. I was about to walk away when Cameron turned, opened the fridge door and pulled out a Powerade. He thrust it at me.

'Here you go. Now, go back to the quarters, I don't want to see you until dinner time.'

I shuffled back to the quarters and gulped down the Powerade. My room was far from being a place of refuge from the heat and anguish outside. An old air-conditioner rattled in the wall and a ceiling fan spun in odd concentric circles, prodding the stifling heat around the room. My cell held a grim story which the men had taken great pleasure in sharing with me. A year earlier, one of the young men in stockcamp had got his hands on one of the Station gun's and shot himself in the head, not more than a metre from where I lay on my sagging stretcher bed. There was still a hole in the wall where the bullet had emerged from the back of his skull. His girlfriend had just broken up with him over the phone.

As I walked over to the kitchen, stockcamp rolled back into the homestead. I was surprised to see them, and also very annoyed. The indignity and humiliation I felt compounded tenfold.

The men were quiet over dinner until Brains piped up in a jeering tone, 'You finding it a bit hard, Kiwi?'

'It's just the heat,' I answered.

'Yeah, well, you just gonna have to harden up then aren't you.'

'What would you know, Brains? You're always riding that motorbike,' Pud said.

'Yeah, well, what would you know about riding the motorbike, Pud?'

The men argued about who did what. I felt even worse.

Ozzie looked at me. 'Don't worry about this lot, mate. If you're finding it hard, you should just leave. There's better work than this, and you can always come back next season if you really want to. It's nicer out here at the start of the year.'

That night I wrestled with the thought of staying on the Station. If I'd had enough money, I would have taken the next bus back to Caloundra. After seeing what lay between the Sunshine Coast and Walhallow, hitchhiking didn't seem like such a good idea. My feet were so blistered from my new boots they were almost too sore to walk on. Every fibre in my body was telling me to leave, and yet a part of me knew I had to stay. I recalled the talks with Mike above the Tattoo Company about going on a journey and becoming a man. I questioned whether such ideals were realistic in the face of adversity. When did courage become plain stupidity?

But giving up? I wasn't the type. I was too proud to turn away, I couldn't take failure and defeat back to the Coast with me. 'I tried' wasn't good enough. I was sick of life pushing me around.

Under the blazing sun, everything was silent except for the cooing of a distant desert pigeon. I gazed out from under the brim of my hat at the dry parched land; a bead of sweat slid down my temple, the dry air stole the moisture from my lungs. Australia. What fresh hell is this? This was the real Australia, the Australia I had come to see and experience—the outback.

'Why do you stay out here if you're finding it so hard, Kiwi?' Chunky asked.

'I don't have anywhere else to be.' I didn't think Chunky could comprehend the discord of my youth, and I certainly didn't see the point in sharing it with anyone.

'You must have somewhere, someone must care about you,' he insisted.

I held my tongue as I gazed out over the barren landscape, at lean cattle that snuffled in the dusty, baked earth for food. A ball of tumbleweed rolled along a barbed wire fence line on the tendrils of a willy-willy. Tormented crows cawed. Overhead, whistling kites and wedge-tailed eagles soared on unseen air currents in search of food. I wasn't sure if life out here was struggling or in harmony. The scene symbolised the struggle I felt inside. A struggle between a lost and lonely emptiness and the search for a more harmonious life, a struggle that had, in some way, been with me since my early teens.

What would I be if I walked away from this? Would I become like my useless stepfather, a man of little strength and no character? The way he had torn my family apart and turned my life upside down ate at me. Would I never be able to know and understand that part of life I wanted to live and feel? My thoughts were swallowing me up like quicksand in the desert. Yet, in all that empty nothingness, all that isolation and solitude, there was a glimmer of solace. I felt that if I stayed and got through it, I could do anything in life.

Daisy yelled at us, 'Come on you lot. Time to get back into those yards.'

The men swore and moaned. 'Oh do we have to?' Chunky whined like a little kid.

'C'mon, shake a leg!' Daisy yelled.

Chunky wasn't getting off lightly today. None of us were. Daisy was under building pressure from Cameron to finish second round. Chunky kicked the dirt in frustration as he walked back to the cruiser.

I shoved my hat into the water trough in the yards, filled it with water, then poured it over myself.

'You're only making it worse for yourself.' Brains glared at me like a mad bull that was about to charge as he walked past.

I was sure Brains had it in for me. He hadn't let up since I arrived. Daisy had stepped in a couple of times to avoid a fight, but I had a feeling I'd have to face off with the guy. I wasn't looking forward to it.

CHAPTER EIGHT

I DON'T THINK YOU SHOULD GO

'Bowed by the weight of centuries he leans upon his hoe and gazes on the ground, the emptiness of ages in his face, and on his back the burden of the world.'
—*Edwin Markham*

Our only contact with the outside world was a phone in a small wooden box on the veranda between the kitchen and the *big house*, the manager's home.

I put a call through to New Zealand for the first time in four months that evening. My father answered.

I'd seen my father half a dozen times in the past seven years and spoken to him the same number of times on the phone. When I told him I was going to Australia, he said: 'You know the Australians don't like New Zealanders much, don't you?' I hadn't felt much like speaking to him after that. A rift had grown between us over the years, and I doubted he would understand what I was out here trying to do. Still, I wanted to let him know I was okay.

'Cows ay? I thought you would be doing something smarter than that. So how long are you going to stay out there?'

'I'm not sure.'

'Well, take care of yourself. Don't do anything silly. We don't want you to die out there. We're all fine back here. Louise is doing better now she has settled in at school and Sam is getting through his apprenticeship.'

My elder brother had been accepted into an aeronautical engineer apprenticeship with Air New Zealand. He had left Christchurch and moved up to Auckland to study before I had left New Zealand. Unfortunately, after our parents' breakup and the subsequent splitting up of the family after my mother's second marriage, I hadn't had much to do with either my brother or sister.

'How are Lesley and Adam?' Lesley was my father's new partner, a young woman he had met in the United Kingdom when he was living there, and Adam was my new baby brother.

'They're good. Adam is growing like a weed.'

'Okay, well, I just wanted to let you know what I was up to and that I'm fine.'

'Well, don't stay out there too long. There's a lot of other stuff you need to think about.'

When I hung up the phone, I felt disappointed. Nothing I did seemed to impress my father. He didn't seem interested in my life. I wondered how he would receive the news if I really did die out here.

I stared at the phone for a moment after hanging up. I thought about Stephanie, and how she was getting on at university. I'd left so suddenly—one day working with a steady income and plans to study business computing, the next on a plane to Australia. Should I call her?

She was coming to the end of her second year at university. Although we hadn't seen much of each other since she moved to Dunedin, we were still close. I recalled her last words: *'I don't think you should go'*. Why had it felt so hard to leave all of a sudden? I didn't know why she didn't want me to go, but I knew she was the person closest to me. She knew just about everything about me. If I'd stayed, stayed for her, I feared ending up like my parents.

* * *

The image of my brother and sister crying when my parents sat us down in our living room and told us they were separating clouded my mind. I was 11 years old, my brother 12 and my sister seven. They had been hurt, but I felt an odd sort of relief that bordered on curiosity. For months our parents had been having full-blown arguments. I could hear them yelling at each other in their bedroom. I had felt a tension with my father that, as a boy, I was unable to understand. Several months earlier my parents had suggested sending me to a boarding school. My brother and sister would remain at home. I hadn't liked the idea at first, but had quietly come around to it. The school offered many extracurricular activities aimed at discovering each individual's talents. My parents thought I would benefit from such schooling. But when the time came, they had changed their minds. Finances were tight.

My childhood had been a good one. As a family, we moved often, which meant my brother and sister and I ended up at half a dozen different schools between New Zealand and Australia. But our lives were blessed by the wild places in which we lived. Our father managed apple orchards in the country, where we grew up among the rows of apple trees on our weekends and summer holidays. We went fishing in highland lakes and hunting for birds and rabbits on our farm. We swam in wild rivers and on beautiful beaches. Life was based around the outdoors. As a child I found that world magical and enchanting.

Shortly after they split up, we moved into Christchurch with our mother and our father moved to Auckland. My siblings and I flew up on separate occasions to visit him. I had wanted to live with my father, but he wasn't settled and was struggling financially, which made it impossible. After living in Auckland for two years, he moved to England to further his new career in business.

For a time, we were fine. Our mother managed the household while working full time and taking care of my siblings and me. Our father paid the mortgage and other expenses as required. He also sent my brother and me some pocket money fortnightly for anything extra we needed.

I started high school and soon made new friends. Most of them also came from broken homes, which gave us a common bond. Fortunately for them, their family situations were more amicable.

I was 14 when my mother remarried. Her need to have a partner and her lack of self-esteem led her into a dysfunctional relationship with an irresponsible, selfish, lazy man. He was a heavy pot smoker and drinker who was of unstable mind and character. I was the first to go, kicked out of home and on to the street after a fight with him. It wasn't the first time either. One night I'd escaped to a friend's place on my bicycle after a fight. Riding through the dark, lonely night, I intended to be strong, but when I arrived found I couldn't hold back the tears. My friend noticed my bruises and invited me to stay.

I had a feeling my life was taking a turn as I walked to a nearby bus stop. A friend of my father's, whom I knew, drove over and picked me up. We went back to collect my clothing and schoolbooks and left.

I began to suffer from depression. The adults—my father, his friend who'd collected me, and my mother—decided it was best I didn't return home. I began thinking it was my fault things had ended up the way they had. I missed my father more than I could tell him. It was in those years I needed his love and support most. I registered with social welfare and began receiving money from the government to cover my living expenses as long as I stayed in school. My grades reflected my inner world, and a deep feeling of loneliness took hold. I had little to do with my brother and sister, and our lives drifted apart. I had less and less to do with my mother. I resented the decisions she'd made.

My parents eventually agreed to sell their house and cut ties. My mother found a place for my brother to live and left Christchurch for Nelson with my stepfather and sister. I worried for my sister's wellbeing. She was only 11, and she couldn't escape the hopelessly argumentative and abusive relationship that was polluting her childhood. Our stepfather steadily annihilated everything our mother had ever worked for. While I tried to keep my own head above water, my brother went into his own silent depression.

A few months after they left Christchurch, I received a phone call from my sister that our stepfather was destroying their new home in fits of rage. I flew up to Nelson for damage control and to evaluate the situation, as things had deteriorated to the extent that our mother had fallen into a cycle of depression herself. On arriving, the first thing that hit me was how vague, distant and confused my mother was. It was like she had given up. I discovered that medicinal treatment with the anti-depressive drug Prozac had considerably changed her frame of mind.

She had also become a heavy pot smoker, I guessed to soothe the toxic, brainwashed relationship between herself and my stepfather. Their home was sparse and temporary looking. Food was scarce, and I glimpsed the shattered remains of plates, bowls and glass cups hurriedly cleared away. I couldn't stand the sight of my stepfather's lying eyes. He attempted to deceive me with a false sense of care and friendship. My sister was clearly unhappy but unable to leave our mother's side. I reported my findings to my father's friend who I was living with in Christchurch. I was asked one very simple, direct question in response: *'Should we remove your sister from the situation?'* The burden of that question on my 16-year-old shoulders nearly crushed me. I knew what had to be done. My father intervened from England and his friend, who I was living with, made arrangements for my sister to stay with a friend of hers in Christchurch. I left after a few days, disheartened and distraught, surviving on a thread of hope.

The following year, my mother and stepfather moved back to Christchurch. My mother had nothing left when they returned. She wanted her children. She promised me my stepfather had changed and wanted to make things work. Despite being warned against it by friends and family, I went to live with them, along with my sister, in the hope of returning to something that resembled a normal life. My brother stayed away. He didn't trust our stepfather, and he was still angry with our mother. It turned out my brother was right. Our stepfather hadn't changed at all.

The first few months went okay; my stepfather appeared to be making a real effort. But I could see tension building as the number of arguments between him and my mother escalated. It was during this time that I met Stephanie. After we first met, we kept in touch mostly by phone, often lost in hours of easy conversation. Eventually, we got together in the safety of a group and over time our feelings grew. Then, I had the final fight with my stepfather. The result of that night changed the course of my life.

After my stepfather finished beating me with a fire poker in front of my mother and my sister, he prepared to flee the scene. My sister phoned the police, and he knew they were on their way. But my car was blocking his in the driveway. I heard him yelling outside while I searched for something to defend myself with. Then I heard something smash. I ran outside to find he had thrown a carjack through the windscreen of my car. He was screaming at me to move it. I started yelling back at him. He jumped in his car and started revving the engine. Then he jammed it in reverse and came straight at me. I was trying to climb into my car without injuring myself on broken glass, when I had to dive from the open door to avoid collision. He hit my car with a shattering crunch. I ran back up to the garage while he rammed my car out of the driveway and onto the street. I grabbed the first thing I saw—a wooden crate full of empty beer bottles. I dashed towards his car with it over my head. I hurled the crate at his windscreen. The crate exploded on impact and shards of glass flew everywhere. To my disappointment it didn't break his windscreen. I think he'd have beaten the life out of me if it had or, perhaps worse, gone to work on me with one of the broken bottles and left me maimed and scarred for life. But I wanted him to be there when the police showed up. I wanted to see them deal to him because I knew he was a coward. The face on the other side of that windscreen haunted me for years to come. It was the face of a man that was about to cross a line from which he could never return. He revved the car's engine, crunched it into gear and drove at me. The vehicle lurched forward in a scream of burning rubber on concrete. Fortunately, I was fast. I dived out of the way and avoided the bumper. He crunched into reverse, and I anticipated a second charge. Instead, he screeched back out of the driveway and screamed off down the street. The flashing lights came up the road just a minute too late. My world was shattered into a thousand pieces strewn across the front seats of my car, smashed and exposed in the middle of the street for all to see. The police took statements and photos of the scene and of me and said they would find him. My mother said she wouldn't have him back.

About a week later, I arrived home from my school work experience program to find all my belongings in the living room with a note in my stepfather's handwriting: GET OUT, YOUR NOT WELCOME HERE! The blood drained from my face as I tried to hold myself together. I felt cold and clammy. I shook with adrenalin and anxiety as I picked up the phone and put a call through to my mother. I didn't know where he was or if I was about to have another confrontation with him. My mother was cold—she confirmed his demands, told me where I could go, and made it clear she didn't want me around when they got home. She hung up. Disbelief, betrayal, hate and anger sliced through me. I couldn't believe I meant so little to my mother; couldn't fathom how she had taken him back after what he did.

My stepfather was eventually apprehended, faced court charges for his assault on me, and was ordered to pay reparation costs for the damage to my vehicle.

The reason for the fight? I had left the light on in my room while I was doing my washing in the laundry. He was worried about the power bill. At least that was the excuse my mother relayed. I knew he was more worried about how he was going to pay for his marijuana and his next drink.

After that night, and after many more long telephone conversations where I conveyed a sense of my new life and found a window of solace, I finally asked Stephanie out. Our relationship blossomed, and we fell into what we believed was love.

* * *

I picked up the receiver and dialled Stephanie's number. I missed our friendship but a part of me was glad to have the distance between us so I could get on with what I most needed to do—making some sense out of life.

Stephanie answered the phone. It was quiet in the background. 'Ben? Oh Ben! How are you?'

'I'm doing okay, I'm working on a cattle station in the Northern Territory now.'

'A cattle station? Why are you working on a cattle station?'

'Well, I needed to get away from everything for a while. I thought I might find some answers out here.'

There was a pause, 'Okay, well I hope you find what you're looking for.'

I knew she didn't understand the point of my being here, and I don't think anyone could have understood how hard it was, so I made life on the Station sound like one big adventure. Rather than attempting to explain how incomprehensibly hot it was, I did my best to give her the impression I was having a good time.

'How are you getting on?' I asked.

'I'm good thanks. I've just finished university for the year. I'm not sure what I'm going to do over the summer yet. I miss you, Ben, how long are you going to stay out there for?'

'I don't know.'

'Well, I think you should come back to New Zealand.'

Strangely enough, the thought was about as enticing as staying on the Station. I didn't want to return to New Zealand and leave the life I was only just beginning to discover.

'Why don't you come over to Australia and stay for a few weeks, we could meet in Brisbane, and you could come up to the Sunshine Coast with me?' I wanted to see her, and I knew how much she loved Australia.

There was silence for a moment. 'I'll see if my Dad can organise the flights,' she said.

Her father worked for Air New Zealand and he got several free flights a year, so I knew it wasn't going to cost her anything to come over if she wanted to. We organised to meet in Brisbane for the New Year. I was looking forward to seeing her again; a little apprehensive about it too. Five months had passed. I was worried about how I would feel when I saw her.

CHAPTER NINE

SURVIVAL

'Defeat may serve as well as victory to shake the soul and let the glory out.'
—Edwin Markham

Joanundah Paddock is 179 square kilometres. There were just over a thousand head of cattle to get from Kelly's Bore, in the western corner of Joanundah, to the yards at No. 14, in the north-western corner of Turkey Plain Paddock, a distance of about 20 kilometres.

It was still dark. Brains rounded up the horses and drove them into the House Yards on the motorbike. The horses were well trained and soon came galloping in, neighing, kicking their back legs in the air and biting at each other. They were 'fresh', Daisy would say.

Daisy drafted off the horses for each of us in stockcamp, giving thought to what we could handle, our riding experience and the horses some men preferred to ride.

We used stock horses for mustering—big, hardy animals with a lot of *life* in them. They came in all sizes and colours, from short and light builds to tall and stocky specimens: white, black, brindle and bay. They could sense a timid rider a mile off.

Soapy's trepidation about riding was known by every man in stockcamp. Every time he climbed into the saddle, he looked nervous as hell, like the horse was about to buck him off. The horse instinctively knew his disposition and gave him a hard time. No matter how much time Soapy spent in the saddle, he remained a hesitant, clumsy and uncoordinated rider who dutifully struggled through this requirement of his job. Luckily for me, I bonded with the horses easily. I was a natural. Other than learning how to handle a horse with confidence, I was comfortable in the saddle from the beginning. It stirred something old in me, as if I had been a horse rider in a past life. The first horse I ever rode at Walhallow was an old bay mare named Cactus, a fitting name for a horse in the desert. Cactus wouldn't harm a fly and she knew how to work with cattle, perfect for a greenhorn like me. The first few times I rode, I followed Daisy while he taught me the art of horse handling, walking cattle out, and what to do during a muster.

On this occasion, I was given a new horse named Agro, a young white gelding. Each horse received a nosebag of grain to boost their energy for the day. Then we saddled up, loaded the horses onto the truck and set off for Joanundah. I sat on the back of the cruiser with Chunky, huddling behind the cab in the cool dampness of the early morning while a glittering blanket of stars shone overhead. The land smelled of dry grass and desert earth sweetened with the night's dew. As we flew down the dirt road, I wondered what the day's muster would bring and what temperatures we would face.

'So, Kiwi, you got plenty of water with you today?' Chunky asked.

'Yeah, I should be right.' I knew it was going to be a tough day.

Chunky knew I was going to suffer no matter how much water I had, and he made a point of reminding me. 'Well, we'll see won't we? It's going to be a *long* day.'

Chunky was from the lush, green and mountainous Atherton Tablelands in tropical north-east Queensland. He was used to the heat and humidity. What's more, he'd been around horses and cattle all his life. He was also a bit of a smart arse, which sometimes got him into trouble, but he was only 16, surprisingly, and he held his own with us older men, so we cut him some slack. His age kept him safe from the real red-blooded macho the rest of us reserved for each other, and which was dealt out on a daily basis in a variety of insults and thrusting remarks engineered to beat a man's morale into bulldust. No man could surrender any ground to the other lest he become a victim of constant harassment and abuse. When those moments arose, and there were many, I had no choice but to partake in this brutish behaviour, claim my ground and fight for respect. Fight or flight was part of life in the outback. This was a constant challenge for me while I struggled with the heat. The heat affected everything I did. The only thing Chunky really suffered from was chafing between his legs and being called Chunky. He wasn't the most agile man in stockcamp, but his determination was fierce. His old man, Harry, balding and well-rounded like his son, also worked on the Station. He took care of the weaner tailing—using his kelpies to train the cattle at the House Yards to walk out and stay in a mob when they were mustered.

We arrived at Kelly's Bore and started unloading the horses. I watched the iron curtain of night give way to the glowing embers of a new day. Like a sauna, the cool dampness of the morning morphed into sticky humid heat. We adjusted our horse's saddles while the flies began to congregate in harassing clouds.

Daisy took up position to instruct stockcamp. 'Get a gut full of water into you. Especially you, Kiwi. You won't be getting any more on the way.'

I gulped back a litre before my stomach resisted, then I strapped on a CamelBak—a small backpack with a one-litre bladder of water. The CamelBaks were reserved for the motorbike man, but I didn't have a quart pot on my saddle like the others, so Daisy threw me the spare, knowing I'd need it.

Agro had a little more life about him than old Cactus. Nothing wrong with that I thought. But on our way to the bore I discovered the horse also had a mind of his own, and he was champing at the bit. The overly eager gelding suddenly took off and, despite my furious tugging at the reins, I went galloping right past Daisy.

'Get that horse under control, Kiwi, or I'll do it for you! And shorten those reins,' Daisy yelled.

I finally slowed the horse and got it back under control. I shortened my reins and trotted Agro over to the other men. They shook their heads, as if I should have known better.

'You should never ride in front of a better horseman than yourself, Kiwi, it's disrespectful,' Daisy advised.

I nodded assent.

The mercury was already nudging 30 degrees. I took small, slow, deliberate sips from my CamelBak and swirled the water in my mouth before swallowing while we waited at Kelly's Bore with a small herd.

The *bat-bat-bat* of the helicopter approaching alerted us to be prepared for the arrival of cattle.

A beast suddenly appeared from out of the bush, followed by another and then another until something that resembled a stampede was heading our way. My heart pounded my chest as I waited for the other men to make a move. Soapy and Chunky calmly walked their horses to one side. I followed suit and walked Agro out of the way to let the cattle gather around the trough. The herd quickly swelled into the hundreds while we held them on the trough. Clem flushed a few latecomers and stubborn beasts out of the surrounding bush. The helicopter disappeared, then reappear through the trees, rotor blades centimetres from branches which shivered with the velocity of the spinning blades. Clem chased a few more beasts out of the bush and spun the helicopter in a 360 above them to stop them dodging back under cover. He gave a couple of stubborn animals a rub with the skids, clouds of dust bellowing outwards and swirling beneath the helicopter.

The last of the stragglers joined the herd, and we let them settle while Clem stood off. Then Daisy gave the order to get the mob moving up the fence line. 'Righto you lot,' he shouted, 'make some noise!' A burst of hoots and shouting erupted from stockcamp. I gave a full-throated yell and the mob slowly moved off the trough and up the fence line. The day's droving was underway.

Pushing up the tail is the least favourable position in a muster. It's dusty, it stinks it's where the flies are worst, and you have to make a nearly constant stream of noise to keep the tail moving. As a greenhorn, this was my slot, along with Soapy and Chunky. Chunky generally moved out to the flank whenever he could.

A few hours after pushing the herd off Kelly's bore, and well before we had made No. 6 Bore (the halfway point of the muster), I was shocked to find I'd emptied my CamelBak. I'd been so worried about suffering from heat exhaustion and dehydration that I hadn't rationed my water supply. By the time we made the bore my mouth was dry, my voice hoarse, my tongue swollen and my eyes stinging from the swirling dust clouds the cattle kicked up.

Survival

The mob was hot and restless and crowded around the trough at No. 6 in a tight compression of bodies; pushing, shoving and jostling for a thirsty drink of water. While we held them, I walked my horse over to Daisy to see if he would spare me a drink. 'Have you drunk all your water already, Kiwi?' he snapped. 'That was meant to last you for the day. Well, you can't have any of mine. Go and ask the other blokes if they'll give you some of theirs.'

I felt pathetic as I walked my horse over to Soapy and Chunky and asked them. Their responses stung with contempt. Water was precious, and every man was in a foul mood because of the slow progress of the morning. Everyone needed their water for later.

Daisy yelled at me, 'Go and get a drink from the turkey's nest if you're thirsty, Kiwi.' He sat motionless in his saddle, whilst all around him the great silence trembled in the heat.

I walked Agro over to him. 'Can you hold my reins so I can go and get a drink then?'

'Be quick then.'

I handed him the reins, climbed the side of the nest and stared at the unappealing murkiness of the water for a moment. A pair of cane toads swam away from the edge of the bank, their partially webbed hind feet stirring the silty bottom as they went. I knelt, broke the veneer of oily, dusty scum that sat on the surface and cupped my hands. I knew what that warm, soupy bore water tasted like, but this wasn't the time to be fussy. I was suffering from dehydration. I knew what the signs of heat exhaustion were, and I didn't want to learn about heatstroke. What mattered now was survival, not enlightenment; not understanding. To stay alive, I needed to drink.

I brought the cloudy, salty liquid to my parched lips. I swallowed a mouthful and my gut tightened in reflexive combat. I wondered what the consequences might be of drinking from the nest even as I dipped my hands in for another mouthful and splashed some over my face and neck. The water was mineral heavy; salty enough to roll a man. The cattle could manage it okay with their four stomachs. I filled my hat and poured water over my head. I would have filled the CamelBak if I could have stomached any more. My thoughts blurred into the heat of the day.

I walked back to Daisy and got back on Agro. He didn't say a word, but I could see the scorn in his eyes, magnified by his spectacles. He thought I was weak, and he was tired of my inability to deal with the climate.

We continued to hold the mob of cattle on the nest where they pushed and nudged each other to get to the trough. Before long, Cameron pulled up in his cruiser. He was in a foul mood again. It seemed every time I saw Cameron he was in a foul mood. I guessed that, yet again, our progress wasn't too good. He growled at me to get off my horse and get in his cruiser. 'Don't let the cattle get past. Just drive at them and beep the horn if you have to!' he yelled impatiently.

The men started to whistle, hoot and yell at the cattle to get them off the trough and moving again. The cattle were stressed and suffering in the heat, and soon they were getting out of hand. A few agitated beasts dodged between Soapy and Chunky. A few more followed as the men tried to contain them. Within seconds a steady stream began funnelling between the horses like sand through an hourglass. A few more seconds and it was a full-blown stampede. Cattle bolted in all directions. A wave charged the cruiser. I jammed it into gear and drove at them, madly beeping the horn in an attempt to contain the herd. Within seconds I was surrounded by the confused stampede. Clem swooped in the helicopter, bending the mob back around to the fence line for the horsemen.

Cameron's face looked like a branding iron that had just been pulled from the fire as he rode over to me shouting, 'Get outta the fuckin' Toyota!'

I had no idea what I'd done wrong, but if I'd had the power to disappear in that moment, I would have done it. I swung open the door and leapt out as Cameron jumped off Agro. He reached me in two steps, grabbed me by the shirt with his left hand and raised his right hand in a tightly clenched fist. I was waiting for the blow to send me back into the cruiser, but something stopped him. Instead, I was subjected to a burst of verbal venom accompanied by sprays of spit, his red face and quivering bottom lip centimetres from mine. Finally, he finished and let go of me. 'And pick up my fuckin' water container!'

I had so much adrenalin pumping through my arteries that my legs nearly collapsed. I turned to the back of the cruiser and noticed the container lying on its side, water spilling from it. I was desperate to ask if

I could fill my CamelBak, but I already knew the answer to my question.

Cameron had a few words with Daisy then shoved Agro's reins back in my hand and screamed off in the cruiser. I knew I hadn't done anything wrong. I knew it was his impatience to get the mob moving off the trough that had caused the cattle to blow out.

'Come on Kiwi,' Daisy said, as I climbed back on Agro. 'Hurry up.' I knew he was under pressure now.

We made a second, more successful, attempt to get the mob off the nest while Clem stood off in the helicopter ready for another blow out.

Soapy and Chunky had become sullen with the day's progress. With not much further to go to No.14 Bore, I left them on the tail and trotted Agro off over the golden Mitchell grass flat to put some space between us and to push some cattle over to the fence line. I probably wouldn't have bothered with the cattle if I had seen Clem out there in the sky.

Agro was only too happy to feel the reins release the bit in his mouth. He quickly got up to a gallop. There's no experience quite like riding a powerful animal when it's galloping as fast as it can. I became one with the horse and its movements. I felt as wild-willed and free as the horse could teach me to be. Heading out around the flank of the mob the wind tore past me and pulled at my Akubra. I forgot about my thirst and my frustration as my blood filled with a dose of adrenaline. A second later Agro stumbled in a hole and disappeared beneath me. Luck and quick reflexes saved me from face-planting into the baking dirt and snapping my neck. Instead, Agro's chest hit the ground with a sickening thud, and we skidded to a stop. As if by some miracle, I stayed in the saddle even as Agro's rear end went up into the air behind me with the momentum of our sudden stop. Agro rolled onto his right flank and onto my right leg. I tried desperately to free myself and get clear as the horse kicked at the air, but my foot was locked in its stirrup iron and the weight of the horse proved too much for me to get out from under. Then Agro rolled right on top of me as he tried to get up. I gasped a breath and tensed my body as hard as I could as I was sandwiched between the ground and 600 kilograms of sinew, muscle and bone. I thought I was going to be crushed to death. Luckily, Agro was only a small horse. It must have only taken him a few seconds to get to his hooves, but it felt like an eternity. Under the pressing weight, something dug deeply and sharply into my lower back.

Clem landed not far away from where I lay on the ground. I watched him running towards me with his water bottle as I lay there.

'That was impressive, Kiwi. Are you alright, mate? Can you stand up?'

I thought my back was broken. I tried to stand up, but my legs collapsed with a shooting pain in my lower back and my head spun with a ringing dizziness. 'No.' I winced with the pain.

'Just rest for a minute, mate. Have you got any water?' Clem asked.

'No.'

'Here take this then, I'll go and get your horse.' Clem dropped his water bottle beside me and ran after Agro. After a minute, I pushed myself into a seated position, then forced myself to stand in a hunched position. Clem came back with Agro and handed me the reins. 'Are you sure you're alright?' He was frowning concern at me. 'Just stay here, mate, and rest under that tree over there. Don't worry about yarding up,' he said, then he was off. I wish I'd listened.

I could hardly walk but forced myself back in the saddle and pointed Agro toward the men and the mob of cattle. Despite the agony I was in, I rode as fast as I could to catch up. That's what a tough bloke would do, I thought. Keep going. Surely, they'd see this heroic display and give me some respect?

Every step Agro took jarred my spine with an excruciating twinge, like part of the saddle had been lodged between two vertebrae. Years later I found out that I had herniated two discs in my lower back; I was lucky I hadn't broken it. I'd just caught up with the tail when everything seemed to happen at once. We got to the north-east corner of Joanundah Paddock where we had to move the cattle through two sets of gates and into the yards in Turkey Plain. The cattle soon moved through the gates. Soapy and Chunky galloped through to yard up. I did my best to catch up but met Cameron at the gates. He was fierce, and I suddenly wished I hadn't got back on the horse. A scathing stampede of swear words came at me. 'Fucking hurry up. Get up there and help them!' he screamed.

I was nearly falling off Agro by the time we got the cattle into the yards. I joined Pud and Chunky where they sat on the ground leaning against the yard rails. I told them about my accident and the severe pain I had in my lower back. I was concerned I needed medical attention and wasn't sure who to speak to with everyone in such foul moods.

Pud finished rolling a cigarette. 'I had a bad one once, couldn't stop this horse, and it was heading straight towards a gate. I thought it was going to run straight into it, but it stopped all of a sudden and sent me flying over it. Thought I was a goner for sure.' Pud spat the dust out of his mouth before lighting his cigarette.

'Yeah, I've fallen off a couple of times too,' Chunky added in his fat kid's voice. 'You get knocked down, and you get knocked back, but you never give up.' I wondered if his old man had taught him that one.

All the men gathered in the hot shade of the trees in the turkey's nest beside the yards for lunch. Clem spoke to me. 'That was a big crash, mate. Are you okay?'

Something resembling surprise tore across Cameron's face and he looked at me.

'I think I'm okay.' I lied. I didn't want to make a big deal out of it right there and then. I didn't realise Clem was encouraging me to speak up while I had the opportunity.

Daisy turned such a malicious glare on me I didn't dare say a word more. His upper lip curled with contempt and a tone filled with venom and blame poured from his mouth. 'No one cares about you out here, Kiwi.'

No one else spoke. The men looked at me and let their eyes fall to the ground. I was dumbfounded. Daisy's words silenced everyone. I hadn't known what tough was until now.

CHAPTER TEN

THE BREAKING AND THE MAKING

'The most glorious moments in your life are not the so-called days of success, but rather those days when out of dejection and despair you feel rise in you a challenge to life, and the promise of future accomplishments.'

—*Gustave Flaubert*

That night I lay on my bed sleepless and in pain, choked by the heat and smothered by the darkness. I felt ragged and run-down, all thought and emotion beaten out of me. I didn't know how I was going to face the dawn.

The following days were the most painful, physically and psychologically, that I had ever experienced.

'No one has any sympathy for you out here, Kiwi. Stop feeling sorry for yourself and get on with it. Hurry up!' Daisy hurled the words at me like spears with merciless vigour in the yards the next day.

The men looked at me with the same contempt and joined the harassment when it suited them. All of them but Pud, who looked ashamed at the other men's behaviour.

'C'mon move faster!' Daisy yelled.

I was working the race with Chunky, encouraging the calves to the branding irons and the knife. Every step I took shot a spasm of pain into my lower back that threatened to fold me in two. Climbing the rails into and out of the yards, knowing I couldn't out-manoeuvre a mad beast, endangered my life.

Cameron pulled up in his cruiser and scrutinised our progress with hard eyes. He walked towards me. 'What's wrong with you?' I felt the scorn in his eyes drill two contemptuous holes through me.

'I've got a sore back,' I said.

I knew Clem would have spoken to him about my riding accident back at the homestead. Or did he? Maybe he hadn't brought it up after Daisy's cold words.

'Sore back? Well, you need to toughen up then. Come on, get moving. You need to keep up with the other men. I heard about your accident; you want to take better care of the horses,' Cameron said, not an ounce of remorse or empathy slipping past his clenched teeth.

I couldn't believe it, the horse was okay, I was the one that was lucky to be alive.

I rode in the horse truck back to the homestead with Pud. I felt like the whole Station was against me. I knew it wasn't right.

'You should leave if you're finding it tough. If you like the work, there's plenty of other stations to get a job on. This isn't the best by a long shot,' Pud said.

I gazed at the setting sun over the scrub-covered landscape, at the empty dirt road ahead of us and at Pud. Wise words for a bushie, I thought. He was trying to save me. I wanted to quit, to just walk away, but I couldn't. He'd been a stockman for four years. It was in his blood. He was what was known as a ringer, his term as a jackaroo had been served. He knew the way the men were acting wasn't fair. He knew it was harsh.

I acknowledged his statement. I didn't know what to say. I'd come this far, if I walked away now, I felt like I might never have the guts to face another challenge this big. I didn't want to spend my life walking away from things every time they got hard.

'At least think about it mate. If you like it out here that much just come back next year at the start of the season when it's easier.' He lit his cigarette and wound down the window.

I didn't really like it at all, I just didn't see any other option.

I spent another night struggling to find a comfortable position on my mattress. I had moved it to the floor to give my back better support.

I suffered through short, fitful stretches of sleep between sweaty heat-intoxicated spasms and crazy dreams of work that became nightmares. I woke myself several times during the night in fits of shouting, confused and thinking I was in the yards being yelled at by the other men to work harder or faster. My pain churned, twisted and writhed within me like a beast with a thousand wounds. Through the long, hot dark hours I was forced to face the shadow side of my personality: anger, aggression, grief, feelings of abandonment and rejection, rage, confusion—dark and shadowy forces whirled around like demons inside me. I began to resent the others. I didn't want to see them, talk to them, listen to them. Starting a new life was proving to be harder than I thought. It was wearing me out. But then something inside me began to stir—an inner voice that said I had the power to change things. Mike's face appeared, and I recalled our final conversation.

* * *

Mike's reply was more pensive than usual when I told him I had settled on a date to leave. 'It's time,' he finally uttered quietly between laboured breaths. 'It's time for you to go. But before you do, I have to give you something.'

Mike opened the draw in the drum table and pulled out a boar's tusk and a miniature carved skull. He grasped each in a fist, closed his eyes and bowed his head. For a moment he was silent. After several long, deep breaths he spoke. 'This boar's tusk,' he said, as he rubbed his fingers over its smooth, ivory coloured surface, 'is the most precious thing I have to give you, Ben. I got it when I was a boy on a hunting trip with my father. It is from the first boar I killed with a knife and my own hands. The boar is my family totem, and a personal totem of mine. To the Gaelic people, boar hunting was a sacred pastime. Irish warriors were likened to boars. They are a symbol of strength and fierceness. This tusk will give you strength and courage.'

Mike shifted his attention to the skull and turned it in his hand. 'This skull has been everywhere with me, it used to keep me safe on the road, and keep danger away by warding off evil spirits. The skull is also sacred to all Gaelic people. They were kept as talismans against evil. Now it will keep you safe and bring you good luck on your journey and on the road ahead. Hold out your hands.'

He placed the tusk on my left palm and the skull on my right. 'Now close your hands. Can you feel the energy in them?'

'I think so.' I wasn't sure.

'Good. Keep them safe, and always keep them with you.'

Mike paused for a moment, as if considering something important. With laboured effort, he got up out of his La-Z-Boy, walked over to one corner of the room and picked up the sword that was standing there. He turned and brought the sword back with him and sat down with it across his lap. The hilt was a golden dragon's head with neck and wings. Flames leapt from its mouth up the blade.

'This sword is for you. You once told me that you used to have dreams when you were a little boy about a giant called Benjamin, Giant Benjamin you called him. You told me he could fly, and he used to help people. Well, this is my last gift to you. You will need this on your final quest. But understand this: the sword's usefulness depends upon the swordsman. You will see on the hilt the initials GB, I don't know why they are there, but I believe this sword is yours. It is a symbolic gift to defend yourself with on the trials that lay on the road ahead. You won't be able to take it with you, but it will be there when you most need it. All you have to do is think about it and remember what I tell you about it: only draw on it in the time of your greatest need. You will know when it is time to use it.'

Mike held the sword out with two hands, and I took it from him. Gripping the dragon's neck, I held up the sword in front of me. I was surprised at the weight of it and realised how strong and fearless a warrior had to be to wield such a weapon—perhaps even a giant. As I held up the sword, a dagger fell out of the bottom of the hilt.

'Ahh, I almost forgot to tell you, always keep something up your sleeve for surprise.'

I picked up the dagger and with a metallic clink slotted it back into the hilt.

'It won't be easy, but nothing worthwhile doing is,' Mike said.

I looked at Mike, unsure of what to say. 'Are you going to be alright?' I asked.

'Don't worry about me, I'll get over there as soon as I can.'

* * *

As I stared into the darkness, I wondered if I would ever see Mike again; wondered if he was okay and if he had made it to Australia.

I got up, turned the light on and started digging through my backpack for the boar's tusk. I knew I had it with me. A spasm of panic took hold when I couldn't find it. I turned my backpack inside out, emptying the contents onto the wooden floor. The tusk fell out, and I picked it up. I sat on my mattress with my back pressed against the wall and held the tusk for a moment, turning it in my hands and rubbing my fingers over its smooth ivory surface while thinking about that night. *'It won't be easy, but nothing worthwhile doing is.'* I got up and sat the boar's tusk on a shelf in my room and murmured to myself, 'Strength and courage.' I channelled my despair into fuelling change. I made the decision that night that I wouldn't just hang in there but that the harder stockcamp became, the better I would become at the job. Better than all of them if that's what they demanded. They would soon see who I really was, and so would I.

I began to observe how the men moved—a sort of slow gait that reserved their energy. I watched closely how they worked; the deliberate movements each of them had learnt and applied as they'd adapted to their particular role in stockcamp. I paid attention to how they spoke and what they talked about. I learnt their thoughts, their views, and their ideas about life and the world. I learnt their ways and became one of them. I knew most people wouldn't be able to sustain themselves out here. I knew the harsh environment: the work, the men, the bush, the climate, the myriad dangers that plagued our days, was too tough for the average man. Extra stockhands came and went.

Clouds passed across the burning pale blue sky like wisps of steam. The humidity pushed 80 percent. I gave silent thanks for every cloud that momentarily covered the sun. The wet season was approaching; it was the *build-up*. Before long, those clouds would bring rains I could only dream of. Then second round would be at its end. It would be time to go home. Until then, dust and sun were all we had.

'Enjoy the clouds but don't expect any rain,' Daisy remarked, when he saw me longingly gazing at them, 'if it rains, treat it as an unexpected gift.'

For some reason, I interpreted a metaphorical expression in Daisy's comment that day; a deeper meaning that lay beyond the physical world that bulldozed its way into a new comprehension of reality: *Appreciate all that you have and accept what you can't change. Change what you can. Then you'll be happy and content.* There was revelation in my suffering. I understood then, that to fully become one with the outback I needed to change some of my ideas about life. Instead of always wanting things to be different, I had to learn to accept some things as they were. To survive, I needed to evolve and adapt. I needed to think like an Aboriginal. I needed to make this land my home. Only then could I truly overcome the climate and learn to manage the work. In that moment, a profound truth unveiled itself to me. What I saw as hard, and at times tyrannical labour, was no longer, it just *was*. What I saw as tough men, became *just* men. Changing my view of one aspect of life seemed to encourage a change in my whole view of life and the world in general. It was a small change, but perhaps one with big consequences. I had a feeling then that what I was searching for might be absorbed in little bits and pieces—not all at once—but that they might add up to something. A bigger, and perhaps truer reality of life. And if I stayed alert and open, and travelled where my heart led, I would find what I was looking for, whatever that was. And so, by burning degrees, I found myself becoming one with that harsh and unforgiving void known as the outback.

CHAPTER ELEVEN

ARE YOU COMING BACK?

'The strongest of all warriors are these two—Time and Patience.'
— *Leo Tolstoy*

West Walhallow Paddock covers 1056 square kilometres. It was home to over 2800 head of cattle. I tightened my horse's girth strap, adjusted the stirrup leathers and climbed into the saddle for the day's muster.

Daisy rode up beside me. 'How you going there, Kiwi?'

'I think I'm starting to get the hang of this riding thing.'

'You'll get there, just remember what I taught you. The horse is only as good as its rider. I just wanted to let you know that Cameron was going to let you go, but I asked him to give you a chance and he has seen you getting better now. So, keep up the hard work.'

'Okay, thanks,' I said. Off he went to take up the lead.

I shortened my reins and manoeuvred Bluey, a white-grey gelding I had been given to ride, through the scrub. I wasn't sure whether to be grateful I still had a job or disappointed Cameron had been considering letting me go. Either way, I was surprised Daisy had stood up for me. I was finally earning a place in stockcamp. It was a strange thing, but I wanted to be liked by these men in the bush; to be seen as worthwhile, accepted, respected. To be one of them. That brotherhood seemed to fill a hole in my life where a family should have been.

After yarding up, we headed for the shade of a small cluster of coolabah trees. The heat of the day shimmered around us in a flock of corellas that streaked the pale sky in a squawking white cloud. A few of the men gathered sticks and kindled a fire for billy tea.

Daisy seemed more relaxed now the season was nearing its end. We'd toiled day in and day out, mustering, drafting, branding. Yet, those long hot days in the yards and in the saddle had begun to trot by and Daisy finally gave us word that we should be finished in two more weeks.

I knew I could relax a few minutes longer after lunch when Daisy pulled out his pouch of tobacco and rolled another cigarette. He compressed it firmly between his lips, lit the end and tilted his head back to inhale a full drag. A few of the other men rolled cigarettes and lay back in the shade. Soapy bum-puffed his smoke.

'So, are you going to come back next year, Kiwi?' Daisy asked.

'He has to get through this season first.' Pud shot a mischievous grin at me.

Soapy and Chunky propped themselves up as they waited for my reply. They seemed as surprised as I that Daisy had asked. Brains sat quietly, his eyes shifting with indifference as he took a drag from his cigarette.

'Don't know,' I replied. Strangely enough I didn't want to disappoint Daisy, even after his harshness, but a sense of pride galloped through my veins. I was worthy of being a stockman. It felt like a privilege and an honour to be asked, as if I had passed some kind of initiation. It made me *want* to come back. But as Pud had said, I had to make it through this season first.

Daisy brushed Pud's teasing aside. 'You'll enjoy it more next year, Kiwi. You've seen the hardest part of it now. The rest of it is more enjoyable and you'll have more time to learn. And we go to rodeos, you'd like to see some of them, wouldn't you?' He pushed his slipping spectacles back up, so they magnified his eyes in the usual unsettling way, but today I sensed a playful flicker in them.

I grinned. 'It sounds good.'

Cameron paid his usual visit to the yards. As he approached, Soapy was clutching his ribs and peeling the toenail off the big toe on his right foot. His eyes were red and wet. The men swallowed smirks and crowded around to acknowledge his misfortune and see his toe.

It started when a calf escaped from the branding race and ran back into the main yard with the cows. 'Catch that calf Soapy and bring it back for branding,' Daisy ordered. Off Soapy trotted. Before he knew it, he was surrounded by several *stirry* cattle. 'Look everyone, Soapy's about to get charged,' Daisy said. Our heads swivelled to see a spasmodic spectacle of uncoordinated movements from Soapy. He performed a little dance before our very eyes; he shuffled to the right then the left in a half-squatted position with his arms out wide like a crab scurrying over sand. As he braced for the impact, he executed an anxious tap dance. The beast ploughed into 100 kilograms of Soapy and carried on straight over the top of him. Brains finally let out a half-mad cackle. Pud shook his head.

'What's wrong with you, Soapy?' Cameron asked, when he saw Soapy.

'Just got charged by a fucking cow didn't I,' Soapy moaned.

Despite the pain we knew he was in, we all started laughing.

'You'll just have to be faster next time then won't you, Soapy.' Cameron flashed a rare grin at the other men while Soapy stared at his toe.

The men roared with laughter.

'Brains you're coming back with me,' Cameron yelled. He turned to me. 'You can come with me too, Ben.'

'So, how're you finding station life, Ben?' Cameron asked, as he floored the accelerator. I was seated between him and Brains. 'Are you coming back next year?' It was odd, but I thought I sensed a tone of respect and understanding in his voice I hadn't heard before.

'He has to get through this season first,' Brains said.

'He'll get through it, Brains. Won't you, Beno?' I was amazed. Cameron was speaking up for me. 'He enjoys it out here. Don't you?' Cameron smiled. It was an awkward smile, not something his face took naturally to, but he had shared it and that seemed a big deal.

'Ahh, yeah?'

I didn't want to agree or disagree to anything just then. In fact, I didn't even want to think about it at that time. Where was this sudden change in their attitudes coming from? Had I created all of this?

Since he was in a talkative mood, I asked him about his life.

'From the Northern Territory, been working with cattle for about 20 years now. Been managing Walhallow for the past five years,' he said matter-of-factly.

I tried to imagine what life out here was like when he was younger and found myself equating his character with the desert—hot, hard, tough and rough.

We talked some more about the Station. I asked about first round and the beginning of the season. He reiterated what Daisy had said: rodeos, campdrafting, and different work to do. 'It's nice and green too,' he said. It was clear to me that they did want me back. I thought Cameron seemed alright after that; still a hard man but alright.

A long, wide, grey sheet fell to earth in the distance. Dusk slid into night. I sat at the entrance to the jackaroos' quarters watching the ominous glow of distant fires. The high-pitched chirp of crickets singing expectantly for the coming rains filled the emptiness with hope. The air smelled of the earth come to life. A time of great change and transformation was beginning in the outback. It seemed like a contradiction, but it felt like there was more life in that empty desert than in a populated city; a sort of energy that moved in and through everything. Something mysterious was at work. I was consoled by the fact that it did rain in the outback. But I learnt the rains didn't cool the land for long. That sacred drop of moisture steamed back up from the baking land and sent the humidity soaring.

'You see any of those black cockatoos out here yet, Kiwi?' Denis leant over the counter at the rec club as if he was about to tell me a secret. He pushed a Powerade towards me. 'It's on me,' he said. He gave me a wink.

I wasn't sure if he was having me on about the black cockatoos. I knew there were white cockatoos, I'd seen them in Queensland.

'They've got the red on their tails; red-tailed black cockatoos they are,' he said. 'I've seen a couple around here lately. You know the rains are coming when they start gathering around the Station. How about those budgies? You see them yet?'

'The green and yellow ones?' I asked, wondering why this old-timer was talking to me about budgies.

'Yeah, yeah that's them. They're beautiful, aren't they?'

I nodded. I'd seen several large flocks of budgerigars around the Station, flying exquisitely through the air, their iridescent feathers flashing and shimmering in the sun as they whirled in dancing ribbons through the sky. I didn't even know they were a flock bird until then and, when I thought about it, it seemed cruel to keep such a free-spirited creature as a pet in a cage. Come to think of it, it was kind of like keeping a person locked in a house. Maybe that was what I had been before I left New Zealand—housed in my own country's culture, locked in a singular way of thinking and viewing life and the world. My life before was beginning to feel insignificant, just a mere stepping-stone. My escape from that cultural prison had given me the freedom to explore and learn who and what I really was.

Daisy rode up to me while we prepared to walk the last mob of weaners out of the House Yards and up to No. 6 Bore for the season.

'How you going, Kiwi?' he asked.

'Good.' Daisy wasn't a man of pleasantries, so I guessed he wanted to tell me something.

'You want to lead this mob?'

I was surprised. I had no experience leading cattle, especially a thousand head of weaners.

'Yeah okay, but I don't know what to do?'

'That's okay, it's easy. Just walk them out slowly. Not too fast otherwise they'll get up to a trot and take off. Make plenty of noise and wave your arm a bit so they know you're there. And most importantly don't let them get past you. If they do, they'll bolt. You have to learn to think like a stockman, Kiwi. Try and work out what those cattle are thinking because that's how you know where to be on your horse. Go on then, get up in the lead and we'll let this mob out of the yards and get them moving.'

I gripped my reins and got in position. Chunky opened the gates and a steady stream of cattle flowed out. Daisy gave me a hand to get the lead under control and steady the flow while the other men came up the flanks, then he peeled off to join them. Slowly, I walked my horse ahead of the mob. I was glad they were cooperating. I wasn't sure how in the hell I was supposed to keep them together otherwise, but it appeared the cattle had responded well to Harry's weaner tailing and they began to follow me. Now and then, an excited beast would try to get past or the lead animals would quicken their pace but, with a yell or a whistle and a wave of my arm as I manoeuvred my horse, they held position. After a while I realised it wasn't so hard being in the lead. In fact, it was pretty enjoyable.

I glanced back at the tail and saw Soapy and Chunky ride up beside Daisy. I saw their lips moving. Soapy shook his head and Chunky stared ahead at me. Neither of them had ever led a mob of cattle before. A word from Daisy saw the men fall back to their posts.

Thick scrub lined either side of the dusty track that led through Bitumen Paddock. We walked all the weaners out of the House Yards and up that road to No. 6 bore. It wasn't easy going on the flanks where Daisy, Pud and Brains worked, or the dusty tail where Soapy and Chunky were working. While I rode along the track, I thought about how much I had improved in every aspect of station life. I felt confident in the saddle, and I was sure of myself in the yards. I worked with a fresh enthusiasm and much enhanced ability compared with my first hot, dusty day on the Station. My strength had increased tenfold; my muscles were hard as iron. I began thinking I'd come back next season. There was something in this life that agreed with me.

Two hours later we had the mob at No. 6 bore.

'Well done, Kiwi. See, I told you it's not so hard.'

Later that week we mustered the last mob from Cattle Creek Paddock to the House Yards for drafting. It would be our final few days in the yards. It had already been a long day when we hit the home straight. I brought my horse to a halt and observed the scene: in the distance, the helicopter flew just above the horizon like a giant insect scouring the bush for food. The sky, broad and reaching beyond the imagination, was painted with every possible shade of salmon, crimson, amber and orange as the sun kissed the horizon like a humongous drop of gold melting into the endless smelter of the outback. Pud rode into the scene on the motorbike, picking his way through the scrub and a sea of golden Mitchell grass. Silhouettes of the men on horseback rode through clouds of dust kicked up by the cattle, hooting and whistling at the mob. Rays of light shone like swords through the haze. It suddenly hit me I could make this way of life my own; that I could forget about the world outside of that desert and vanish into the raw, real, simplicity of a life in the wilderness.

I felt alive. I hoped to never forget the profound beauty of that moment; I hoped it would echo through eternity.

I was riding Brigalow, a tall black gelding. Earlier in the day Daisy had swapped horses with me because Brigalow had gone lame. The horse had injured its hoof. Brigalow was Daisy's favourite horse, he rode him every muster, and he had given me strict instructions to take it easy on him. I was pushing up the tail. While we made our way along the southern fence line of Cattle Creek Paddock, an old cow bailed up. It turned to face me. I rode at it shouting to get it moving. The cattle are normally intimidated enough by a man on a horse. Instead of moving back into the mob, the beast lowered its head and charged. It hit Brigalow square in the chest. The horse reared up as it stepped back from the blow. I was caught off guard. I thought I was going to be thrown from the saddle, but I managed to hold on and regain my balance. Brains was lagging on the tail. When he saw what was happening, he rode his horse directly at the old cow. Outnumbered, the beast snorted, tossed its head and bolted back into the mob.

'Come on, Kiwi, get this fuckin' tail moving,' Brains snarled.

'Why don't you do some work,' I growled back through gritted teeth.

A few days earlier Brains had tried to pick a fight with me. I hadn't backed down and the other men thought I knew something about fighting to pull a stunt like that. I had just called Brains' bluff. Or so I thought until the other men told me what a dogged scrapper he was. I knew then that I might not be able to bluff him again.

I was no fighter. I didn't like it. I'd been in street fights back home, in self-defence and in defence of mates. I'd learnt how to throw a good punch and make it hit its mark, but it wasn't who I was. Back then, I had listened to Mike's stories of the fights he had been in when he was a gang member and painted them as heroic feats. Once he had described in detail, taking down six men that had turned up at his house to deliver a severe message to him. He walked outside and met them in his front yard. They surrounded him. One by one, he broke noses, teeth, jaws, ribs, snapped arms and legs back at their joints and watched as the men limped away. He was in his prime then, and he had a fierceness in him that I would never have. But Mike never went looking for fights. He emphasised the point by sharing with me a story about his best friend who had been stabbed in the neck with a broken bottle at a bar over a passing comment; how he had watched him die in his arms in less than a minute. But back then, fighting was a newfound vent for the anger I carried inside. It felt good to let it out. Fortunately, Mike had drummed into me what a waste of time and talent fighting was. That it didn't prove anything, and the only thing anyone got out of it was broken bones, scares, disfigurement and maiming. Most fights nearly always involved alcohol and started over something that wasn't worth fighting about. He'd always impressed on me that I was smarter than that. That life was too valuable to throw it away scrapping in the dirt with men that weren't very intelligent. The fight with my stepfather had left me scared about fighting a man that doesn't know when to stop. I feared equally being badly beaten and being pushed into beating someone until they couldn't fight back. I didn't want to be pushed that far; I was afraid of that animal inside of me.

'Don't get smart to me,' Brains said, his voice full of venom. 'I'll smash ya head in.'

Anger rose in me. I tensed, ready to fight him, and stared into his eyes. That was the last straw for Brains. He rode his horse straight into Brigalow's left flank and my leg. 'You wanna fight do ya?'

The image of my stepfather's face the night I thought he would kill me screamed through my mind. I jerked at Brigalow's reins and the horse backed up. My heart was thumping, my blood was pumping. I wanted to finish it right there and then.

Daisy came from out of nowhere, riding straight into the side of Brains' horse with a thunk. 'You wanna fight, Brains? You can fight me,' he bellowed.

Brains nearly jumped clear out of his saddle, then he straightened his back and pushed his head forward. 'I'll fight you.'

Daisy's right hook connected with Brains' jaw, squarely across his left cheek. Brains' head swivelled then returned to face Daisy. He was as red as a branding iron. The surrounding air seemed to tense to exploding point as the two men glared at each other, then Brains spun his horse about and trotted off. I heard him swearing and noticed he was starting to cry.

'Go and do some work and don't make me come back here again or there'll be hell to pay,' Daisy yelled at his back. He turned to me, 'Don't worry about him, Kiwi. He's just upset he has to ride a horse today.' He trotted away.

It was dark by the time we made the House Yards later that evening. Overhead, the stars spoke of parallel worlds in the moon-less sky. Distant storm clouds billowed ominously over the Tablelands, illuminated now and then as Thor struck his anvil in the hot night. I knew I had found the last frontier.

CHAPTER TWELVE

BACK TO THE SUNSHINE COAST

'March on. Do not tarry. To go forward is to move toward perfection. March on, and fear not the thorns, or the sharp stones on life's path.'

—*Khalil Gibran*

I shook Cameron's hand before I got out of the cruiser at Barkly Homestead. It had been a long, drowsy drive down the Tablelands Highway seated between him and Brains. I could hardly believe that Brains and I were the last two men from stockcamp to leave the Station for the season. Daisy and Pud would be staying on over the wet.

'So, you're coming back next year?' Cameron asked in his sharp but now mellow voice.

'I'll be back,' I said, as I shook his hand.

Brains let out a manic chuckle. 'The Kiwi likes it!'

I'm not quite sure why I said it. Maybe I really did think I would be back, maybe it was just the easiest thing to say at that moment. Whatever the answer was I had the feeling, at least when I said it, that I needed to come back.

I grabbed my pack and waved as they drove off. It was early in the afternoon. I turned and looked at the sign of the thirsty sweating camel that signified Barkly Homestead and walked inside. I had a few hours to kill before the coach to Mt Isa arrived. I dumped my pack, strode over to the counter and asked Kris for a beer. He reeled in his distant gaze to focus on me. 'So, you survived then? Didn't think ya would; not many people do. Looks like I owe Ozzie some money next time I see him then,' Kris said, as he slid a beer across the counter.

'Money?'

'Yeah, we put a wager on to see if you'd make it to the end of the season. I betted against you.'

'Thanks mate.'

'Don't worry, mate. I lost, not you.'

I nodded, pulled out a stool and sat at the bar.

'How'd ya find it then?' Kris asked, while he polished a glass.

'Bloody hot.'

'You wait until the wet season hits. Then it gets hot.' He threw the bar cloth over his shoulder and walked off. 'The beer's on me.'

It was just after midnight when the Greyhound coach from Darwin pulled into Barkly Homestead. I yelled goodbye to Kris before I strolled out the door of the roadhouse.

'We'll see ya next year then?' Kris called out.

I glanced back and nodded. 'Enjoy the wet season.'

I swung my pack into the undercarriage then climbed aboard the coach. The driver pulled back onto the dark desert highway, and we rolled away into the sultry night. I put in my earphones and gazed out the window into the blackness. It wasn't until then that I stepped out of that world and back into the one I was returning to. What I didn't know just then, and wouldn't know until many years later, was that I had left one foot firmly planted in that other world, the consequences of which would change the course of my life. Mike had told me that anything was possible, and I wanted to prove to myself that anything *was* possible. For me, that was a freedom I could only dream of. As the bus traversed the dark continent, I realised I had to believe in myself before anything could be possible; I had to free myself. The outback seemed to be a good test of whether a man believed in himself or not. My head lulled with exhaustion, and I closed my heavy eyes.

I arrived back on the Sunshine Coast on December 16. Biruta met me at the bus station in Caloundra. 'So, you came back in one piece then?' she said, after releasing me from her motherly hug.

'Only just.'

I began recounting my adventure in the outback from the day I arrived. Biruta was impressed.

'It sounds like you enjoyed it?'

'I don't know if enjoyed is quite the right word.' We both laughed.

'Time for a holiday now?'

'It's time to hang up my boots.'

Everything was just the way I had left it in the beach shack. It was like returning home, a feeling I hadn't experienced in years. While I looked at the bleached shells and gnarled pieces of driftwood I had collected on my walks along Golden Beach, I was shuttled back to my first sunny weeks on the Sunshine Coast. How could two months feel like a lifetime? What had happened to time out there in the centre of Australia?

As I unpacked, I unwrapped a small piece of cloth protecting a gidgee stone I'd found at a set of yards on some remote part of the Station. I turned the stone slowly in my hand, rubbing its glossy hard surface. A gidgee stone is an ochre-red chiselled stone that's been baked extra hard and shiny by the intense sun of the outback. That gidgee stone seemed to be a marker; a token from the new world, and a portal back to it.

Stephanie flew over from New Zealand just before the New Year. A flood of forgotten memories and emotions surged through me when I saw her.

'Hi.' She smiled, almost shyly, I thought.

'Hi.' I smiled back at her, and we hugged. 'How was the flight?'

'Good, how are you?'

'I'm good, thanks.' I felt awkward, as if a pane of glass separated us.

We caught the train into the city and made our way to the hotel I had booked. On the way, Stephanie handed me a small parcel. 'Merry Christmas.'

'Wow, thanks.' I felt terrible. I hadn't even thought of getting her a Christmas present.

I opened the perfectly folded paper to find a small magnetic chess set inside. It was stylish and compact, made of a matt finished metal, perfect for travelling. I recalled how well she knew me; how similar our tastes were.

Over the weeks that followed I took Stephanie to the places on the Sunshine Coast I had fallen in love with, in particular Noosa and the National Park that covered the headland in subtropical rainforest, tumbling over boulders and down into secluded bays. The Park was home to an exquisite variety of wildlife that I knew would impress her: koalas, goannas, snakes, huge spiders, and the colourful rainbow lorikeets that squawk and screech, flying swiftly through the trees while kookaburras laugh at the sunset. We spent long days on the white sandy shores of Golden Beach, exploring with picnic lunches, and lounging in the beach shack.

'When are you coming back to New Zealand?' Stephanie asked one evening back at the beach shack.

'I don't know.' I had been avoiding the awkward conversation, but I really did have no idea. All I knew was that I had been given an intriguing insight into a world I hadn't known before, and I wasn't about to let it go.

A few nights earlier I'd had a vivid dream that I had returned to New Zealand but once I was there, I couldn't get back to Australia. Strange, invisible bonds held me captive. I felt trapped, cornered, and tricked. The premonition scared me. Part of me was afraid to return in case my dream came true. I had decided to accept it as a warning from my subconscious.

She gazed at me. In the mirrors of her eyes, I could see my own sadness, trembling loneliness and fear of the unknown. It wasn't that I didn't want to be with her. I just couldn't go back and face everything else that came with her.

Stephanie's disappointment and my distance tore apart our last days together. I knew it was my fault. Part of me no longer had time for *us*. I didn't want her to be a part of my new life. She was a reminder, albeit a good one, of a miserable past. A past that I wished to bury.

'Take care, Ben. I hope you find what you're looking for,' she said, as we sat in the departure lounge. Tears clouded the blue sky of her eyes like a storm was approaching. She wiped them away. I was lost for words. 'I'm sorry this didn't work out, that your holiday wasn't… what you hoped it would be. I'm sorry I can't come back.'

A sad, half-smile shaped her soft lips as the last call for her flight was announced. 'I've got to go.'

My heart sunk into a lake of despair as I watched her walk away; even in that final moment, I wasn't able to tell her how much she meant to me. I'd just lost my best friend.

It was the last week in February when I boarded the bus to the Northern Territory. Through the dusty, desert kilometres I reflected with a sort of melancholy upon the past two months on the Sunshine Coast. A part of me yearned to make it my home. Its comfortable, homely coastal lifestyle churned the deep waters of belonging within me. But I had begun to feel a hunger, a gnawing dissatisfaction with the answers provided by comfort, materialism and scientific progress. A hunger that came from the wildness of the outback and a craving for the inner life that it had sparked. I deeply regretted pushing Stephanie away. I had missed her company dearly after she left. I doubted we'd ever be together again. I reclined in my seat and closed the curtains on that chapter of my life. My thoughts drifted into a lingering uncertainty about what lay ahead. I had no sure ideas or dreams. I just knew I wanted a life—the kind I could look back on one day and know I'd lived it well.

CHAPTER THIRTEEN

YEAR OF THE OUTBACK

'In my solitude I have pondered much on the incomprehensible subjects of space, eternity, life and death.'
—Alfred Russel Wallace

'So, why'd you come back?' Ozzie gave me a perplexed look, as if to question my sanity.

'I wanted to see what the place looked like after the wet season.' I didn't try to explain to Ozzie the quest I was on; I didn't think he would understand.

I had big expectations of what the Territory was going to look like after months of rain; it didn't disappoint. What lay before me was the most wild and beautiful scene of solitude I had ever witnessed. Below the cockpit of the Cessna, the dusty, arid landscape I left had morphed into a sea of emerald-green that reached to the distant horizon. Milky-brown threads of flooded creeks criss-crossed the plains through wooded glades where they swelled into small lakes and wetlands. Flocks of magpie geese flew across the landscape in black and white chevrons among pale blue-grey lines of brolgas.

I was fortunate Cameron had sent Ozzie to collect me from Barkly Homestead in the Cessna; most of the men had never flown in the plane before. I took it as a token of his respect and appreciation that I had returned.

The season began with a medley of new men from across the country: New South Wales, South Australia, and Tasmania. They were young, fit and champing at the bit. The newly formed stockcamp bonded with a variety of jobs: kilometres upon kilometres of fencing, scrub clearing, painting, repairing bores, building yards and other odd jobs around the homestead like mowing the lawns and gardening. A photo of me working in the sheds at this time was later published in the R.M. Williams *OUTBACK* magazine as part of a story about Colonial Agriculture, the company that leased the Station. Walhallow was the company's largest breeding station with 36,000 head and its only station in the Northern Territory.

Over the weeks and months that followed, I watched the new men learn the hard, honest lifestyle of the stockman. Several stockhands came and went. For the men that stayed, station life gradually became the lifeblood of each of them as the land moulded and hardened them to meet its needs and demands. Eventually, stockcamp became a fine-tuned beef-processing machine. We worked the Station all hours of the day, all days of the week. We mustered paddock after paddock, churning tens of thousands of head of cattle through the yards, branding thousands of calves and weaners.

Under the watchful eye of Daisy, my skill and confidence as a stockman quickly grew in all aspects of station life. I became one of the most skilled men in stockcamp: an accomplished rider, professional fencer, effective musterer and an expert in the yards with the cattle. One day I asked Daisy why he was so hard on me the previous year. He apologised and explained that he had to know I was going to stick around before he taught me anything. Too many blokes came out here and left after only a few weeks. Because I had stayed, he had taught me how to survive: in the bush, in the yards with the animals, and in stockcamp with the men. He had toughened me up and made a stockman out of me because he had to. At times he put pressure on the other men, yet I never saw him be so consistently hard or push anyone as much as he did me, as if he knew I always had more to give. I had to remind myself not to take his treatment personally at times. He had a job to do, or he had Cameron to answer to. Daisy was a tyrant when he was against you and, as I found out, an army when he was on your side. I was accepted into the stockcamp pack.

Daisy's determination to find out just what I was made of pushed me to my very limits. As a reward, he gave me opportunities and responsibilities the other men weren't permitted. Any complaints from the men that I was receiving special treatment was soon hushed. Daisy believed I had a head stockman in me.

After Pud left the Station, I took over the job of the motorbike man. It was one of the best things that could have happened to me. It gave me freedom and solitude, and I savoured every moment.

Every day I traversed hundreds of kilometres of untouched wilderness, checking fence lines and mustering. I crossed vast plains, pressed through scrub-covered country and swampy woodlands, and cut along red, rocky ridges and escarpments to take in breathtaking views of a grand scale. I discovered dry creek beds and explored their carved paths to waterholes. I rode through the vast open spaces of the downs country where the grass brushed the handlebars on my motorbike.

Out there, scattered ghost gums, prickly acacia, turpentine wattle and spinifex bordered golden oceans of Mitchell grass that rolled and undulated into the big, cloudless blue dream of the arching skies forming the roof of the Barkly Tablelands.

As the motorbike man, I spent a lot of time working with Clem, who was in his second year as Walhallow's mustering pilot. We got along. He remembered my horse riding accident in Joanundah the previous season and the treatment I had received. He seemed to respect that I had returned despite it. We quickly became an effective mustering team.

Clem taught me the art of the muster—how the helicopter and the bike worked in harmony, sweeping paddocks simultaneously, using speed and positioning during yarding up. Clem was always patient with me and his skill as a mustering pilot never ceased to impress. He was a fearless flyer, and his aerobatic prowess privileged me to the most incredible mustering scenes. I watched him chase animals over the flat, flying just metres above them before rounding on them and giving them a rub with the skids. With mind-boggling velocity, he could swoop down to push a mob along, then accelerate back into the sky. He raced over treetops then disappeared among them, rotor blades spinning centimetres from branches. Hammerhead turns, quick stops, steep approaches, 180's, 360's, zigzags; I watched the helicopter yaw, pitch, and roll as Clem pushed hundreds of head of cattle through the bush, across deep creek beds and watering holes, over the plains and into the yards.

I learnt to control the bike with reflex, skill and intuition to move the maddest cattle in the scrub, and I had to be alert, nimble and surefooted to clown the animals that refused to move for bike or helicopter.

I learnt how to *throw* a beast; how to pull a half ton animal off balance and hobble it so that it could be dealt with later. Throwing a beast involved getting close enough to get hold of its tail and then yanking it towards its charging head to pull it off balance. I had close shaves, twisting, bending, smashing and bashing my body like a rag doll coming off the bike in more ways and more times than I can remember. I hit logs, rocks and termite mounds hidden in the long grass. I flew over creek beds that appeared out of nowhere. I chased dingoes away from calves mid-muster, had near misses with kangaroos, and nasty moments with deadly snakes. Often, I courted danger because danger was one of the few things strong enough to help me forget my past.

Stockcamp was allowed time off the Station to compete in campdraft and rodeo events. I became a competent campdrafter and rode a bullock in the biggest rodeo event in the Northern Territory—the Brunette Races. Chunky gave me some of the least encouraging words imaginable before such a ride. 'Well, if there's one thing you can be sure of, Kiwi, the ground will always catch you.' Thanks, Chunky.

Station workers from all over the country came together to compete at the campdrafting events held in the Northern Territory. Campdrafting involves riding into a small yard called the *camp* containing six to eight steers or heifers, cutting out one beast then manoeuvring it to the front of the camp. The rider blocks and turns the beast two or three times to prove to the judge that they have the beast under control. The rider then calls for the gate. Once the gate to the main yard, or arena, opens the rider works the beast around a figure of eight course, often at full gallop, manoeuvring inside and outside of the beast to steer it around the course. The course is completed when the beast is guided through two cones—the *gate*. The rider has less than a minute to perform the entire round. Points are accumulated through each stage of the process but only awarded if the round is successfully completed by putting the beast through the final cones. I enjoyed the sport as much for its horsemanship and the chance to compete against other stockman from around the country, as for the chance to get back in the saddle.

Cameron chose a small, agile and sure-footed bay mare named Arcadia for me to compete with in the campdrafting events. She had a white stripe between her eyes and a white sock on her right hind leg. The mare knew how to campdraft because Cameron had spent time training her. After competing in several drafts with Arcadia, I learnt how to handle the lively horse and we became an effective team.

It was at the Tennant Creek campdraft and rodeo, in November, when I was introduced as 'New Zealand's best campdrafter' by the commentator, Rod. It was more of a practical joke than any truth that I was aware of, but it was the best run I ever had in a campdraft, and I was applauded heartily by the small crowd of seasoned veterans who watched from around the arena. The irony was that I tied equal third with my old foe, Brains, who now worked at Brunette Downs Station. To decide the winner, one man was to ride again. Brains was chosen and was awarded an extra point for a successful run. I was heartily disappointed with the outcome, but it was a fair decider. He could have just as easily missed out. That evening Brains found me at the rodeo and bought me a beer, congratulating me on my run. He confided in me that he was nervous as hell about stuffing up his run and losing to me. We made our peace.

I finally met Elvis, a charming young man with a beaming smile of white teeth, thin as a blade of Mitchell grass, yet one of the most dexterous stockmen I'd ever seen work in stockcamp. We got along well. Elvis' brother, Warren, also joined stockcamp for a time but it wasn't long before the two men went walkabout.

The men suffered body breaking injuries through the first round. Accident prone Soapy broke his collarbone when he was thrown off his horse early in the season. Ronnie was admitted to hospital with ongoing health problems from his heavy drinking life as a Queensland sheep station cook. He often used to tell me he was 'fucked'. I could see it. Soapy took over as Station cook while his collar bone healed. Chunky was knocked unconscious by a gate that a cow jumped into while loading the road train. He was out for several months after the incident with jaw and tooth reconstruction and plastic surgery. Our Tasmanian had to have his forehead stapled up after being head butted in a mad cow ride at a rodeo. Daisy caught a hoof blow to the head while breaking in the new geldings. Together, they proved station work was the most dangerous occupation in the country, with the highest rate of injuries and fatalities.

The wretched heat of the outback slowly gave way to winter dry season days; days bitten with pale skies stretching away over the parched wilderness. Towards the end of first round, the respect I'd hard won from the men early in the season began to evaporate. Several of the men in stockcamp, even Daisy, at times, became resentful and began to criticise my absence from yard work. As the motorbike man I was doing the 'bludger's job'.

One afternoon, on my way back to the homestead after checking a paddock's fence lines, I stopped in Creswell Paddock to offer help. Stockcamp were branding calves from a freshly mustered mob. They were just finishing up when I got there.

'Here's blister,' said the Tasmanian.

'What do you mean?' I asked.

'Shows up when all the hard work's done.' A few of the men murmured in agreement.

A hit of adrenalin galloped through my veins, I wanted to grab him by his shirt and put his nose on the other side of his face to remind him of his place.

Daisy caught my glare and was quick to growl at the men. 'Stop ginning around you lot and get on with it.' He turned to me. 'There's a couple of old cows in the yard over there, Kiwi, grab the axe off the back of the cruiser and take care of them. We'll be over in a minute to drag them into the turkey's nest.'

I knew what Daisy was doing, I nodded assent and walked over to the cruiser to get the axe. I picked it up and clenched the wooden stock in my hand, the muscles in my arm felt as strong and hard as the wood. This was a chance to release some frustration.

Though an axe or a sledgehammer was the usual way of things, I never felt good about finishing a beast off that way. Some of the old cows were on their last legs when they hit the yards. Their wizened, decrepit, bony bodies couldn't handle the stress and it was often enough to finish them off. They'd lie down and couldn't get back up. There was nothing for it but to end their days. It wasn't a nice thing to do, but we didn't waste bullets out here, not unless Soapy was shooting.

The first blow sent the cow's head down into a salivating mess and its back legs started to kick in spasms. A couple more blows and it all stopped. I hit the old cow a few extra times to make sure it was definitely dead, caving in its skull a little more with each blow. Brutal? Yes. But life in the outback was brutal. The brutality taught me the value of life, and how to survive.

When I returned to the Station, I had been hoping to bury my past in the vast empty landscape that surrounded me. I wanted to knock it on the head like the cow and be done with it. But I was beginning to realise that I could no more knock my past on its head and bury it than I could change it. It was irrevocably a part of me.

Daisy brought the cruiser around. We chained the carcasses by the back legs and dragged them off to the turkey's nest, depositing them next to swollen, baking bodies, half decayed beasts, bleached bones and dry hides of long deceased animals. It was a stinking graveyard of carrion.

I wandered back to the bike, jumped on the kick start and took off down the dirt road into the watercolours of the late afternoon. The golden ocean of the Tablelands seemed to reach beyond time and space, putting everything in perspective again.

I was contemplating leaving the Station to make my way back over to the east coast and dive into the Coral Sea when one of the borerunner positions became available. Being a borerunner was the last thing I had on my mind when I returned to the Station. The job held responsibility and entailed spending a lot of time on my own, but it exercised a freedom that couldn't be experienced in any other aspect of station life, other than checking fence lines on the motorbike.

Denis took me out on the run to teach me the new position, and how to survive on my own. There were two bore runs on the Station which were split into three-day cycles. In those three days I would cover hundreds of kilometres and service half the Station's bores, visiting every bore on my round twice a week. There were 90 bores in total. All ran mono pumps that were sunk hundreds of metres into the ground to pump up the water. The other half of the Station's bores were taken care of by Andy, a young chap my own age from Canberra. I didn't know it then, but Andy and I were to become good friends.

While I learnt about the bore run from Denis, we chatted at length about life in the outback, its transcendent scenes and the life-changing experiences that could only transpire from spending time in the heart of that vast empty wilderness. We also spoke at length about life in general. At one moment Denis was talking about the outback and how he thought it was God's cathedral, then, in the next breath he was asking me to make sure he was buried in a coffin with a life-size picture of Julia Roberts on top of him. I wasn't sure if he was being serious or not. He was the driest comedian I'd ever encountered, and sarcasm was one of his specialties. Yet he was one of the most interesting characters I'd ever met.

Denis had morphed from a runaway youth to a dust-covered drover in the far north, experiencing the brutality of the Congo along the way. He still harboured bitter memories of a war fought and lost in Rhodesia, which had seen so much destruction of the land and the wildlife that roamed the veld. For him, the vast, lonely, beautiful Barkly Tablelands had become a sanctuary from that useless, man-made horror. He was sunburned to a cinder and removed cancerous growths from his skin with a razor blade.

His crass ways and outspoken manner aside, I thought of Denis as the old gentleman of the outback. He was a man who cared; who had understanding and a wisdom that came from a rare knowledge of life.

One day Denis told me about the pearling industry up in the Top End and how the pearl farms stretched west, through the remote Kimberley, all the way to a place called Broome, in Western Australia. I was fascinated. Working on a pearl farm in some other remote part of Australia gilded my romantic ideas of a life at sea. I determined I would get there one day.

It was during those months in the wilderness on the bore run that I had my 21st birthday. I quietly celebrated the occasion at a rodeo at

Daly Waters, which claimed to be Australia's most remote pub. Andy asked me if I could be anywhere that day where would I choose to be. I told him I'd choose to be right where I was.

I watched the men struggle through second round as the furnace of the outback smelted their mettle and the land became cracked and barren. Entire paddocks turned into little more than dust in the blistering heat. Daisy wanted my assistance—they needed me. I told them no.

As the months on the run passed, I observed the dramatic cycle of the seasons in the outback; a great synthesis of beginnings and endings, comings and goings, death and rebirth. If there was one thing I could be certain of in life, it was change.

One day I found myself gazing over the landscape that had once been so tormentingly harsh and saw an uncommon beauty in it all. Those few magic moments set the inhospitable hours with diamond minutes. Where the sudden recognition of all this reckless beauty came from, born out of such a harsh and unforgiving environment, I wasn't sure. Perhaps it was the time of year, but it seemed more likely that the way I viewed it had changed. The way I viewed everything was beginning to change.

Like a seed taking root and sprouting leaves, I felt a growing awareness of life and what it meant to be alive. That awareness flourished in the absolute silence and solitude of the outback, a silence that was so complete and unparalleled that a deep peace began to resonate within me. A process of healing had begun. I pondered life's mysteries, reassessed my frame of mind and imagined what sort of life I might like to live moving forward. As those golden days passed with never a cloud, I learnt to smile at the dark forebodings of days gone by. I was assuming a newer—and perhaps truer—perspective of things.

Some days I wondered if life had ceased to exist outside of the wilderness that had become my cradle, or if I wanted to return to that life. As I gazed out across a timeless landscape, it became harder to comprehend that outside of that immense and quiet interior, there was a world fretting over its business: confused and complicated cities of traffic and pollution, constant noise and endless hordes of people rushing to and fro like economic tidal waves.

But man is a social creature, not made to spend a life alone roaming the wilderness, forever searching.

Something in me cracked. It wasn't one of my finest days. A lingering niggle that I couldn't shake, something old and yet something new that I hadn't accepted, had been bothering me for most of the day. Unable to decipher what it was, my patience waned in the shadow of the question.

Earlier that day, I had replaced three belts on three different bores. I was trying to run another onto the head of a bore the way Denis had shown me when it came off the head and whipped my upper thigh at high velocity. It was a trigger that decoded in a split second the mood that had been with me all day, translating into anger. I clasped at the inside of my upper thigh where blood seeped through my shredded jeans from a throbbing wound just below my groin. Wincing with the pain, I stomped over to the motor and shut it down. I picked up my tools, threw them in my toolbox then hurled a belt and rags out over the flat and screamed, 'Why the fuck am I out here? Why is this my fucking life?' I cursed the sky as if expecting an answer. But the wilderness just sucked my pathetic screams into the vacuum of its silence, making me feel insignificant. Through tears, I cast my gaze over the empty landscape; a mixture of new beginnings and ends contained within an hourglass. The emptiness reminded me of the empty, hollow space I felt inside when I first arrived. I still didn't know what was missing from that space, or how I would fill it. I felt like a marionette. I looked back up to the sky and spoke softly, 'I am in your hands now.'

When I saw the cow in the nest at Bore No. 16, in Benmara Paddock, later that day the anger that had been triggered earlier sparked into a rage the likes of which I had never known. It was my greatest fear.

The cow had broken a pipe, which I had already fixed several times before. The pipe fed precious water from the bore to the turkey's nest. The water continuously flowing from the broken pipe had yet again eroded the side of the nest and pooled on the ground in a filthy mixture of mud, slush and cow shit. I'd tried several times to chase the stupid animal out. I had even succeeded in doing so, but it insisted on jumping back into that little oasis.

When I saw the mess, I backtracked to the cruiser and dug out a roll of tape from my toolbox. I broke a suitable branch off a nearby tree and taped my knife to it in the manner of a spear, then I began chasing that cow around the turkey's nest like a madman. I was going to fix that beast once and for all. I hurled my crude spear and struck the poor animal several times. Bleeding from its wounds and enraged by my attacks, it charged. I nimbly stepped aside on the deep grassy bank. I felt like a matador, like a wild man after food.

But it was a real madness that had taken over me as I ran through the tall grass, bush, reeds, trees, mud and water screaming in pursuit of my prey. I stung the beast a few times more. Luckily for that cow it finally got the message. It bolted from the nest and didn't look back. It never came back.

The realisation of what I had done to that poor beast dawned like a red sky in the morning. I felt a deep remorse. I was forced to acknowledge the destructiveness of my anger. Although it had been useful in the past for survival, the destructive force needed taming. I didn't feel proud or good about what I had tried to do. It wasn't brave or tough or clever. It was stupid and, when I thought about it, I wasn't sure who was more stupid; me for getting angry about having to fix the pipe, or the cow for breaking it? After all, it didn't know what it was doing. It was just a poor dumb animal that had no knowledge of human virtue or morality. I, on the other hand, had no excuses.

Yet, strangely, I experienced a feeling of liberation and release that day. As if a burden had been lifted from my shoulders, I felt lighter than I had done in a long time; I was finally free of invisible shackles that had held me for years. I'd let go of something: anger that had been brewing in me at stockcamp for their rejection, anger and resentment that came from my stepfather's cowardly acts and mistreatment of myself and my family when I was too young to do anything about it, anger at my mother for letting it happen, and anger at my father for not being there to help. Anger, that went all the way back to my parent's separation and the unnecessary destruction that had resulted. I had been carrying all of it on my shoulders for a long time.

CHAPTER FOURTEEN
REALISATION

'The world is all gates, all opportunities, strings of tension waiting to be struck.'
—*Ralph Waldo Emerson*

After 10 long months in the wilderness, I gave Cameron a month's notice of my intention to leave the Station. When he asked why I wasn't staying over the wet season as I'd indicated I would, I simply told him I wanted to explore the rest of Australia. He accepted my month's resignation with understanding and, it seemed, some regret.

The thought of leaving the Station tugged at a fresh part of me that had come to love and admire the outback and the rugged determination of the people that lived in its stoic isolation. I knew, even then, that the experiences of the past year had changed me irrevocably.

It was November 29 when all station hands worked half a day then packed up and made for Barkly Homestead for the Walhallow Christmas party. I didn't care for the party, but I was obliged to attend. I watched the festive celebrations from the sidelines where I sat in conversation with Denis. After the isolating months I had spent on the motorbike, and later as one of the borerunners, I no longer felt a part of stockcamp. While the men laughed and drunk and joked, my thoughts bore me away on the wings of a giddy uncertainty for the road ahead and a drunken excitement for my freedom.

One by one, the men left the Station as the days to Christmas counted down. Eventually, the Homestead became a quiet and lonely place.

The first wet season rains began to fall in spasms over the bone-dry Tablelands. I felt relieved that my days out on the bore run were drawing to a close. The change in the seasons signified the end of a cycle and the beginning of a new one, not just in nature but within me. I understood then that my own life would always have such cycles: times of growth and dissolution, times of birth and renewal, dormancy, times of harmony, celebration, times of strife and upheaval. Now was a time to be reborn, with a new idea about life.

The rains became more frequent, washing my thoughts away in torrents over the dry land. Those areas of the Station receiving heavier rain than others quickly transformed the land into a giant patchwork quilt of verdure and ochre. The desert country sprung back to life at an astonishing rate; green shoots emerged from baked earth and naked branches on a monumental scale, the cattle began to move off the bores. I detoured waterlogged roads, turned back from flooded tracks and raced ahead of brooding storm clouds carried on brisk winds. Those storms spoke of life in a profound text as they released their sweet loads. The smell of fresh rain reminded my soul that all was not forsaken; life was beginning again.

Then came the dry storms—tremendous thunder and lightning displays that tore the air to shreds but released no rain. Fires tortured the dryer parts of the Station as the thirsty land awaited the monsoon. I went out with Chunky, Denis, Chris and Cameron to fight the biggest bush fires I had ever seen. Two separate fires had collided in savage combat in Larry's Paddock and built into a firestorm that tore the night apart on a cataclysmic scale. We started back burning and bulldozing firebreaks in a futile attempt to contain the blaze. The fire's ravenous consumption of the bush, the bang, crackle and hiss of its life, the heat expelled by trees exploding into flames and the choking smoke left in its wake was something I would never forget. I watched a billowing wall of smoke kilometres long claw at a blood-red sky. I observed snakes, lizards, kangaroos, cattle and birds, scatter and slither, bolt and bounce or fly for their lives. The fires scorched and charred hundreds of square kilometres of bush. Little more than termite mounds were left standing. Skeletons of trees lay in piles of silver-grey ash upon the black earth in perfect silhouettes of their former selves, as if they had been vaporised the moment the fires hit them. Dozens of willy willy's waltzed across the carbonised country by day, twisting great black snakes into the sky for weeks. But soon those thirsty, burnt tracts of land would be replenished. The annual transformation of the outback would take place and along with it, new people would come to replace the old. All the events and memories of the previous season would be forgotten. That was the way of the bush.

We were gearing up to fight another fire in South Horse Paddock, but it had advanced so quickly that it was beyond our means. I sat on the veranda outside my quarters that evening in awe of the ominous sunset glow of that fire, where it burned in the fading light forty kilometres from the homestead.

The blackness of night framed distant storms that danced in a corroboree of flashing spears and ominous bulging figures in the sky. Thunder rolled across the plains like giant waves punishing a distant shoreline. The excited, throbbing ring of insects electrified the still, humid night. A light breeze began to collect, moving the oppressive air, transporting the irrefutable smell of fresh rain. The breeze quickly intensified and cooled rapidly. Within seconds a shower of lightning erupted from a monstrous cloud bank that had crept up on the homestead. The full fury of the storm was unleashed as it passed overhead. I struggled to make out the other buildings around the homestead as a black deluge poured from the sky. Between thunderous blows from the storm, I could hear the Homestead's generator growling like a wild beast caged in its corrugated iron shed. Bats flew madly about searching for shelter in a strobe of lightning. The monsoonal rains were upon us.

I was still watching the storm from my veranda at 9:30pm when Cameron ran over to my quarters. 'Beno!' he shouted above the thunder of rain on the tin roof. 'I need you to jump in your cruiser and drive down the highway to our southern boundary and check if you can still see any glow from the fire in South Horse Paddock. If you can't see anything, just come back and go to bed. If you can, come and let me know.'

I ran to the cruiser through gusts of warm rain and jumped in, slamming the door after me as another gust hit. I turned the key and slowly backed out from under the shed. The rain was pelting down so hard that dark, humid night, it sounded like stones hitting the cab roof as I drove up the muddy road from the homestead to the highway. Something felt different, though I couldn't say what. I slowly edged the cruiser up to the junction and stared up and down the highway into the gloomy downpour. The wipers heaved rivers of water from the windscreen as sheets of rain bounced off the bonnet. Slowly, I pulled out and changed into a higher gear, the headlights cutting two swords of light through the storm. I could hardly see 50 metres down the road.

Suddenly, the headlights caught a dark, sleek object moving onto the road. I hit the brakes, sliding to a halt while a huge, black-headed python slithered across the road, its shiny wet body reflecting ominously in the cruiser's lights. In the seconds that it took for the snake to cross the road I seemed to fall into a trance. It was as if the serpent had wrapped itself around my mind, cutting me off from the outside world as the storm intensified around me. A feeling of complete solitude and oneness came over me. Time slowed until it felt like the whole universe had stopped while I watched the snake cross. A flash of lightning, a crack of thunder; in a microsecond my consciousness seemed to merge with that of the storm. A myriad of images flashed before me; past storms and associations going back lifetimes—a patchwork of genetic memories flashed through my mind. My thoughts shifted, and I felt a growing awareness of the millions of drops of rain that were pelting down around me. Each drop seemed to contain within it the memory of a day spent toiling endlessly under the desert sun. Every drop, now representing a drop of sweat I had sacrificed to that place, was being offered back to me. I had never known that something so empty could contain so much. Another flash of lightning followed by a tremendous clap of thunder jerked me out of the trance.

I collected my thoughts, drove to the southern boundary and gazed into the night. There was no glow on the horizon. The rains had quenched the hungry flames and South Horse Paddock was saved.

I left Walhallow Station in the early hours of the next morning. The long-awaited journey back to the eastern seaboard began with Mick in his old Valiant ute.

REALISATION

Mick was real bushie; a scruffy old stockman from Queensland with a short beard, thick mop of longish dark-brown hair, and burnt-henna eyes sunken deep into his head from a life in the outback. He'd been taking care of the homestead's gardens for the past few months and was now on his way back to Mt Isa where his brother lived. It was the end of the second week in December.

'So, what did you learn out here, Kiwi?' Mick asked, as we rolled down the highway.

I stared out the window for a moment and watched as kilometre upon endless kilometre of scrub and downs country ebbed slowly past, taking with it the life I'd lived so intensely for the past year. I was leaving my old identity out there, buried in the desert forever, and heading back to the coast with the genesis of a new one. I had lost all excitement about leaving the Station. 'I guess there's no hurry.'

Mick laughed. 'You're not getting all philosophical on me, are you?'

I dragged my thoughts back to the reality of heading back to the coast and thought about Mick's question. What had I learnt from my stay in the outback?

I'd learnt how to push myself beyond anything I thought possible. I'd learnt how to believe in myself. Daisy, in spite of his apparent lack of empathy for the men who worked under him, had instilled in me the confidence of a man who knows his own strength, both of mind and body. Daisy's relentless pushing had unlocked something; awakened something dormant, hiding like a sleeping giant in the recesses of my being that may have otherwise never been awoken.

Mick was staring at me, waiting for my answer. As if reading my thoughts, he raised his eyebrows. 'Daisy's a bit hard on the men, isn't he? I heard some of them complained to Cameron about him.'

'I heard.'

I knew Daisy's harsh ways better than any man I ever saw go through that camp. But in a way, their complaints had settled any doubts in my mind that his harsh treatment of me might have been misplaced. Maybe all the men felt it at times, but sometimes it was hard to know if you weren't losing your mind in a place like that. In the end, Cameron fired Daisy for his mistreatment of the men.

'It takes a lot of determination to survive out here, Kiwi. You need a reason, and I guess you must've had a pretty good one to stay out here as long as you did. Many of these guys wouldn't be out here if they didn't have to be. Most of them don't function properly in normal society. They've all got stories to tell. But life out here teaches you things that you can't learn any other way, no matter where you come from.'

Mick was right. There were many reasons the men made their way to the stations of the outback. Some came for the experience, some to save money, and some to straighten out and stay out of trouble. Others came to escape society for a while. For a few it was punishment rather than serving time in a correctional facility. For some of those men, it became their way of life. Whatever the reason, I would never forget those wild men—the salt of that red earth.

Station life had prepared me for the world in ways that most other men would never know. It had awakened my instincts and sharpened my senses. The lessons I had learnt in the wilderness, beyond the comfortable confines of the institutions, were invaluable. I was beginning to understand that we will never know our true selves if we do not push ourselves past our perceived limits and self-imposed boundaries. There is no reward for anyone who turns away from a challenge.

Mick grabbed his pouch of tobacco and rolled a clumsy, oversized cigarette while he drove. I watched some of the tobacco fall out of the end and onto his lap as he fumbled his lighter. He was in no hurry in this heat. He had resigned himself years ago to the fact that there was no point in rushing things. I sat back and closed my eyes, full of the clarity that comes from exhaustion and achievement. I fell into a comfortable, free moment of tired, thoughtless bliss, safe in the knowledge that a part of me would always be comfortable and at one with that vast and mysterious interior.

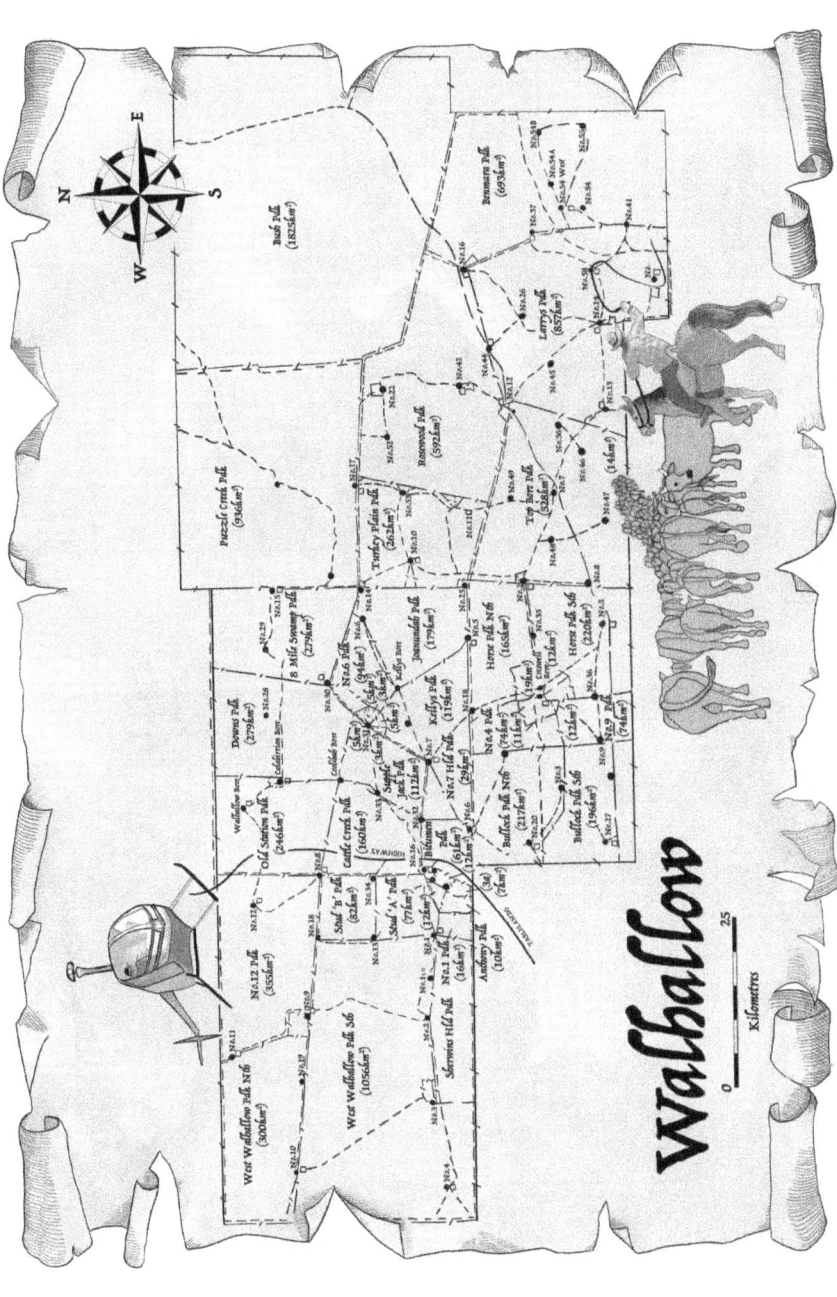

Lining up Walhallow airstrip, 16th October 2002.

Weaner cradle at the House Yards where I started my first day of work.

Branding trailer in tow, taken while sitting on the back of the cruiser.

Kelly's Bore, Joanundah Paddock, riding Agro the day I came off him.

Flying from Barkly Homestead to Walhallow with Ozzie in the Cessna, February 2003. Barkly Tablelands—the great transformation after the wet season.

Getting a killer. I'm at the head of the beast, beginning to skin.

Heading out for a muster with the bull catcher.

Pushing cattle up through the race yards to be drafted, No 7 yards, Kelly's Paddock. I'm in the foreground.

Willy-willy in No. 7 yards, Kelly's Paddock.

Loading road trains early in the morning at No. 7 yards, Kelly's Paddock.

Cameron's pride and joy, Walhallow's road train—Georgina Drover.

Riding a clean skin at No. 14 yards, Soapy (left) holding a jacket and Tim behind the rails shooing the young beast out while I hang on—practice for the Brunette Races.

Camp at No. 12.

Narrowly avoiding a mad cow in the first of two turns around the tree. Taken by Daisy at No. 12 yards—nearly a year after being called Gumboot Man at the same yards.

Moving the Puzzle Creek mob from No. 14 to No. 30, 8 Mile Swamp Paddock.

Mustering Turkey Plain Paddock, taken by Clem from the helicopter. I am on the motorbike, centre of photo.

Up in the helicopter with Clem, moving cattle into No. 1 yards, Sherwins Paddock.

Walhallow Homestead, July 2003, taken from the helicopter with Clem.

Checking endless fence lines under the big sky country, taken in North Bullock Paddock.

Typical early start at the Homestead. Work shed in foreground. Men's quarters, where I stayed, in the background.

Bullock ride at Brunette Downs Races, June 2003.

New Zealand's best campdrafter, taken at the Tennant Creek Rodeo and Campdraft, November 2003.

PART TWO

CHAPTER FIFTEEN
COOLUM BEACH

'You must live in the present, launch yourself on every wave, find your eternity in each moment.'
—Henry David Thoreau

The huge breaker came slowly and majestically, gaining volume and velocity as it advanced, until it assumed a clear watery arch which sparkled in the bright sun. I watched him take off down the building face on his longboard, smoothly, effortlessly, almost elegantly. The upper edge of the wave lipped gently and fell over him with a roar that seemed as though the heart of the ocean was broken in the crash of the tumultuous foaming water. Then, suddenly, like being fired from a gun, he shot from the barrel of the wave.

He rode his board right up to the beach and stepped off, as if he had just been for a quick paddle. Prancing up the shore, he smiled at me. 'Beat that.'

* * *

I moved out of the beach shack soon after arriving back in Caloundra. Biruta was an amazing help. She organised a place for me to stay with her son, Andrew, and his friend, Mason, at a beachside apartment overlooking the Coral Sea in Coolum Beach.

I had met Andrew once before, a year earlier, when he had visited Biruta. He was a six-foot, blonde-haired, blue-eyed dive instructor who had been working up in Cairns. His favourite sayings were: 'It's all good' and 'Right on.' Andrew had spent most of his adult life travelling and he wasn't about to stop.

Both Andrew and Mason were working at One Realty for Andrew's older brother, James. Mason worked in marketing, and Andrew ran errands. The two men were like chalk and cheese but had been good friends since they were in high school.

Thanks to Andrew, it wasn't long before I also had a job with One Realty. Every morning at 6:00 am, I cleaned the showroom windows and swept and vacuumed the showroom floors and offices. I also completed maintenance jobs on rental properties: everything from fixing roofs and gutters, mowing lawns and gardening, to small plumbing and carpentry jobs.

Andrew and I also assembled the property For Sale signs. We had a small office set up in our garage below the apartment dedicated to this purpose. It contained a sign-printing machine, stacks of plastic signboards, and a computer that was programmed to transfer the sign writing onto huge rolls of glossy black or white plastic tape for us to adhere to the One Realty signboards. When the signs were ready, we loaded them into the work truck with wooden stakes and erected them on the front lawns of the properties that were for sale.

Having been busy with work every hour of the day for the past year on the station, I now found a space opening in my days, in my mind, and in my life. I experienced a quickening of thought, insight, and understanding as I melded what I had learnt in the outback with the everyday. With my attention free from a long preoccupation, and that chapter of my life now complete, new possibilities took shape.

I started surfing. Morning, noon and night, I carved the sculptured waves that rolled and curled into the beautiful bay below the apartment. Every day I awoke to steep, rocky headlands at either end of the bay framing the clear, turquoise waters of the Coral Sea in a perfect picture of paradise. The deep, yellow-sand shoreline banked into pandanus palms, horsetail she-oaks and the road that the apartment sat beside. I soon developed a love and respect for surfing. The ocean was a myriad new world of possibility, rich in enigmas about which I knew very little. I was caught in rips and side currents. I got speared, rolled, dumped, and tumbled. I saw turtles surface for air and watched stingrays swimming below. Surfing was how I met Joseph.

One evening, as I trudged down the sand bank onto the beach, I noticed an older man whom I hadn't seen before. He stretched his athletic limbs in Zenist poses as he gazed out to sea. His beard and head of hair were quicksilver. A longboard lay beside him. I felt an overwhelming urge to say hello.

'I like it when it's like this and there's nobody else in the bay,' I said.

'Yes, it's my favourite time of year too. Do you live near here?' His voice was calm, relaxed, and composed.

'Just across the road.' I pointed at the apartment. 'But I'm from New Zealand.'

'Thought I heard a bit of a twang. I live just across the road too, up that way.' He pointed towards another group of apartments. 'So, you're travelling then?'

'I've just spent the last year working on a cattle station in the Northern Territory.'

'Cattle station?' He stared at me and frowned. His grey-blue eyes matched the colour of the ocean behind him. 'Not many people would choose to go and work on a cattle station. Too hard. I bet you learnt a thing or two about life out there. You can learn a thing or two about life from surfing, too.'

I thought about what he said for a moment, then asked him what it was like to surf on a longboard.

'It's fantastic, especially on days like today, when the waves aren't so big. Would you like to have a go?'

'Sure.'

He picked up his board and handed it to me. I passed him mine.

'Our journeys in life are much like waves: opportunities that roll under us, lift us up for a moment for an elevated view of what life can be like and then drop us back down to where we were if we don't take them,' he said suddenly. He turned his grey-blue gaze to the sea. 'There's no getting them back once they've passed. Of course, it takes courage to jump on those waves when they come, and sometimes you don't have much time to think about it either. After that, there's no looking back—no knowing what the ride ahead will be like either, or where it will take you. You don't know when it will finish or what you'll find along the way. All you can do is focus on what is happening right in front of you. Surfing teaches you to be in the moment and to let go of everything else that isn't helping you right then. But you can be sure of one thing.'

'What's that?' I asked.

'Well, if you dive off halfway, you're in for a washing machine of a ride.' His silver beard shook with laughter, as if he was recalling a distant memory. 'But, like the waves and the storms that produce the swell that makes them, the energy and the opportunities of your life will eventually all pass you by if you don't launch yourself on them when you have the chance. So, the better you get at surfing, the bigger the opportunities you can surf. Shall we?' He smiled. 'By the way, my name is Joseph, but you can call me Joe.'

He gripped my extended arm firmly, shaking it like a piece of spaghetti.

I struggled to keep up with Joe as he navigated his way through the waves. He knew every current, submerged rock, the bank and curl of the waves and where they would break. Beyond the breakers, I sat up with my legs dangling. The rhythmic rise and fall of the ocean swell delivered a moment of transcendent freedom. I thought about what Joe had said. It was an odd thing to say out of the blue, but it made a lot of sense. Opportunities came and went. It would be up to me to jump on them whenever I could to make an interesting life. I'd never know what lay ahead. I'd just have to accept what came. Sometimes things wouldn't work out and the ride might get a bit rough, but it was a lot better than not taking opportunities at all.

I counted the sets as a storm moved in and showers began to fall. Lightning flashed around us, and thunder reverberated off the cliffs like bellowing giants. It was just me, Joe, and the bay. Droplets of rain hammered the sea's warm surface like gravel falling from the sky. My back grew cold as the rain flicked at my skin while my legs hung, insulated in the warm water.

Joe took off down a building face. I watched, impressed at how well he could manoeuvre my board. I quickly followed on the longboard, which sat in firm and stable confidence on the wave. I grinned. A new journey was underway.

I waved goodbye to Joe, and I watched as he lightly sprung up the beach. He stopped at the bottom of the track to the road, turned to me and called out, 'See you down here again soon, Ben.' He disappeared up the track.

Shortly after I met Joe, I met Rebel Clair. She was a carefree, fun and light-hearted local who worked at the café next to One Realty. She had long, light-brown hair, brown eyes and legs like a supermodel. She was as tall as me. We hung out at the beach and went out on the town. Coolum was a sleepy seaside village, but that didn't stop us from hitting the main haunts—the Surf Club and a funky corner club called Sol Bar, which occasionally had live local bands. When we felt like travelling, we headed up to Noosa or down to Mooloolaba. Hanging out with Rebel reminded me of the softer, more intimate pleasures of life.

The heady summer days of new scenes and surfing quickly passed into spectacular late summer storms. One in particular, a huge low pressure system that had made its way down the coast from a dissipating cyclone in the tropical north, sent savage weather and gigantic waves thundering into the bay. Soon after the skies cleared, surfers tackled the enormous dark breakers that peeled around the point and into the bay like colossal arms, clawing at the foreshore. My curiosity at their bravery and thirst for the thrill of big wave surfing got the better of me. I was drawn to the beach to observe toy men bobbing on flimsy boards as silty tons of water heaved and crashed around them in foaming, boiling, eddying rips. The suck of the waves punishing the shoreline had stripped the beach of sand and rocks poked through like Galapagos tortoise shells.

One surfer caught my attention. He seemed to be paddling for his life as a wave built like a grey mountain behind him. He was dangerously close to the cliffs on the point. Ahead of him, waves smashed into the rocks, obliterating anything they caught in their watery grasp. As the crest of the wave picked him up for its final punishing blow, he jumped to his feet and raced forward down the steep, dark, foam-streaked slope before disappearing into the thunder of its giant foaming barrel.

I anxiously waited to see his board churn through the wave, a sure sign he was in the water and getting dragged towards the rocks, when he shot from the barrel.

As the surfer came closer to the beach, I recognised it was Joe. He was grinning from ear to ear. I laughed, bedazzled by his skill and composure. I hadn't seen him for several weeks.

'Not surfing today?'

'I would get killed out there,' I said, feeling defeated by my fear of the waves.

'You don't know that—you haven't tried it yet.' I knew he was right.

'I'll try in a day or two.'

'Just remember what I told you about opportunities, Ben. They can pass you by if you don't take them while you have the chance. Why don't you come up to my place for a cup of tea? I need to warm up.'

'Sure.' I felt bad. Joe had invited me over to his place for tea and to talk about life whenever I felt like it. I had never taken the opportunity. I was too young to see the openness of his heart then. After the savageness of my stepfather and my father's absence in my life, I held a deep distrust in older men.

Joe lived alone. Artwork splashed the walls of his living room with abstract colour. A calm energy that I wasn't familiar with pervaded his apartment.

'There you go.' Joe handed me a hot cup of herbal tea. 'So, what have you been up to, Ben?'

'Working, surfing, and I met a girl. It's been nice having someone to hang out with.'

'It sounds like you're enjoying life on the Coast, not getting too comfortable, are we?'

'I could easily stay.'

'Well, you must do whatever makes you happy.'

'What makes you think I should be doing anything else?' I asked. I was wondering why he had put so much emphasis on opportunities since I met him.

'I travelled a lot when I was younger. My life has taken me all over the world and I don't regret a bit of it. Now I'm older, I don't like to move so much—don't have the energy anymore. I never had a family of my own to worry about, but I don't get lonely either. There are plenty of other people in this world that need taking care of.'

I had a think about what Joe was trying to tell me.

'The wanderer's danger is to find comfort, Ben. Out there, the path of infinite possibilities awaits you. But something tells me you worked all that out in the outback? Am I right? Don't wait too long to catch your next wave or it'll pass you by. All this will be waiting here for you when you get back. That's if you come back.'

Joe's last words cut right to the heart of the matter. Mike had told me the same thing. I thought of Mike and wondered how he was getting on. And maybe Joe was right; maybe I was getting a little too comfortable on the Coast. I had only just begun to see life, and I knew I still wasn't done with my journey. I had a great desire to travel. The Sunshine Coast would still be here when I got back, just like Christchurch would be if I wanted it.

'See you again soon, Joe.' I left his place and went for a long walk along the beach, caught in a visceral mood between what I had awakened in my head and my heart in the outback, and a yearning to belong.

Autumn in Coolum Beach wove a lonely thread into the serape of busy summer days. I often found myself alone in the bay, sitting on my surfboard in quiet contemplation. I became intimately attached to the bay. I observed its seasonal moods, from sunrise to sunset and deep into the starry nights. I shared with it my most intimate thoughts. As I rose and fell on the breathing swell, it seemed almost as if we became one.

I strolled along the shoreline in the warm, early autumn rains, taking interest in the way the waves shifted the sands along the foreshore. The swish and the swirl, the splash and the spray, seemed to calm a growing restlessness I felt. The coast was always changing, would always change and yet, would always be beautiful. I scooped up colourful shells and sculptured corals that painted and framed the scenes of far-off exotic locations and unknown adventures. I knew I had to open myself to the change that opportunity brings, uncomfortable as it could sometimes be. That was what made life beautiful.

Then, one night, I found myself looking at some of my station gear: my spurs, my faithful old Akubra, my trusty Ian Harold riding boots and Wrangler jeans—the threads of an experience that had changed my life. Was I forgetting what I had learnt in the outback?

Early in May, I ventured up to Double Island Point to camp and surf and to unplug the blockage of my dreams. Double Island Point lay two hours north of the Sunshine Coast. Empty beaches and native bush unravelled into the horizon.

I spent hours surfing in a small bay I found on the Point. The shoreline was rocky, with just a wisp of sand from where I launched into the water. Steep, bush-clad cliffs towered above the beach. The last evening came as I sat on the rocks and gazed over Rainbow Beach. I studied the arching coastline—a huge yellow-white crescent of sand dunes that disappeared into the distance, shrubbery greens and flowering trees lining the foreshore. Just off the coast, Fraser Island sparkled like an emerald jewel. I had made up my mind to leave.

I had barely knocked on Joe's door when it swung open. 'I've been expecting you,' he said. 'Come in.'

I took a seat in Joe's living room and gazed out to sea. The view struck me. 'I never noticed what a great view of the bay you have.'

'Yes, it's a nice view.' Joe smiled, and his eyes rested on me. 'We all notice the details and beauty in everything just before we make a major change. It's the mind clinging to what is safe and familiar. It's also the tearing of the soul's connection to place and people and it's longing to belong. It's often enough to keep people in jobs they don't like, relationships they've outgrown, and even in towns or countries they should leave. The uncertainty or the challenge can become overwhelming, and you become afraid that you won't find anything better. But life is fluid and always changing. You need to learn to experience the *flow*, which can only happen when you truly let go and allow life to show you the way. The soul needs to explore, learn, and grow, Ben, and that requires some discomfort and courage. So, I take it you're leaving.'

'How did you know?' I was still thinking about what Joe had said about noticing the beauty in everything just as it's ending. I knew then there would always be reasons to stay when it was time to go. I wondered about the mysterious *flow*.

'It wasn't half-obvious.'

'Well, I've decided to buy a car and drive around Australia.'

'You know, Ben, the greatest danger in life is *not* taking the adventure. All this *will* be waiting here for you when you get back. I can see your uncertainty in the road ahead, but that's just life testing you, to see if you're ready. You are crossing another threshold. If it were easy following our dreams, everyone would be doing it. Most people will choose the safe, well-trodden path. This is your chance to do something different with your life. Use your imagination, your courage, and your brains to blaze your own trail into a life of adventure, entrepreneurism or humanitarianism, whatever you desire. All of us are afraid of failure, but we mustn't forget to embrace the lessons we learn from such experiences. Just remember, the years of your youth will not wait for you. Spend them wisely.' I suddenly felt ashamed I hadn't asked Joe more about his life.

'I'm glad I met you, Joe. I hope when I get back, we can go surfing again.'

'You'll have to get a lot better before you can keep up with me.'

Joe and I both laughed. 'Just remember, Ben, there's an ocean full of opportunities out there. You just need to go and find them. That's the adventure. Keep your mind and heart open and accept what comes.'

CHAPTER SIXTEEN
SETTING OUT

'The man who goes alone can start today.'
—Henry David Thoreau

Rebel pushed her head through the open window of my car and pressed her lips against mine. The warm, soft seconds of that touch reminded me of the simple, pleasurable comforts I was leaving behind and a connection that I still craved.

'Take care out there, Ben. It's a big country. It's going to take you a while to see it all. I hear Western Australia's nice.' Her casual smile dismissed any sign of emotion, but I could see the clouds through the windows of her eyes. 'Let me know when you get back.' She waved as I drove off.

I didn't know when I was going to make it back to the Sunshine Coast. I had no idea how long it would take to drive around Australia. As I drove down the street, I recalled Mike telling me how he had always travelled alone on his motorcycle. Rarely did he have company with him. Then I remembered the second gift he had given me that last cold night I saw him before I left. The skull. He had taken it everywhere with him on the road. He'd told me: 'This skull has been everywhere with me. It used to keep me safe on the road, and keep danger away by warding off evil spirits. Now it will keep you safe and bring you good luck on your journey and on the road ahead.' I was in awe of his foresight.

I pulled over and dug the skull out of my backpack. I held it for a moment, then hung it from the rear-view mirror so that it was gazing ahead to ward off danger. I pulled my silver, 1984 XF Ford Falcon back onto the road and opened up the 4.1 litre straight 6 that sat under the bonnet. With a jerk, the machine accelerated with primal freedom.

I made it to River Heads in Hervey Bay and jumped aboard the ferry to Fraser Island with my backpack. Fraser Island is the largest sand island in the world. The earliest known name of the island is *K'gari*, in the Butchulla people's language (pronounced *Gurri*). It means paradise.

I disembarked at Wangoolba Creek and surveyed a deep sandy track lined with ruts which disappeared into the jungle that covered the island, then set off at a trot for the beginning of the Fraser Island Great Walk. It was a hot and humid day. As I trudged up and down hill-sized sand dunes that rose from the water like giant leatherback turtles, I caught glimpses of the Coral Sea and the long bleached sandy shores of the island. Wompoo fruit-doves, rosellas and lorikeets called from the rainforest canopy.

Several hours later, I discovered Lake Garawongera, set among scribbly gums, Moreton Bay ash and foxtail ferns. I dumped my pack on the sandy shoreline, gathered kindling for a fire, and made camp. Sulphur-crested cockatoos squawked and danced in head-bobbing, crest-raising displays. Kookaburras laughed with deranged excitement. There wasn't another soul around. I sat, watched, and listened from fading sky blue through carmine and indigo into star-studded black. The hot whisper of flames and glow of embers filled me with wonder about the road ahead. I contemplated how life was made up of choices; how a single choice could change the whole direction of my life. I gazed through the treetops at the glittering, starry blanket above me. In a microsecond, I was transported back to my first nights on the cattle station. Without that experience, I knew I wouldn't be here now. I averted my gaze to the lake's glassy surface. Like an astronomical mirror, it reflected the glittering cosmos. In that moment, it seemed I could have stepped off the shoreline, plunged into eternity, and discovered the secrets of the universe.

After seven days hiking through the heart of the island, over colossal sand dunes and through sub-tropical rainforest; swimming alone in stunning crystal-clear freshwater lakes; sighting dingoes, goannas, snakes, and scores of beautiful parrots and other bird life, I finally made it back to Eastern Beach. I caught the ferry back to the mainland with the fever of adventure in my blood.

Rolling meadows dotted with towering eucalypts lined the winding road west. I thought about the people I'd left behind—my friends and family and the kilometres and years between them and me. If there was only one thing I wanted to come from my journey around Australia, it was to prove to myself that anything was possible on the road of life.

It was in that moment that I realised just how precious my life was, and how lucky I was to still be alive. I had so nearly given it up; thrown it away in a desperate, fleeting moment of suicidal depression. As if to emphasise the point, from out of nowhere, the faces and names of the youths I had known in and out of high school that hadn't made it through those dark days and nights swam like ghosts through my mind. There was the troubled 15-year-old boy in my English class who drove into a rock wall at the bottom of the Port Hills at 100 kilometres an hour, nothing recognisable was left of the vehicle; a close friend's best mate whom I'd hung out with many times that sucked his life from a can of lighter fluid at 16, found lying on his bed cold and blue staring at the ceiling; my new friend outside of school who I thought had his life together, but who left it on the train tracks at 17; and the 19-year-old girl I met through my flatmate, and became friends with shortly before I left New Zealand, who hung herself a few months later. They all called from the recesses of my mind, along with my own demons, telling me how lucky I was, screaming what a waste of their young lives those decisions had been. If only someone could have been there to guide them through that dark and perilous moment... and the next.

It was late in the afternoon when I turned off the highway and down a dirt road toward Cania Gorge National Park. I drove into the campground just in time to see a small crowd gathered around a kaleidoscope of brightly coloured birds.

The bird feeder's name was Old Jim. He was wearing an Akubra, blue jeans and a khaki shirt with Cania Gorge embroidered on the left chest. His boots were of the brown leather bushman's style, making me feel at home. He described the birds and their habits while he fed them. With a disarming smile, he encouraged several people with a handful of seed each to join in. Old Jim saw me waiting patiently off to one side, no doubt with a big stupid grin on my face, and walked over. He gave me a nod and a smile. 'You look like you want to feed the birds too, mate.' He was a real bushie.

I cupped my hand, and he dropped a handful of seed into it.

'Now just stand there and they'll come and land on you.' Old Jim grinned, then stood aside.

A flock of rainbow lorikeets descended upon me in a technicoloured cloak, flashing their spectacular green, blue, yellow, orange and red feathers. A king parrot landed on my arm and pushed some lorikeets out of the way. He was an impressive parrot, twice the size of the lorikeets, with a brilliant red front and head and bright green back and wings. The lorikeets decided to wait their turn on my head. A few young children that had been impatient to join in the feeding frenzy looked at me and ran back to their parents, overwhelmed by the show. Sociable little grey apostle birds ran around my feet, chattering in a harsh grating and scolding manner, happily collecting the seed that spilt onto the ground.

Old Jim walked over and handed me a small piece of meat. 'Now hide this quickly, that kookaburra there is already watching us. He's clever. He knows what's going on.'

I started to feel a little uncomfortable with the crowd's attention on me, but I did as Old Jim asked. I folded my fingers over the piece of meat just before the kookaburra landed on my arm. The bird cocked its head, gave me a sharp eye, then turned back to my closed fist. Old Jim gave me a nod. I opened my hand. In deft and honed movement, the kookaburra seized the piece of meat like it was a live prey. It threw its head back and swallowed it in a single gulp. Understanding the game was over, the kookaburra flew back to its perch.

I spent the rest of the week exploring Cania Gorge: walking, climbing, fishing, and learning about the local ecology. I was preparing to leave the park when I met Old Jim again.

I was seated at a park bench in a small clearing by Lake Cania, immersed in a book on Queensland's national parks and plotting out the next stage of my journey, when I heard a rustling nearby. I looked up to see Old Jim pushing his way through some bushes and into the clearing. He was holding a bucket.

'G'day Jim. You caught me by surprise there, mate,' I called out.

'Sorry about that. Didn't mean to sneak up on you like that. Just been looking for yabbies in the creek there.'

'Yabbies?'

'Yeah, freshwater crayfish. They're small blue things.' Old Jim held up his bucket for me to observe the critters. 'Say, I didn't catch your name the other day?'

'It's Ben.'

'Nice to meet you, Ben. You just on holiday then?'

'I just started driving around Australia. I'm going to see as much of it as I can, the national parks in particular.'

'Ahh, good on you, mate. You've got the right idea there. Once there was a time when many a lad like you could be seen following his star across the countryside. Yes, and girls too. I guess it just became too dangerous for many. Still, I think more young people should be out exploring the country. It really helps to open your mind, and this is an amazing country. These people that just visit the cities are missing the real Australia and a big important part of life I reckon. So, where're you planning to go next?'

'I was just looking at Expedition National Park in my book here, and Carnarvon Gorge sounds interesting.'

'Okay, both good choices. Just a word of advice—watch yourself around Expedition National Park because you get a few yahoos out there off the stations sometimes. Carnarvon Gorge is an amazing place. You'll enjoy yourself out there, so make sure you stay a while if you can.'

'Do you know Australia well?' I asked, hoping he might share some more insights with me.

Old Jim laughed. 'Not well enough mate. If I had my way, I would be off travelling the country right now, but the missus doesn't like to move so much now. You're going to have a lot of fun. I drove around Australia when I was 20, best thing I ever did, and I've been meaning to do it again ever since. That's how I ended up out here, actually, and I couldn't be happier. There's a lot to learn and see out there, so take care, but take risks too. We all encounter obstacles on the road, but once you learn to overcome them, you can go anywhere and do anything. Well, you take care of yourself out there and enjoy your travels. This journey you're on will change you. Just wait and see.'

CHAPTER SEVENTEEN
CARNARVON GORGE

'There is in my nature, me thinks, a singular yearning toward all wildness.'
—*Henry David Thoreau*

Small cattle stations lined the winding dirt road into Carnarvon Gorge. Ahead, sheer ivory escarpments fell from eucalyptus-green plateaus and ridges into a maze of ravines that tumbled into the surrounding savannah.

I drove into the campground at Takarakka and paid for a campsite. The host handed me a map and a handful of brochures. Caravans, motorhomes, and four-wheel drives littered the busy grounds amidst a hive of human activity. The smell of barbequed meat filled the air. I set up camp, then jumped back into the Falcon with my map and headed off up the Gorge. There was just enough daylight left to get in a short walk.

The road climbed over a steep jump-up, followed the curve of an extinguished ridgeline and dropped back down through a gully past the Carnarvon Gorge Wilderness Lodge. Just over the next jump-up, on the next bend in the road, I saw the parking bay at the head of the Aboriginal Cultural Trail.

I was about to pull into the carpark when, from out of nowhere, a white station wagon came skidding around the corner and towards me at high speed in a pendulum of tail slides. The dark-haired girl driving the vehicle shot me a wide-eyed glance, flicked an apologetic hand over the steering wheel, then changed down gears and tore off in a cloud of amber dust. Inexplicably, in the two seconds I had glimpsed of her, I wondered if she was single and whether she was staying in the park.

Surely, she was travelling with her boyfriend and was late for their dinner date? I tried to shake the idea from my head.

I followed the meandering trail through open eucalypt forest. Plaques set on top of wooden posts were placed at intervals along the trail. The plaques stood in front of different plants and trees and gave their names and uses to the Aboriginal peoples. I stopped at one where a tall palm overhung the trail: Carnarvon Gorge Cabbage Palm—*Livistona nitida*. The growing point was called *heart of palm* and used as a food source. Further on, I came to another in front of a plant called a Macrozamia—*Macrozamia Moorei*. Several of the ancient cycads grew into explosions of sharp fronds like fireworks detonating a few metres off the ground. At the centre of some of the plants grew large clusters of nuts. The nuts were poisonous and full of carcinogens, but they were used as a viable food source, only after a lengthy treatment process to rid the nuts of their toxins. These plants barely grew a foot a century. I suddenly realised that what I saw as a wilderness was a plentiful garden to more knowledgeable eyes.

The trail undulated beneath towering white-trunked spotted gums, past truck-sized sandstone boulders, and arrived at Baloon Cave. Before me, stencilled onto a smooth white rock face that was sheltered from sun and rain, was some of the first primitive records of ancient man. For the first time, it struck me that I was walking on land that had been home to an ancient society of people for thousands, perhaps tens of thousands, of years. People who had lived and learnt and evolved in harmony with the landscape. A part of me suddenly felt ashamed by my ignorance of Australia's Indigenous history. Another part of me felt my first real connection to the country in the wonder and magic of those earthy, sacred ochre stencils of hands and stone tools.

The cave's name originated from the Aboriginal word *baloon*, meaning *stone axe*. The stencils on the rock face were about 500 years old, yet the red and orange ochres leapt off the white sandstone overhang in sharp definition.

I was about to turn back when I noticed a steep, narrow, barely visible path to the left of the cave. It wasn't part of the main track, but I decided to explore it. After a few minutes climbing, I came to a small clearing and an outcrop above the cave called the Goombangie Cliffs. The view stole my heart in a single breath. Before me, a wilderness of forest sprawled into the Gorge and over the ranges, hugging escarpments and tumbling over ridges in green cascades. Silvery-yellow shafts of sunlight pierced the treetops beyond the outcrop. The earth-tree-rock ambrosia of the Gorge tingled through my body. I'd arrived somewhere special.

When I got back to camp, I heard through the bush telegraph there was a talk about the Gorge being held at a small gathering place called the Platypus Circle. I located the site on my map, not far from where I was camped, and joined a small gathering crowd.

A dark-haired girl dressed in a khaki uniform sat on a log off to one side under an enormous old gum tree. Her posture exuded calm confidence and quiet determination. Her back was straight, her legs crossed, and her hands rested in her lap. The people assembling in the Platypus Circle responded warmly to her amiable, self-assured smile as she greeted them. With fated exhilaration, I realised suddenly that I recognised her. It was the girl in the white station wagon I had seen earlier. I quickly concluded that she had been racing back to the campground to prepare for her talk. I took a seat on the ground, unsure if she recognised me, and waited for her talk to begin.

Claudia introduced herself and welcomed everyone. She was one of the Australian Bush Guides based at Takarakka. She briefly described the geology of the gorge, some of her favourite flora and fauna that lived in its seclusion, and the walks that were available. Her sales pitch on the advantages of taking a guided tour of the Gorge over walking it alone was convincing, but she also offered tips for those who preferred to explore the Gorge on their own.

I waited while several groups enquired about guided walks. I had questions about an overnight walk I planned to start in the morning. I also wanted to find out if Claudia recognised me from our earlier brush with danger. Slowly, the crowd dispersed.

Claudia smiled and tilted her head to one side in a quizzical expression. Dark, shoulder-length hair framed her delicate, elfish beauty. She was a small girl, but strong looking.

'Hi,' I blurted out. She didn't appear to recognise me.

'Hi.' Her tawny-brown eyes urged the question I had come to ask.

'Ahh, there's a walk,' I stumbled over my words in awkward shyness, 'I was wanting to find out about the walk… up to Battleship Spur.'

'Sure, so you're planning on going up there then?' Her lips curled around the words in an amused smile.

'Yep.'

'Alone?'

'Yep.'

'Okay, have you done any big walks before?'

'Yep.'

'Okay… What do you want to know about it then?'

'Well, I was just wondering if it's worthwhile, and it mentions here that I need to let a park ranger know I'm doing the walk.' I pointed at my map of the Gorge in as dignified a manner as I could.

'It's definitely worth it, and you can find a park ranger at the Parks and Wildlife Visitor Centre which is three kilometres further up the Gorge from here on the road you came in on.' She finished with a smile that could have sunk a battleship.

'Okay, thanks very much.' I stood there for an awkward moment, gazing into her eyes and lost in her smile. I wanted to say more, but what could I say? That I just got here, and I was travelling on my own and needed a friend? Did she want to hang out, get a drink maybe?

I became aware of several people nearby that appeared to be waiting to speak with her.

'Can I help you with anything else?' Claudia frowned.

The thorny realisation of my gauche behaviour jolted my senses. 'Ahh, no, I think that's all. Thank you.' I turned and wandered back to my tent, kicking at the dirt for not being more confident. I hoped I'd get another chance to speak with her.

My campsite felt empty and void of company as I gazed about the campground, envious of the families, friends, and couples that shared the evening. I decided to head up to the Carnarvon Gorge Wilderness Lodge for dinner.

The amber-eyed windows of the Lodge's restaurant were warm and welcoming. I seated myself at a table. Scattered around the spacious restaurant, at several other tables, were older couples and young families. Chestnut and coffee-coloured hardwoods formed the main structures, countertops, doors and furnishings. It felt like a homely mountain cabin. A young waitress with short auburn hair, mahogany eyes and a cavalier (but not impolite) attitude appeared and took my order. Twenty minutes later, a prime rib steak and roasted vegetables appeared in front of me. After weeks of pasta and tinned food, my mouth watered in slobbery profusion as I shovelled down the fresh fare. I wiped the last of the gravy off my plate with a dinner roll, then walked into the small country-style bar that was attached to the restaurant. I was the only customer. The young waitress that had served me earlier reappeared behind the bar. Before I'd even had a chance to ask for a drink, she shot me with a direct question: 'So, what are you doing out here?' Her voice was sharp and slightly abrasive.

'I've come to see the national park and do the walks,' I said, a little taken aback.

'You've come out here by yourself?'

'Yep.'

'Why would you do that?'

'I like the bush, and I'm driving around Australia,' I replied.

'Don't you get lonely?'

'Been fine so far.' I half-lied.

'Where have you been then?'

'I started out from the Sunshine Coast, and I've been to Fraser Island and Cania Gorge,' I said, warming to the conversation. There was no curtsying around formalities, just the familiar tone of two old friends. Perhaps too familiar, but I hadn't spoken to many people over the past few weeks. Any new friend was surely a good friend to have.

'You should apply for work here if you like the bush so much. Two of our guides just left and we need another one.'

'You mean, they're looking for guides right now?'

'I don't know if they're looking, but we need one so you should talk to our head guide, Wayne. He'll know.'

'Where can I find Wayne?' The chance of living in a stunning national park and spending time with Claudia instantly paved the road ahead.

'He's out night spotting now. You'll have to wait until he gets back, so you should have a beer.' A beer appeared in front of me. 'My name's Annie.'

'Pleased to meet you, Annie. I'm Ben.' I started to pass her money for the beer.

'Pleased to meet you too, Ben, it's on me,' Annie said, flashing a smile and disappearing back into the restaurant.

A large painting of a friendly, wise, old, enigmatic looking Aboriginal man hanging on the wall beside the bar above a single couch caught my attention. The man looked important, and I wondered who he was.

Just as I was about to call Annie for another beer, a grey-haired, bearded man of average height and build with an intelligent face appeared behind the bar. Annie followed him in and pointed towards me. It was Wayne.

'Annie tells me you're interested in becoming a guide.' He busied himself with some work behind the bar.

'Yes, very interested.'

Wayne quietly continued for a minute. Finally, he looked up, offered an unassuming smile and humbly held out his hand. 'Wayne. Sorry, been a long day. Do you have any experience as a guide?' His nut-brown eyes pierced me with a sagacity that made me acutely aware of my lack of experience.

I shook his hand. 'Ben, and no, but I spent a year on a cattle station in the Northern Territory and I'm exploring Australia's national parks at the moment.'

The mention of cattle station and my open-ended exploration of Australia's national parks seemed to rouse his curiosity and deflect any previous misgivings.

'Okay, so you wouldn't mind staying here for a while?'

'Not at all.'

Wayne was quiet for a moment. 'Well, we might be looking for someone. I'll have to speak to our manager, Trish, first, so I can't promise you anything. Have you got a résumé?'

'I can get it to you tomorrow if you like.'

'That would be good. I'll have a look at it and pass it on to Trish. It's getting late in the season now, though, she may not want to train anyone new up.' He said goodnight and left.

Annie reappeared. 'How did it go?' she eagerly asked.

'Good. I think.' I suspected she had been waiting around the corner and listening to the whole conversation.

'It did. Don't worry about Wayne. He's had a long day. You're going to be a nature guide now. You'll have to get used to living with all of us then.'

'Living with all of you? We'll see. I haven't got the job yet.'

'No, but you will. We need someone else. Are you coming night spotting with us tonight? A few of us are going out when we finish work. You should come. It'll be fun.'

I nodded. I was thinking of Claudia again and wondered if she'd be there.

'Cool. I finish in half an hour. See you then,' Annie chirped, and disappeared back into the restaurant.

I walked outside and took a seat at one of the tables that were scattered around a large deck. The magic of the Gorge took me by surprise once again—in the evening call of the kookaburra, the echidna scratching in the undergrowth, the dull thump of kangaroo and wallaby on the lawns around the lodge, and the scatter of lizards and other small marsupials in the leaf litter below the deck. The eerie calls of owls pierced the crisp mountain air and flew through the forest like winged warnings, defied by the guttural screeches of possums. Another world came to life after nightfall. I felt hopeful about staying in the Gorge and working as a wilderness guide.

CHAPTER EIGHTEEN

BATTLESHIP SPUR

'One of the first conditions of happiness is that the link between Man and Nature shall not be broken.'

— Leo Tolstoy

I handed my résumé to Wayne early the following morning and explained my plans to hike up to Battleship Spur. I told him I would drop in and check about work in a couple of days.

Further up the dirt road that winds its way through towering white sandstone escarpments I found the Kooramindangie Plain and the park's Visitor Centre. Kooramindangie means *kangaroos here*. As if to validate the name, large eastern grey kangaroos lay under ancient trees that were scattered over several, mostly cleared, acres of flat land that made up the national park's main campground. Pretty-faced wallabies scattered in startled shyness at my early appearance. The white stripe running down either side of their face made it easy to identify them. This was where the main walk up the Gorge began.

I stopped by the Visitor Centre and spoke to the park ranger on duty. After entering my name and contact details into a register, I set off on the Boolimba Bluff Trail—Boolimba means *on right hand*. The thousand step ascent into the sky unfolded through the crisp mountain air into the lookout on the northern escarpment at the two-kilometre-wide mouth of the Gorge. Rolling savannah, brigalow and station country marched eastward into the morning sun. I struggled to discern the lines of the Wilderness Lodge, concealed within the forest below. Like a battlement sitting above the Lodge, the southern escarpment of the Gorge mouth struck out in the white precipice cliffs of Warrumbah Bluff—Warrumbah means *on left hand*. From the two battlements that guarded the entrance the terrain gradually rose into the sky, into vast plateaus known as The Ranch and Consuelo Tableland. There was enough wilderness to keep me busy for months, years even.

I met Wayne on the main track up the Gorge. He was taking a guided walk to a place called Moss Gardens.

'You may as well join us, Ben,' Wayne offered.

'You don't mind?'

'No, it'll give you a chance to see what guiding is all about. That way you can make up your mind if it's for you or not.'

I joined Wayne's party of two and we continued up the broad dirt path. From time to time, the path leapfrogged the clear, sparkling waters of Carnarvon Creek in a series of large, flat, half-submerged stepping-stones. Splashes of yellow wattle flowers and river sheoaks lined the creek's banks.

The two ladies Wayne was guiding wanted to know why I had such a big pack with me.

'Going up to Battleship Spur for the night,' I explained.

'You're brave going up there on your own,' remarked one of the ladies.

I noticed Wayne grinning. He seemed to be observing my ability to respond to the two women. He then indulged the women's fascination of the seemingly perilous journey ahead of me.

'Best view of the Gorge in the whole park. That's if you make it up there. I haven't been up there for a while, but it's a real backcountry walk. The track isn't well defined, and it's quite steep in places. You need to be skilled and experienced in the arts of the bushman, and you need to have the tranquillity of spirit to accept the consequences of your decisions.' Wayne's voice was soft, almost whimsical, I thought, and he shared his candid advice with a friendly smile, but I could sense the seriousness of what he was saying. I knew not to take anything for granted in the wilderness.

Wayne described the local ecology, geology and geography of the Gorge. On our eighth creek crossing we came to another track that forked off to the left, to the smaller Violet Gorge.

Tree ferns, ancient king orchids, and fig trees with their roots ensnaring colossal sandstone boulders lined the gorge and bordered a small creek that trickled down from somewhere far above. The starkness of contrast to the open eucalypt forest we had been walking through all morning caught me by surprise.

As we started around a bend, the track climbed then descended and we crossed the stream again. Wayne suddenly stopped, knelt by the stream, and pointed to a tiny purple flower. 'In the dew of little things the heart finds its morning and is refreshed. It's a violet, you don't see them very often.' He nudged the little flower. 'You never know what you'll find in here.'

We stepped up a newly erected boardwalk and into an amphitheatre of velvety moss walls. Liverworts, hornworts and fishbone ferns shelved the green carpet in erratic waves and bouquets. A small waterfall cascaded over a slab of rock from a narrow chasm in front of us, falling several metres into a clear shallow pool that became the stream we had followed in. The resounding splash of water into the pool was spellbinding.

'Welcome to Moss Gardens,' Wayne said.

'This place is incredible,' exclaimed the ladies.

I nodded, at once hypnotised by the magical micro-world that encompassed us.

'Yes, the natural beauty here is quite unique,' Wayne said. 'The water you can see seeping out of the moss-covered walls is thousands of years old. It has spent all that time slowly percolating through the porous sandstone from the tablelands above. Here it hits an impervious layer of rock and is forced out of the porous stone. What doesn't re-appear as springs in places like this, trickles down to the Great Artesian Basin. It's quite intriguing if you think about it, we're actually looking at the past dripping out of the walls, perhaps from a time when this place looked quite different. This whole park was a sacred place to the local Aboriginal tribes that used to live in this region. They used it as a corridor to travel across the ranges, and places like this were used for special men's or women's ceremonies, like initiations. It's easy to see why.'

Wayne took off his pack and dug out morning tea: coffee, tea, sugar, powdered milk, water, biscuits, a Trangia stove, lighter and gas. 'Biscuit anyone?'

Wayne was quiet while we sipped our tea or coffee. Other than answering a few questions from the ladies and myself about Moss Gardens and the Gorge, he seemed to encourage the silence.

After a while I decided to move on.

'Going so soon?' Wayne asked.

'I'd like to make Battleship Spur before nightfall,' I replied, acutely aware that I had broken the spell of the meditative capsule we sat in.

Wayne smiled. 'Make sure you take your time at the Art Gallery, Ben. Cathedral Cave is good too. The rock art in the Gorge is world famous for its sheer scale and complexity.'

'I will. Thanks for a great morning. I'll come and find you at the Lodge tomorrow.'

I pulled my hat down to protect my eyes from the glare of the sun back on the main track. The golden, fate-filled morning wasn't lost on me. Woven into the string of coincidental, yet crucial, meetings that had unravelled since my arrival in the Gorge was a thread of destiny that I couldn't ignore. I recalled what Joe had said about the *flow* back on the Sunshine Coast. Perhaps this was what he meant when he spoke about that mysterious force? Each chance meeting had imparted its own sliver of information. Something, somewhere, was trying to speak to me.

An hour later I arrived at Aljon Falls. Beside the cascading spring, a steep passage of steps carved a trail into Wards Canyon.

I walked past giant king ferns—*Angiopteris evecta*. The Mesozoic limbs of the ferns which towered over me in a perennial green wave of bipinnate leaves were close to extinction. Angiopteris Ravine was the last surviving place of the fern in central Queensland. Walking beside the ferns gave me the impression I had taken a step back in time.

I took a seat on an enormous, weathered tree trunk that had fallen into the canyon decades earlier. A cool draft funnelled its way past me from somewhere deeper in the canyon. The faint, mellifluous echo of water splashing into an out-of-sight pool, beyond an area that had been cordoned off, filled the canyon with a spellbinding presence. The area was known as the Freezing Chamber, aptly named for its temperature even during the long hot summer months.

In the latter part of World War One, four German brothers: Ernest, Walter, Archie and Thomas Ward, lived in here as recluses, avoiding conscription. The brothers hunted koalas, possums and kangaroos. They stored food and the pelts of their hunt in the cool recesses of the canyon's interior.

I found myself cast into another world—a magic that connected the physical to the supernatural like an invisible river. It harboured an energy I didn't understand.

The loud squawk of a native bird pulled me from my meditations. Battleship Spur pressed in on my thoughts. I didn't like the idea of trying to navigate my way along a backcountry track in the dark, especially if it was as tricky as Wayne had described.

A chalky, white sandstone wall sixty metres long displayed a vast and impressive array of rock art at the Art Gallery. Red, white and orange ochre stencils, paintings and engravings splashed the sandstone in a poignant reminder of the rich culture that had thrived in the Central Highlands before the arrival of Europeans.

Stencilling, a form of art where the pigment is blown from the mouth of the artist in a fine spray over the object it is meant to depict, formed a large part of the artwork that covered the wall in hands, emu feet and boomerangs. Nets and coolamons (a bark container used to collect food and water) were painted with the use of bark brushes. Vulva's, the female's reproductive organ, were engraved deep into the stone. Millennia of stories spilled from the sacred wall in an ancient odyssey of rites and rituals.

I paused often along the boardwalk in quiet recognition and awe of the site. The scale and complexity, the colours and the shapes, wrapped me in reverential arms. Sentient beings had spent countless hours marking the sandstone, trying to convey a sense of their life, values and the natural world in a story for future generations—sacred ceremonies, Songlines, storytelling—the real Australia lay bare before me.

The width of the Gorge ranged from 40 to 400 metres. The sun climbed through the blue sky. I walked beneath the fronded shadows of towering cabbage tree palms, stands of ancient forest and navigated boulder-strewn creek crossings. I gauged the time of day and quickened my pace. I still had a long distance to cover.

As the precipice walls of the Gorge expanded then contracted around Carnarvon Creek, the track hugged the left flank. Cathedral Cave materialised. It was larger than the Art Gallery and overhung a long boardwalk in a huge, curling ivory wave. Hundreds more engravings, paintings and stencils stretched across its walls in a story that could only be measured in millennia. It was Queensland's largest habitation shelter. Engravings extended one metre below ground.

The significance of that scope of time stretched beyond my comprehension. The remnants of the cultural journey that stood before me was old. Very old. Yet the rock art was symbolic and reminiscent of the long story all humans share. A story that, through Aboriginal culture, had reached the modern world. I knew my own ancestors had left rock paintings in caves, in other parts of the world, in their own attempt to convey a sense of place and time and share their own stories. Trying to comprehend the long journey from then to now drew my being into the earth. It was as if my feet were putting down roots to taste and recall the connection I had lost. That close connection to the land and nature spirits was something that had been discarded and forgotten, displaced by science and technology, and the tyranny of consumerism.

I followed a dry creek bed to the mouth of Boowinda Gorge—yet another branch in the maze of side gorges that fed into Carnarvon Gorge. Boowinda means *thunder*. A great stone face guarded the entrance of the gorge. Strange how we attribute human qualities to images in nature.

The gorge was dark and cool. Basalt boulders cobbled its sandy bottom, and fig trees clung to its sides at queer angles. In places, the basalt bed extended into deep cliff-base undercuts. Tree ferns sprouted sporadically from its base, towering above me in viridescent fireworks. The passage was timeless and curving; the way ahead and behind dissolved into emerald and ivory. Above, only a brushstroke of blue.

After about an hour of walking, I came to a large boulder in the middle of the gorge with an arrow carved into it. The arrow pointed up a steep narrow gully, marking the beginning of the ascent to Battleship Spur. I took out my map and carefully reviewed the notes. The description fit. If only I could pull out a map of life, I thought, and check to see if

I was headed in the right direction. Perhaps I could learn to listen to my intuition, and my heart, as the compasses to guide me through life.

The rocky gully went straight up for 100 metres at a 45-degree angle. I clutched at roots and branches and pulled myself up to an open, yellow-grassed woodland. I began navigating the track—more of an animal pad. In some places, I was sceptical of it being a trail at all. Occasionally, I passed a ribbon nailed to a tree as the climb levelled out and then ascended again.

The trail became better defined as it ascended through a rocky section and through different layers of time. I stopped and peered through enormous old iron bark trees to take in the growing panorama. Elation nearly swept me off the ranges. The olivine, cream and golden folds, twists and undulations, pinnacles, domes, mesas and cliffs described freedom better than I ever could. Enchantment swallowed me.

Late in the afternoon I came to a large area of the mountainside that was covered in jagged shards of black basalt. The rocks had warmed in the sun and radiated a stifling heat. The basalt was the crumbling remains of an ancient volcanic eruption that had covered thousands of square kilometres.

Beyond the crumbling remains of lava, the trail regressed into a goat track as it skirted a steep ridge. Boards of wood, wedged into the ridge and braced by star pickets, kept the track from crumbling away where it curled around rocky outcrops. I took slow, deliberate steps, ensuring the safest footing. I didn't want to find out how long it would take a search and rescue party to find me if I tripped, fell, and rolled down the slope into a broken heap.

Finally, a sheer rocky face presented itself before me. I studied it for foot and hand holds—a few spindly roots protruded at increments. I scanned the area around the rock face for other options. There weren't any. With a nip of courage, I reached out and grabbed hold of the first sturdy looking root and gave it a tug, then began pulling myself up. Finally, with adrenalin pumping effort, I crawled onto a flatter part of the track along a razorback ridge.

A small clearing encircled by a tight grove of trees marked the campsite on Battleship Spur. I dumped my pack on the ground by a large stone cairn near the lookout. A small plastic container sat on top of the cairn. I picked it up and opened it. Inside was a rolled-up notebook. The pages were full of the names and comments left by the people who had made the climb to the lookout. One of the pages read: *You made it!* I laughed to myself. Somehow, it felt like the message had been written for me.

I placed the notebook back in the container and sat it on the stone cairn, then sauntered to the lookout. A thousand metres below, Carnarvon Gorge curved and twisted eastward to the horizon, the silver-green thread of its creek curled through the precipice passage like an enormous olive python. Eucalypt forest clambered over the ranges and escarpments. Silence perched on the lookout, then took flight upon a collecting breeze and the far-off cry of some bird. Shadows advanced in the Gorge, leaning off the cliffs into the forest below. It would be getting dark at the Lodge.

I sat, lost in that view, in the clouds of my lone journey, adrift in quiet contemplation. Time slid through the hourglass, curling rose-gold around the trees at the edge of the clearing. I realised I was lonely; had been terribly lonely, inside, for a very long time. The incredible, terrible beauty of that moment squeezed tears from eyes that ran down my cheeks and fell into the Gorge below to join Carnarvon Creek. I could hardly believe I had found myself in such a beautiful time and place. I wanted to share it with someone.

Like a flock of flamingos taking to the sky, the white precipice sandstone walls of the Gorge turned fiery pink at sunrise. I packed up camp, eager to get back to the Lodge and find Wayne. There was no doubt in my mind that there was something sacred about the land I was in, and something I felt I had come here to learn.

Annie chattered incessantly behind the bar that evening.

'Maybe you're a bit strange,' she said. The frown that creased her brow didn't successfully hide the mischief in her eyes.

'How old are you?' I asked her.

'I'm 19, but I came out here because my sister was working here, and home was boring.'

'Why am I strange then?'

'You know, because you're travelling alone. Nobody does that. How was Battleship Spur, did you get scared up there by yourself? Lonely?'

'It was amazing.'

'I'm jealous now. I've never been up there before. Maybe you can take me sometime?'

'Maybe. I'm going over to the A-Frame to listen to Wayne's slideshow about the Gorge.'

'You should ask him if you're a guide yet.'

'I'm sure he'll let me know when he's ready.'

Wayne was busy stoking a fire in a huge stone hearth. 'Hi Ben. You made it to Battleship Spur and back then. Did you enjoy it?'

'Amazing.'

'Well, that's good. The spirits must have left you alone then.' Wayne smiled.

'Spirits?'

A small group of guests walked in. 'I have to get the slideshow ready now,' Wayne said, leaving my query about the spirits hanging. 'You're welcome to stay and watch if you like.'

Wayne clicked through projector slides as he delivered his speech about the Gorge, explaining to the recently arrived guests the advantages and enjoyment they could derive from taking a guided walk during their stay at the Lodge. After joining Wayne for the walk to Moss Gardens, and then walking the rest of the Gorge alone, I could now appreciate the benefits of a guided walk.

I envisioned myself standing there, talking to the guests and selling guided tours, as Wayne reeled off statistics: 200 species of birds, 90 species of reptile, 60 mammal species, 20 species of bats and amphibians, as well as a dozen fish and turtle species. The park's plethora of fauna was only magnified by its vast collection of flora, 23 species of which were rare and endangered. Forty different ecosystems, nine of which were also endangered, survived in the hidden chasms and deep ravines.

I waited while the guests quizzed Wayne about walks. As they drifted away, I approached Wayne. He looked up from his walk register and caught me with trusting eyes. 'So, how would you like to be a guide, Ben?'

CHAPTER NINETEEN
WILDERNESS GUIDE

'I went to the woods because I wished to live deliberately, to front only the essential facts of life, and see if I could not learn what it had to teach, and not, when I came to die, discover that I had not lived.'

—*Henry David Thoreau*

'I told you you'd get the job,' Annie squealed when she saw me. 'The uniform suits you. Are you happy?'

Annie's elation was contagious. I gave her the thumbs up. The corners of my mouth were nearly touching my ears. 'Does it look like I'm happy? Well, I better get going. Wayne is waiting for me.'

Rob was the Lodge's maintenance man—a short weedy fellow with a mullet and coppery skin that was creased and lined as deeply as the Gorge. One of his jobs was to drive the tour groups up to the Visitor Centre where several guided walks started. 'The Kimberley is *God's country*,' he said to me. 'If you like it here, you're going to love it up there.' He'd spent his life in remote parts of Australia.

Wayne drew the guests' attention to geographical points of interest as we rattled along the dirt road in the minibus. I took notes. Outside the front of the Visitor Centre, we scanned a large topographical map of the national park and surrounding area.

With practised, precise movements, Wayne articulated the significance of the park and its main points of interest with thrusts of his bamboo walking pole. Circling the general highland area, he explained how the park was a major water catchment and valuable part of the Queensland Sandstone Belt, which is known as the *Home of the Rivers*. The headwaters of six rivers began life in the park. Three of these rivers eventually joined to form the Fitzroy River which, after traversing hundreds of kilometres, emptied itself into the Pacific Ocean via Rockhampton on Queensland's central east coast. The other three rivers fed into the Murray-Darling Basin, an area which is responsible for draining one seventh of Australia's land mass. These waters eventually made their way into the Murray River, Australia's longest river at 2375 kilometres, which stretches all the way to the Southern Ocean near Adelaide.

Wayne briefed the walking party on the localities of the other sections that made up the national park. This region of the Great Dividing Range ran roughly north-west to south-east. There was Mt Moffat and Salvator Rosa to the north-west, Ka Ka Mundi to the south and Moolayember to the south-east. Moolayember was still an untouched wilderness. Mt Moffat and Salvator Rosa had succumbed to early European settlement and still ran cattle.

The land was gazetted as a national park in 1932 and had grown considerably in size since its formation. It now covered 298,000 hectares, 66,000 of which made up the Carnarvon Gorge section of the park.

Wayne finished by informing the group that the Gorge carved a 30-kilometre path through the plateau. We would be covering about one third of it this morning.

Inside the Visitor Centre, we inspected jars containing preserved specimens of poisonous snakes, spiders, lizards and amphibians, the likes of which might be encountered in the Gorge. The specimens were submerged in ethyl alcohol and filled long shelves. An impressive, lifelike miniature scale model of Carnarvon Gorge sat in the centre of the room under a large plastic display case. Wayne pointed out Moss Gardens, our destination for the morning.

We set off up the main track at a modest pace. I scribbled notes on flora and fauna while Wayne guided the group. I was glad of the previous opportunity to join him to Moss Gardens because I knew what to expect when we got there.

That afternoon I moved into one of several pale green portable accommodation blocks, known as dongers, which were the staff living quarters. The dongers were nestled in a large clearing beside Carnarvon Creek, a few minutes' walk from the Lodge. They were considerably more comfortable than the dongers on Walhallow. Each building comprised of four rooms, shared amenities, and a balcony running the length of the building both front and back. Wayne and Rob lived in their own single bedroom dongers. Another, much older building sat in the back corner of the clearing. It was the old Country Women's Association (CWA) cottage. It had once served as a gathering place, social network, and holiday accommodation for the isolated families of local stations. It was now a social common room for the Lodge staff.

A sculpture of a very tall, slender Aboriginal man holding a long spear in his left hand stood beside the deck of the Lodge. His gaze pierced the dark forest like a sentinel, keeping watch over the lodgers. The restaurant deck was the guided walk meeting point. I met Wayne, and we waited for two guests that had booked an early morning walk to the platypus viewing area.

Shoulder-high spear grass lined the wide dirt track that twisted and wound its way beneath towering spotted gums. With instructed stealth and silence, we waited above a small pond where platypuses were most commonly sighted. In whispered tones, Wayne described the shy platypus, its unusual habits and how to spot the wary creature.

'The platypus is one of only two egg-laying mammals in the world, both of which are endemic to Australia. The other is the echidna, which is also found in the Gorge. They're known as monotremes and are the link between reptiles and modern mammals,' Wayne said.

'What exactly are we looking for?' asked one of the guests in a southern American drawl.

'Well, the platypus is semi-aquatic. It's a duckbilled, web-footed, toothless, beaver-tailed, fur-covered creature with a venomous spur on each of its hind legs, which it uses for combat with other platypuses. It's about the size of a large rat.'

Bewilderment bulged from our guests' eyes. I had the feeling they thought Wayne was joking with them.

Undeterred, Wayne continued with the baffling facts. 'The platypus suckles its young, which it hides in a deep burrow just above the water line. Dusk and dawn are the platypus' most active times...'

Just then, a small ripple broke the surface of the pool. 'Platypus!' Wayne hissed.

We froze as a creature no bigger than a large rodent paddled along the surface of the pond. It briefly lifted its bill, then dived. Within a minute the creature reappeared then dived again.

'It's foraging for food,' Wayne said, taking the opportunity to describe how the platypus hunts. 'It does this by picking up tiny electrical pulses through the tip of its bill, which small fish and other invertebrates, like shrimp and yabbies, give off when they move.'

A piercing 'kork ork ork ork' burst from the branches of a tree above us. We all shot our attention into the pendulous leafy limbs of the tree. A large grey bird with long wings and tail, and a tremendous bill, stared back at us. I noticed the skin surrounding the eyes was a brilliant red. Wayne swiftly identify the raucous intruder. 'That's a channel-billed cuckoo. A rare sight. It's the largest cuckoo in the world,' he said, suppressed excitement spilling from his lips. 'This particular cuckoo lays its eggs in other bird's nests, namely crows, magpies or currawongs, so their young are reared with the host's chicks. All the responsibility of raring their young is passed on. The poor little magpie must wonder why it has such a large and unsightly presence in its nest. Funnily enough they don't seem to mind. The Gorge is part of the cuckoo's summer feeding grounds where they annually migrate from New Guinea and the Celebes, but I've only seen one here once before, so we're very lucky.'

The platypus reappeared, dived, surfaced again then swam upstream. While we waited to see if it would come back and forage in the pond, a rock wallaby stirred in the gully beyond the pond. 'Ahh look, another rare sight,' Wayne said, as he pointed in the direction of the illusive creature so we could all see it.

We said goodbye to our guests at the Lodge then departed for the guides' room.

'I don't like to disappoint people like that but it's part of the job sometimes, unfortunately.'

'Why do you think they were disappointed?' I thought we'd had a great morning.

'I could sense it. They wanted to see more of the platypus. But you can't always expect nature to come out dancing and doing somersaults on queue. Some people seem to understand that; others don't. When people are paying to see something it's always good if they see what they have paid for. It makes our job more enjoyable too. Some of the people you will meet have come a long way to see the Gorge and the wildlife here, like those Americans have, and they may never come this way again. Night spotting is much the same—sometimes you see lots of wildlife and lots of activity, other times you don't see much at all. If it's really bad, I offer the guests a refund. Now, let me show you where we keep everything.'

Wayne opened the door to a small wooden building that resembled an old backcountry cabin. Shafts of light streamed through the windows, picking up particles of dust in the dimly lit room. It felt like an old treasure hunter's lair.

The cabin was full of guiding equipment: backpacks, first aid kits, bird identification guides, binoculars, radios and the bamboo poles we encouraged our guests to use. We went through the use of spotlights and the need to keep their batteries fully recharged for night spotting trips, packing adequate morning tea for half and full day walks and the supplies I would need for different sized groups.

'You can use the computer too if there's anything you'd like to research. It's a bit old, and the internet isn't great, but it does the job,' Wayne said in sheepish amusement as he brushed the dust off the monitor. We walked over to a large basin. 'This is where we do the washing up. We re-use everything we can. You'll need to replenish stocks from time to time as well. You can find everything in the restaurant's storeroom. I usually ask the chefs before I take anything. What do you think so far?'

'I like it.'

'There's a lot to learn, so don't expect to know everything at once. The Gorge will teach you something new every day. I'm still learning, and I've been working in these parts for 17 years.'

CHAPTER TWENTY

THE WEAVINGS OF NATURE

'This world is but canvas to our imaginations.'
—*Henry David Thoreau*

From an early age, I had recognised a connection with nature, a mystical thread moving beyond mind and heart, connecting me to some mysterious, unknown element.

The day I saw Claudia I had been reminded of that connection; reminded of a waking vision I had had in the hills of Akaroa, in New Zealand, when I was a boy.

It was a warm summer afternoon. After several days of being stuck with my brother, sister and cousins whom we were holidaying with, I found myself wanting to escape all the noise and energy.

I found a dirt track and followed its winding path into the hills. After an hour of climbing, I came to a stream. Caught by an alluring energy, I stopped and sat on the ground between the track and the stream. Native bush lined the banks and encroached on the track. The water, rocks, trees and air seemed to vibrate in a suffusion of brilliant, sparkling light. Suddenly, a profound energy welled up inside of me and the image of a girl appeared in my mind. Many years later, I had taken Stephanie into those same hills—as if to self-fulfil a prophecy; to find an answer to a question—but neither the energy, nor the answer, was there. Listening to Claudia talk at Takarakka the evening I met her, and feeling the energy I had felt from the Gorge over the past weeks, I felt like I was meant to be here.

'Do you know Claudia?' I asked Annie, trying in vain not to draw attention to my question.

'Of course, everyone knows Claudia. She's a guide. She usually comes up here for a beer. You like her, don't you?'

'Um, she seems nice. How often does she come up here?' I asked, my cover blown.

'Most nights, but I haven't seen her for a while. She's probably been busy. We could go down and see her if you like? She lives in a caravan at Takarakka.'

'Yeah okay,' I said dumbly.

The following afternoon I drove Annie down to Takarakka. She knocked on Claudia's caravan door. The door flew open and Claudia stood, wide-eyed. She stared at me and then at Annie, and her surprise melted into that beautiful, warm smile.

'Hi Annie.' Claudia turned to me, her eyes narrowed in a confused frown. 'Hi…?'

'Hi Claudia. I thought we'd come over and say hello and introduce Ben to you. He's our new wilderness guide. You'll probably see him out guiding now he's one of you.'

'Wilderness guide?' Claudia cocked her head in question, her expression shifting from confusion to a mix of suspicion and bewilderment. Sheepishly, I looked at my boots and then back at Claudia and smiled.

'You asked about the walk up to Battleship Spur the other day, didn't you?'

'Yep.'

'How did you go?'

'Fantastic, just like you said.'

'Yeah, it's a pretty special place alright. I haven't been up there in a while, but I'd like to visit it again. Would you both like a tea or coffee then?'

'Coffee,' Annie replied.

'And how about you, Ben?'

'Coffee's fine, thanks.'

We sat down on a couple of foldout chairs around a small firepit outside the caravan while Claudia rustled up a few coffees.

'So, you're planning on staying for a while, Ben?' Claudia called from her caravan.

'Seems that way.'

'Have you worked as a guide before?'

'No, first time.'

'Really?' Claudia's tone was more piqued than surprised. She came out of the caravan and handed Annie and me a coffee.

'Yep.'

'What else has been happening, Claudia?' Annie interrupted the awkward conversation with shrewd preciseness.

'Oh, the usual, guiding people up the Gorge, spotting wildlife. I had a couple of fantastic glides the other night.'

'Glides? You go gliding in the forest? At night?' I was baffled.

Annie and Claudia looked at each other and laughed like a pair of kookaburras. 'Yes, of course, from one tree to the next. It's quite a thrill actually once you get the hang of it,' Claudia said, her amusement spilling into another round of convulsive giggling.

'You should see the look on your face,' Claudia said, wiping the tears from her eyes. 'No, not me, silly. The yellow-bellied gliders. They are just one of the nocturnal mammals we see when we go night spotting. Last night I saw one glide 50 metres between two spotted gums. I said to my tour group: *It doesn't' get any better than that, folks*. They all cheered.'

'Seriously? I have to see one of these gliders.' I was amazed an animal that wasn't a bird could fly so far, or glide.

Annie piped up, 'It sounds like you two need to get together sometime and go night spotting then. As for me, I need to get back to the lodge for work.' Annie started nodding her head and rolling her eyes at me.

'It was nice to meet you again, Claudia.'

'You too, Ben, see you up at the Lodge for a beer sometime?'

'Sure.'

Over the following weeks I immersed myself in a forest of information about Carnarvon National Park, the central Queensland highlands and the region's rich cultural history. My passionate enthusiasm for the Gorge, new friends, and new life unfolded in the pages of geography and geology, flora and fauna, culture and history. Spiritual connotations and philosophical phrases seemed to unlock within me a vast storehouse of insights about subjects I had never contemplated and questions I had never asked: what is the purpose of living, what did it mean to be alive?

Wayne was a walking library of knowledge. To assist me with my studies, he dropped enthusiastic piles of books and papers by my room. If it weren't for Wayne's impeccable ability as a guide, I would have mistaken him for a recluse. He tactfully avoided the other employees of the Lodge unless his presence was required. His quiet demeanour provoked the passionate, deep thinker within him. His reclusive behaviour aroused my curiosity. After some investigation, I discovered he was often busy observing life through the lens of his camera.

'I have an environmental photo library and photography service on the internet,' Wayne said, handing me a business card. The name read: EcoPix.

'I wasn't always a guide. I have a master's degree in Research Science. I found it a bit boring, though. I enjoy my photography more. It allows me to spend a lot of time in nature, which I relish.' His burning but calm and patient passion for nature shone from his youthful, unassuming nut-brown eyes.

He glanced at the Minolta SLR camera I had bought to document my travels around Australia. 'There's quite an art to capturing a moment in a single frame. It takes dedication and patience. You will do well early in your photography career if you can learn these things. Sometimes you think you have taken a good photo, and then you find out after you develop the negative that it isn't. Sometimes you get lucky and a photo comes out better than you expected. My new digital camera takes a lot of the guess work out, but it still takes keen observation and practice to capture those magical moments, much like life.'

'How do you mean, Wayne?'

'Well, the camera lens has a way of changing perspective. Just as with life, you can choose to either zoom in or zoom out on a subject. Over time you work out what's worth focusing on and what isn't. Once you have mastered this, you begin to experiment with the elements that are worthy of your time and attention. Somewhere in there you will find what works best for you, and then you learn to apply that knowledge. Even then you don't always get it right. But it's all about perspective. When that happens to me, I just remind myself to get back to nature, and it all makes sense. Life is predictable and random, all at once. It's always changing on you just when you think you know something about it. We're all playing the same game; the better you are at applying what you've learnt in the past the further along you'll get and the easier things will be in the future. And sometimes you just have to let go, accept, and enjoy life for what it is. But I think you know that already.'

Wayne and I piled into the Lodge's minibus with our guests and their day packs for my first Ultimate Full Day Walk. It was early September. I was now competent in guiding on most of the other walks we offered: Mickey Creek Walk, Nature Trail Experience, Moss Gardens, Aboriginal Cultural Trail and Boolimba Bluff.

Rob dropped us off at the Visitor Centre and gave me a nod. 'Good luck Ben.' I was anxious. It was my first full day walk, and I'd be taking charge as far as Moss Gardens.

Wayne reeled off his speech at the Visitor Centre. Our guests were suitably impressed. I knew they would be expecting a lot for the day. When Wayne had finished, he turned to me, 'Okay, Ben, you can take it from here.' He gave me a confident smile and nod.

Ten pairs of eyes shifted their focus to me. For a moment, I shrivelled under their expectant gaze. Then I summoned a nervous smile and took a deep breath. 'All right folks if you'd like to follow me, we'll head off to the first creek crossing,' I announced with unexpected gusto. The group picked up their heels, swung their bamboo walking poles in time with their gait, and we marched towards the sparkling moat of Carnarvon Creek.

Wayne herded the group from behind. In staccato spurts I reeled off the facts and figures I had memorised over the past month. Now and then, Wayne spliced succinct snippets to broaden my knowledge and meld my delivery.

Wayne rallied our group at Moss Gardens, and we pushed on for Big Bend, stopping at Wards Canyon, the Art Gallery and Cathedral Cave along the way.

Through the course of the morning Wayne painted a story of how the Gorge was formed. Three main layers of sedimentary sandstone made up the escarpments that surrounded us. The first was the Clematis sandstone—the underlying, pinkish, sandstone layer. It was laid down in the Triassic Period 252–201 million years ago, deposited by rivers into a huge inland basin when Australia was still joined to Gondwana. Above that the white precipice sandstone, which formed the steep walls of the gorge, was laid down in the Jurassic Period 201–145 million years ago. From 145–66 million years ago, during the Cretaceous Period, two bands of sandstone formed on top of the precipice layer, known as the Hutton and Evergreen layers. They had been eroded into the shelves that retreated up into the tablelands far above where a thin basalt cap covered the land. The lava flows that formed the cap happened about 28 million years ago. These had originated in the earth's mantle, 60 kilometres below the surface. The Buckland had been the main flow, which originally covered some 15,000 square kilometres, originating from The Steeple in the Mt Moffatt section of the park. Wayne explained how during the Tertiary Period, some 66–2 million years ago, uplifting had caused cracks and other faults in the sandstone, which, with the help of wind and water, had then eroded into the gorges that we were walking through today.

Wayne loved bird spotting, and he knew a great deal of the birds in the Gorge by sight and sound. While we walked down the main track, he pointed out white-throated treecreepers, variegated fairy-wrens, eastern yellow robins and willie wagtails. Yellow-tailed black cockatoos called plaintively as they flew above the treetops, and red-winged parrots quietly fossicked in the canopy. Along the creek we spotted pied cormorants, their outstretched wings drying feathers in the sun. White-faced herons, dusky moorhens and azure kingfishers poked, prodded and dived among the reeds in small pools in search of fish and invertebrates. Occasionally, Wayne mimicked the calls of birds in fluted whistles and chattering chirps while I referenced the bird finder for their descriptions to show the bird enthusiasts in our group. I had volumes to learn before I would be as comprehensive and entertaining a guide as Wayne.

Big Bend was the furthest our guided walks ventured up the Gorge. It was the end of the track for most of the visitors to the park unless a special request to venture further was made. I encouraged our group to sit at the wooden park benches by Carnarvon Creek while Wayne unpacked their lunches. We prepared a billy-tea then sat on the smooth boulders that lined the creek under a tremendous overhang of white precipice sandstone.

'How are you going, Ben? Still enjoying it?' Wayne asked.

'If every day is this good, I won't want to leave. The Gorge gets more interesting the more I see and learn about it.'

'Yes, it has that effect on a lot of people. When you get to know the Gorge, the Gorge will get to know you.' Wayne said it in a way that made me think I had yet to find out what the Gorge really was. 'And remember, it's good if you can just have normal conversations with people too. It's not all about the facts. Facts get boring. Remember to *discover with*, rather than *lecture to*. You'll learn to understand the dynamics of the groups you guide and tailor your tour to suit their needs. Sometimes it's good if you just let people walk alone in silence too, the same way you would if you were out walking on your own. Presence is needed to become aware of the beauty, the majesty, and the sacredness of nature.'

I reclined on my elbows and watched the sun's reflection off Carnarvon Creek dance like angels upon the white sandstone wall above us. That angel light seemed to penetrate and permeate every atom in my body. I fell in love with the Gorge in that moment, and I accepted the *flow* that had entered my life. If God offers man the choice between repose and truth, I chose truth.

That evening, I prepared tea, coffee, biscuits and soft drinks in the A-Frame. I stoked up the fire and tested the slide projector.

The gathering crowd of newly arrived guests slowly swelled to daunting numbers. Finally, the last patron took his seat. I had never addressed a large crowd of strangers before. I hadn't even seen Wayne deal with a gathering of this size—twenty-three faces stared expectantly back at me. I'd secretly been hoping that only a handful of guests would show up for my first Carnarvon Gorge Wilderness Lodge welcome and slideshow presentation. 'Good luck.' Wayne smiled bashfully. He slipped aside to dim the lights.

With a *click-shuffle, click-shuffle*, I slowly flicked through the slides: images of Moss Gardens, the Amphitheatre, Wards Canyon and the Art Gallery. Stunning wildlife and breathtaking views from different escarpments around the Gorge flashed in a consortium of portraits that endeavoured to portray the personality of the Gorge and hook the new arrivals. I peddled the indisputable benefits of taking a guided tour with an experienced and knowledgeable leader.

Wayne turned up the lights and took questions and bookings.

'How'd I go?' I asked Wayne, after our guests had drifted off.

'Well, I'd have gone for a guided walk with you.'

'Yeah?'

'Sure. It was a big group tonight, so you did well. We have a busy day tomorrow. It's starting with an early booking for a sunrise walk up to Clematis Ridge. You'll like this one. After that we have a Mickey Creek walk, then a night spotting walk. Well done.'

The morning was cool, damp and dark. A light fog hung in finger-like wisps among the trees around the lodge. The eerie, wailing cry of a bird resounded somewhere in the forest, not far from the restaurant deck.

'That's a bush stone-curlew. I haven't heard one of them around here for a while. If we're lucky we might see it,' Wayne said. We were waiting for our guests to arrive for their walk up to Clematis Ridge for sunrise.

'That's a curious sound it makes,' I remarked.

'Yes, it's a mysterious sort of bird. It has long legs, large eyes and a short beak with greyish plumage that's streaked around the neck. You'll probably see one around here early in the morning before one of your sunrise walks. Our guests might scare this one off.'

I tried to imagine the bird. Its call was another exotic sound that added to the mysteriousness of the Gorge.

Our guests arrived sleepy-eyed. We trudged into the early morning gloom with our torches, slicing beams of light through the forest. From the Nature Trail, we ascended a rocky, grassed ridge on a narrow, barely noticeable path. Dawn pushed back the bewitched cloak of night in a symphony of bird song and chatter that began to wake the quiet wilderness. The loud, distinct, onomatopoeic call of the Currawong flew in looping wingbeats through the forest.

We topped the ridge shortly before sunrise. Wayne guided the way to a large, flat rocky outcrop. The view to the east, over the Arcadia Valley, was unobscured. Below us, the entrance to the Gorge opened its arms to the rising sun and surrounding savannah like the gates to a utopian city. A forest of eucalyptus reached for the sky, marching south in solidarity with the white precipice cliffs of Moolayember Gorge.

I assisted Wayne with tea and coffee while the sun peeled back the dark shadows from the labyrinth below in a wash of salmon-pink, brilliant orange and flame-red. I had to pinch myself.

While I sipped tea and chatted with our guests, Wayne poked around car-sized boulders scattered along the ridge. 'Ahh, here it is,' he called out. 'Come and have a look at this.' I wandered over with our guests. There, under the sheltered overhang of a boulder, were two stencil handprints.

'Keep your eyes peeled, Ben. You just never know what you'll discover in the Gorge. You might even find something no one knows about.'

I led the afternoon Mickey Creek Walk. Wayne tagged along, insistent upon being treated as one of the guests while he evaluated my skill in quiet recognition of my growing confidence as a nature guide. I pointed out flora and fauna and articulated their names, uses and habits.

In Warrumbah Gorge, I reverted to following Wayne. There was a whole other ecosystem to learn about in the cool confines of the ravine. Wayne pointed out a myriad of life that was rarely seen: whirligig beetles and water-striders swam in dizzying loops over the water's surface in small pools. Fish-eating spiders crouched motionless on small boulders. Tusked frogs hid in small nooks and crannies. I found a curious looking creature that looked like a very small snake. I collected it in my hands and showed Wayne.

'Where did you find him?'

'Just here on the rocks.' Our tour group compressed into a tight circle of bodies around us.

'Good spotting. Look folks, Ben's found a Burton's Legless Lizard.'

'A legless what?' I replied in bewilderment.

The Weavings Of Nature

'It's a lizard, related to the skink family, you can tell by looking at its head.'

The legless lizard was slow and felt cold. After showing our guests, I took it out of the chasm and released it under the warm forest canopy.

That evening Wayne and I prepared for my first night spotting tour.

'Night spotting can be one of the most exciting walks we take, but it all depends on how active the wildlife is because there isn't much else to see at night.'

I was excited about seeing the nocturnal movements of the gorge—especially the gliders. I wondered if I'd see Claudia with one of her groups. Several weeks had passed in a whirl of guide training since I visited her with Annie, yet the magnetic draw I felt to her hadn't dissipated. It bound my thoughts to her like an invisible thread of energy that wove an intricate web through every magical, living element of the Gorge.

'Here, take this.' Wayne passed me a huge spotlight and a motorbike battery. I attached the spotlight leads to the battery terminals and put the battery in my backpack while he gathered torches for our guests.

'Are you sure these won't blind the poor creatures?'

'It's not their eyes I'm worried about. It's our guests' eyes that aren't so good.' Wayne handed me a handful of torches. 'They'll want these so they can see where they're walking. No good for spotting, though.'

Wayne described the habits of the nocturnal creatures in the Gorge to our expectant guests as we ambled along the Aboriginal Cultural Trail.

'The gliders drink the sap from the eucalypt trees.' Wayne aimed his spotlight at the oozing cuts on the trunk of a nearby spotted gum. 'They glide from tree to tree with the help of a membrane, which runs from their front elbow to their back ankle—a thin flap of fur covered skin. They use their tail as a rudder to steer themselves.'

'How many different gliders are there in the Gorge?' asked one of our guests.

'The greater glider and the yellow-bellied glider are the most active around here. The greater glider is the largest of the glider family in Australia. It can grow up to a metre in length and is grey and white in colour. The yellow-bellied glider is slightly smaller and, as its name suggests, has a buttermilk-coloured belly. The rest of the body is brown.

They are gregarious creatures. To the untrained eye, they resemble a possum.'

A harsh guttural screech cut the air. I slowly waved my spotlight through the treetops in the direction of the noise to see if I could pick up the eye shine of the active creature.

'There! Looks like a yellow-bellied glider, Wayne, it's on the move in the high branches of that spotted gum just across the gully there.'

'Nice spotting, Ben. Just hold the light slightly off it, that way we won't blind it and distract its movements.'

I held the light slightly ahead of the glider while Wayne instructed our guests to follow my torch beam with their eyes to where the glider was crawling along the branch.

'Okay, quiet now folks. It looks like it's going to jump. We don't want to disturb it.'

The group's excitement quietened into suppressed murmurs of anticipation. The glider stopped, shuffled into a seated position, and appeared to make an assessment of the scene in preparation for jumping. Suddenly, it leapt from the branch and spread its legs wide apart, like a man in a wingsuit. It soared through the air with the might of a magic flying rug, steering itself with rotary like movements of its tail. Its swift descent was briefly slowed with the creature assuming a vertical parachute-like profile just before it latched onto a trunk with abrupt accuracy. It was a whopping 50 metre jump. The glider scrambled up the trunk. I was dumfounded.

A cheer went up. 'Amazing!' cried our guests.

'Watch the boobook owls, folks.' Wayne waved his spotlight in the direction of two boobook owls that were perched in nearby trees. The owls bobbed and swivelled their heads in excited 'boo-book' chants. 'They're waiting for one of the gliders to make a fatal mistake.' The owls made several low passes at another glider as it scrambled along a branch, swooping in fearless attacks just centimetres above its head.

'The boobook owl is a small brown hawk-owl with greenish-yellow eyes set in a large facial mask with pale margins. They nest in hollows of old habitat trees and hunt beetles and possums. The boobook and barking owls are the most common owls seen in the Gorge. The barking owl's voice is a deep 'wook wook' similar to a low muffled bark of a dog. You'll probably hear them in the treetops around the Lodge tonight. The Gorge is also home to a less common and more secluded species, the powerful owl, which is a large owl with a relatively small head and a rounded tail. It's dark grey to dark grey-brown above, with white barring, and off-white below with distinctive dark chevrons. The eyes are yellow. The legs are feathered, and the yellow-orange feet are massive, with sharp talons. Powerful owls are the largest of the Australian nocturnal birds. These owls have a very large territory, perhaps only one or two might live in an area the size of the Gorge. All the owls have a taste for gliders.'

We continued along the track and spotted several other species of wildlife: brush tailed possums, swamp wallabies, and a tawny frogmouth. I spotted another yellow-bellied glider on the move.

'Look here everybody, another yellow-bellied glider, and it looks like it's about to jump!' My fervent eagerness to catch the spectacle startled the guests into a confused spin of bodies and heads as I waggled my spotlight at the creature.

As if on cue, the glider took to the air. Its vector was straight towards us. With an audible *whoosh* it soared above our heads. In a clap of fur, flesh and claws, the stunt-glider latched onto a trunk several metres ahead of us. The creature paused, eyed its spectators, then scrambled into the branches. A roar of delight burst from our guests in a spirited applause of the close encounter. I recalled Claudia's words the day I met her at her caravan with Annie, when she addressed her group after a good show: 'It doesn't get any better than that, folks.'

CHAPTER TWENTY-ONE

SACRED JOURNEYS

'Faeries, come take me out of this dull world, for I would ride with you upon the wind, run on the top of the dishevelled tide, and dance upon the mountains like a flame!'

—*William Butler Yeats*

Wayne had planned a trip for us to the Devil's Signpost to make good use of our free morning. 'It's good to go exploring,' he said. 'Not enough people truly explore life. And the real thirst for life can only come from walking with death.'

The Devil's Signpost is a steep pinnacle of rock on the northern end of Clematis Ridge. It protrudes from the ridge like a giant pointed tooth.

Wayne knocked on my door early. He seemed disappointed. 'Good morning, Ben. Trish has asked me to come into work to take a late booking on a guided walk to Moss Gardens. Sorry, I won't be able to come with you, but I can give you some directions to get to the Devil's Signpost if you want to head up by yourself?'

Had he planned this? Perhaps it was a test? I thought I'd had my fair share of walking with death in the outback, not to mention my youth. I was the thirstiest I'd ever been for life. Surely, he wouldn't send me off on my own to a place called the Devil's Signpost?

'Really? You can't get out of it?' I pushed the point.

'No, I already tried. It's a shame. I was looking forward to taking you up there. If you go, just be careful, it gets quite steep, and you'll be on your own.'

'Okay.'

Wayne gave me instructions on how to find the start of the track. 'Just follow your nose after that, you can't miss it.' It sounded easy enough.

I sprung across the sparkling waters of Carnarvon Creek and along the Nature Trail to find the unmarked track to Clematis Ridge. The track climbed gradually through the crisp mountain air, up past the sunrise lookout and along a razorback ridge where it became better defined. From towering gum trees, the falsetto calls of currawongs sped me on my way, as if some urgent matter of nature was calling. The track continued to ascend through the warm morning light and after about an hour of climbing my sight stretched through the open forest to smaller ridges and vales below.

I caught my first glimpse of the Devil at the top of the next ridge. I slowed my pace, in awe of its mysterious presence. The hairs on the back of my neck pricked up. Funny how some places have that effect.

The track slowly curled east then west, following the graceful arcs of the ridge north. The pinnacle vanished then reappeared, gaining presence with every step taken into its dominion.

I came upon the towering monolith like a pilgrim to a sacred minaret. Like an enigmatic sentinel, the dark protrusion guarded the inner sanctum of the Gorge. Beyond the pinnacle's searching gaze, the land tumbled away through open forest to the golden savannah below. Slowly, carefully, I circumnavigated the Devil, weary of the deep fractures and fissures in its foundations that gave me the impression it was heaved up by the earth like a foreign body being expelled from the fires of hell. The peak rose high above me, steep and challenging. I resolved to climb to the top and began searching for a place to launch my ascent. The view would be superb if I could make it.

I found a likely path and started up. A light breeze picked up. Was it the usual morning winds? Probably. With simian ease, I climbed halfway to the top of the pinnacle, then paused to rest and take in the view. My palms were sweaty, and the cool sandstone felt slippery. A sudden gust of wind pushed me like an invisible arm. I reached out to grasp hold of the rock when, without warning, my left foothold sheared off. A crumbly old piece of sandstone fell and shattered on the rocks below. My heart threw itself against the wall of my chest in palpitating thumps. I peered down the sheer precipice below. *'Be careful, Ben. You'll be on your own.'* Wayne's words spiralled through my brain. I had no wish to tempt the Devil and end up at the bottom of one of the deep fissures below. I flattened myself against the cool stone, clinging to the side of the pinnacle like a giant spider. When I'd collected my thoughts and the pounding in my chest had settled, I reassessed the climb. Reason duelled with resolution: not today, not today.

A warmer, friendlier gust of wind assisted my long strides back to the Lodge with the triumphant calls of birds chasing me. I was thirsty for life. The Gorge demanded respect. The map in my brain of its intricate workings was growing like the complexity of my understanding of life. One thing was clear—respect all living things.

With grace and agility, I navigated the rugged decent back to the Lodge for my afternoon Mickey Creek Walk, springing over exposed roots and rocks, as if my boots had wings. Youth coursed through my arteries, elemental desire spurred me over the terrain, the magic of the Gorge collected me in a giant's grasp and rushed me forward through time and space.

Wayne found me when I got back. 'How did you go?'

'I think you know very well how I went.'

'Oh? What do you mean?'

'There's something going on up there, some kind of spirit guarding that place or something,' I replied, in a flurry of nervous excitement.

'Ah, you met the spirit. I think we have more to talk about now, but all in good time. In the meantime, start listening to the Gorge, not with your ears but with your heart. Learn to see with your mind. Open yourself to the possibility of things you don't yet understand or cannot comprehend.'

When I learnt to listen, truly listen, I discovered something behind the external forms of beauty, something I couldn't name, something ineffable, some deep, inner, holy essence shining through in my own presence.

A few days later Wayne came to me. 'I've persuaded Trish into letting me take you up to The Ranch. I told her it would be useful as part of your guide training in case someone ever wants to do a walk up there.'

A growing respect for Wayne's calm, patient, and accepting approach to life and toward me as mentor and teacher had prized open the clamped treasure chest of my being. I learnt to trust him in a time when trusting people didn't come easy for me. Perhaps I saw something of myself in him, or things I wished to see in myself. The quiet rewards of his time and knowledge for my progress and enthusiasm as a guide weren't lost on me. I felt honoured.

We ascended a barely visible track near the top of the Mickey Creek trail. As we climbed past Warrumbah Bluff, the trail branched into animal pads. Wayne pointed to a piece of pink ribbon tied to a random tree. 'We need to keep an eye out for these now. You probably saw a few on the way up to Battleship Spur.' After a while we couldn't locate any pink ribbons and were left to navigate our way along the ever-shifting animal pads. Higher up, we pushed through thickets of scrub and along an ancient layer of rock called Hell Hole Shelf. After two hours of climbing, clutching at tussock grass and scrambling over rocks, we climbed up onto The Ranch. I stood beside Wayne, and together we gazed out over the wilderness below: Clematis Ridge climbed out of the earth like the long tail of a crocodile, its back ascending to the north, to the Devil's Signpost. Boolimba Bluff, which sat at the top of the white precipice sandstone, stood far below us in the mouth of the Gorge. Beyond the sacred bluff, the escarpments gently shelved away up into Jimmy's Shelf and the Bulkanoo Cliffs. There, on that heavenly plateau, lay the Consuelo Tableland.

Wayne pointed to a giant white mahogany near the escarpment we stood on. 'Local Aborigines refer to these trees as *Maigal*. There is a small forest of them on the Consuelo Tableland which holds mythological significance with the creation of *Budhanbil*—the Milky Way. Some trees measure up to eight metres around the girth. Legend has it, the fierce Goori Goori bird had its nest in the loftiest of these trees. Aborigines claim the people decided to punish this bird for its practice of luring away and eating disobedient children. One night its nest was set alight while it slept and, when the bird awoke with its leg on fire, it flew westward through the night sky leaving an arch of sparks and burning feathers, which became the Milky Way.'

'I'd like to learn more about the Aboriginal culture. I find it fascinating. Their stories bring the landscape to life in a meaningful and magical way.'

'You will learn, Ben. All in good time. Well, shall we?' Wayne asked.

'Let's.' I returned his gracious, unassuming smile, and we started pushing our way through knee-deep kangaroo grass that covered the plateau in a sumptuous golden blanket.

Wayne pointed out several species of trees that didn't grow down in the Gorge, then he suddenly stopped. 'Do you hear that?' I paused to listen. A faint rustling nearby caught my attention. A loud squeal pierced the air and two enormous black pigs, followed by three piglets, charged from the undergrowth several metres away. I flashed a mischievous grin at Wayne. 'I'm going to catch one of the piglets,' I shouted, and took off after them. I was hot on their heels when they vanished under a barrier of scrub. I began poking around, trying to see through the bushes, listening, and peering under them. I couldn't see or hear anything. Then it occurred to me that the intimidated beasts might launch a defensive charge. I broke off the chase and trudged back over the plateau to where I left Wayne.

I couldn't find him. Had I lost my bearings? I hadn't chased after the pigs that far, had I? I called out but no reply came. Perhaps he was busy silently observing a rare bird? I didn't want to spook a possible rare sighting, so I kept walking in the general direction I thought he would be.

A rustling nearby pricked the hairs on the back of my neck. I turned, expecting to see the pigs scrambling through the undergrowth when I noticed a tree move. The leafy, sasquatch-like figure leapt forward and ran towards me, waving its arms and screaming, 'Ooga booga, ooga booga booga!' I turned to run, caught my boot on a log that was hidden in the long grass and fell backwards. I put up my arms to fend off the monster.

'Haha, you should have seen the look on your face!' Wayne convulsed with laughter like a tree being shaken by the wind—it was good laughter, honest and kind, and with no malice in it. He pulled the leafy branches out of his shirt.

'What was that for?' I shouted testily, embarrassed at my buffoonish sprawling. I was still recovering from the shock as I clambered to my feet. I brushed myself off.

'Just seeing if you're ready to deal with any spirits you encounter up here.' Wayne said.

'You're going to have to tell me more about these spirits. Everyone seems to know about them except me,' I replied, determined to get an answer this time.

'Any luck with the pigs?' Wayne enquired, deflecting the subject once again.

'No, they vanished into the bush,' I mumbled, a stab of disappointment piercing my pride.

'Maybe they weren't really there?' Wayne chuckled.

We hiked to the eastern edge of the plateau then doubled back towards its southern escarpment. Our view encompassed the untouched, sprawling wilderness of Moolayember Gorge. A tranquil, almost unnatural, presence settled over the plateau like an invisible blanket.

As if nature had waved its wand, Wayne began telling me about the Aboriginal spirits that resided in the ranges. 'The Ranch is known as a home of Aboriginal spirits. It's rarely visited by humans. You might've heard from some of the staff at the Lodge that it's a place best kept away from when *Dhoongaburra*, or misty rain and fog, settles on the tablelands. Local Aborigines respectfully avoid these elevated lands during these times, believing this to be a sign that the spirits inhabiting these areas are particularly active. The spirits are known as Jun-Judies—small long-limbed hairy people with an ape-like appearance who live in seclusion throughout the belt.'

Annie had told me about Jun-Judies. She liked to talk about them to scare me before I went off exploring on my own, as I did often.

'There are many other spirits that live in the ranges. They include the Eunjies—powerful malevolent spirits that can occasionally be heard calling 'Eunjie-Eunjie' at night. They are far-ranging, shape-shifting spirits, often avian, who frequently visit certain known escarpments and burial caves. Goori-Gooris and Yakajahs are a spirit type people of the night. The former tends to be of a non-physical appearance while the more tangible Yakajahs can be heard moving around in the bush, just out of campfire light range.'

I was glad none of them had bothered me on Battleship Spur.

We came to a rocky outcrop shaded by a large mahogany tree on the southern edge of the plateau. Wayne took off his pack and foraged through it. 'Brumbies, feral cattle and pigs inhabit much of the impassable country below,' he explained, while he peeled an orange. 'Unfortunately, they do a lot of damage to the native flora and fauna of the region. It's a constant battle for the park rangers to keep their numbers in check.'

I recalled a wild scene I observed one day on the station. A small herd of brumbies out in Bush Paddock had run ahead of the cruiser while I was investigating a fire. I imagined chasing wild cattle through the country below on horseback, hunting pigs and making camp in secluded pockets of the Gorge.

'So, Ben, how long do you intend on travelling for?'

'I'm not sure, but as long as it takes me to see Australia I guess.'

'I think it's good to spend some time on the road, you work a lot of stuff out when you get away from people and cities. Balance is the peace we are all looking for but few of us find. You don't mind being on your own?'

'I don't mind my own company, I'm used to it.' I half-lied.

I didn't see the point in telling people that I got quite lonely at times. It seemed a necessary part of my journey and, for the most part, the good times outweighed the lonely spells.

'What do your parents think of what you're doing?'

'Oh, they think it's good.'

'Do you see much of them?'

'My parents broke up when I was 11. I left home when I was 16. I haven't seen much of either of them since then.'

'That must have been hard?'

'It was. It doesn't' bother me so much now.'

I didn't like dragging up my past. How could I encapsulate my youth in a few short sentences?

* * *

I ended up in a variety of fostering arrangements until I was old enough to live on my own. By then, I viewed most adults with a suspicious distrust, and I had learnt to rely only on myself. My flimsy salvation was in praying to a God I didn't know—pleading with him that things would somehow get better—and in my tender young relationship with Stephanie. God never made any promises, but sometimes it seemed he could make miracles happen. I had no idea what to expect from a relationship. Despite the limited help that was available through social services and a few adults that offered me their friendship and a helping hand, I drifted helplessly into a black hole of depression. I grew distant, reckless and lonely. In the withdrawals of depression, I gradually alienated myself from everything that had once been friendly and familiar as my life and mind spiralled into a dark internal void. My good friends drifted away as my search for a release from the pain and loneliness squandered hours and days with my new stoner mates—delinquents and vagabonds in similar situations; some of them totally lost. I learnt about blue uniforms, handcuffs and court hearings. I felt like a victim; like I didn't have any control over what was happening in my life.

My brother's attempt on his own life smashed home the shocking reality of the dark, silent cloak of suffering we shared. Yet, we rarely caught up or discussed what had happened or opened up about what we were going through. Heavy nights and days spent contemplating my own demise circled like winged wraiths. Driving alone from Stephanie's place back to the empty room of my foster care tore at my soul with jagged steel and shattered glass as I contemplated speeding off the road into a power pole or off a bridge. Other times an overdose of some description seemed more suitable. Anything to end the bitter, worthlessness I felt inside. It had turned into a monster I didn't know how to deal with. Fortunately, I held on.

I never believed Stephanie would ever stick around, but she did. She lived in a respectable suburb, came from a close-knit family, and enjoyed the benefits of good friends and social support networks. The months of our relationship blossomed into an inseparable friendship. That first experience of love filled the dark void in my life with light, but it also scared me. It was something I had no control over, and I knew it had the power to tear what was left of me apart. The dark and the light of it; the ferocity and the tenderness of it; the way it unmade me as it was made. I became a part of her family. Stephanie's parents welcomed me into their home. It helped me. In a way, they became my new family and a foundation in my life.

When Stephanie wanted to meet my own family, and I sensed her parents did also, a stab of shame and spike of embarrassment pierced me. My father lived in another city, over a thousand kilometres away. I had little, if anything, to do with my mother because her state of mental health was damaging to those closest to her.

There were things about my family I never shared with Stephanie—like my mother's repeated and almost successful suicide attempts. I never shared with her my own suicidal thoughts; never mentioned any of my problems beyond what she could see on the surface. I knew she didn't understand what it was to be broken, and I knew I couldn't expect her too. I knew the cold, hard, unfair sharp edges of life. She could see the weight I carried on my shoulders. I was sick and tired of it all. It was killing me.

When you shove off from the bright bank of life into the black lake of depression in a sinking raft, your mind tells you there is no possibility of making it back to the shore. The void sucks you in like a vacuum and the chemical imbalance in your brain drowns your ability to reason as the psyche fractures and then splinters into the long dark night of the soul. Unless a light appears on the horizon somewhere to help you navigate those still, deep, life sapping waters, it's easy to slip below the surface. Mike reassured me that things wouldn't always be the way I thought they would. He provided the channel markers, safe water marks, and the isolated danger marks that helped me navigate the beginning of that change. Mike captained the foundering raft of my soul across that dark lake, pointing me towards clearer waters and a new destination. Up until then, I hadn't thought much about travelling.

In 2001 Stephanie left Christchurch for Otago University—New Zealand's oldest and most prestigious institution. She resided at Knox College, where only the affluent, influential, and best sports or intellectuals boarded. Set on 27 rolling landscaped acres opposite the botanical gardens, the institution recreated and retained some of the feeling and traditions of Oxford and Cambridge College. Her departure was a hard blow. She faced a new life, and she wanted her space. I respected that, but I was envious of her privilege. Our relationship rapidly deteriorated under the pressure of distance and Stephanie's new lifestyle. It was clear to me that we were headed down different paths. It tore my heart in half.

Most of the people I knew from high school had gone off to university. They appeared to know what they wanted to do, or to be. University proclaimed to offer the student the promise of a better life. It seemed like the normal thing to do—the right thing to do, but it didn't feel that way for me. University felt out of reach, and I began to feel that I was getting left behind in a world that demanded conformity. I had no idea what I wanted to do or to be. I envied my peers whom had access to such privilege. Their lives seemed so much easier, more fun, more interesting and happier than mine. Having good family support seemed to make all the difference. Those people appeared to have the world at their feet.

When I visited Stephanie, I found the imposing building, and what it stood for, intimidating and out of reach. When I saw the hall where she ate her meals with the other students, I was instantly transported to Hogwarts. What a magical life, I thought. Stephanie's parents were friends with the Master of the College. Those imposing doors opened freely for her, and I was jealous. Our relationship finally ended with a fight at her College.

It came to a head at Stephanie's formal. I collected Lee, Stephanie's new college friend's boyfriend, from Lincoln University in Christchurch and we hit the road for Dunedin for the weekend. We were both excited to see our partners, but anxiety also formed an uncomfortable question mark in the back of my mind. Stephanie and I hadn't been getting on for the past few weeks. Trying to keep a relationship alive through a telephone was proving to be conflicted. I suspected she was moving on. The four-hour drive gave Lee and me time to become acquainted. Through the winding, twisting, undulating hours, our conversation opened our hearts to the fact that we were both facing the same heartbreaking dilemma.

Formal night bustled in lavish gowns and opulent dresses of gold and snow white, scarlet and jet black, twirling and curtsying in the arms of tuxedos and bow ties in flowing affairs like a fairy tale ball. Floral perfumes and heady colognes moved in invisible waves through the hall, swirling around admirers and clutching partners. The gorgeous elite and beautiful privileged frolicked and played in dreams of future fame and power, wealth and intellectual recognition. Lee commented on the pomp and ostentatious display. I agreed, we were not of this class, and we made it known. Lee straightened his back, lifted his chin, and walked stiffly back and forth, nodding left and right in pretentious seriousness. I balled with laughter at his impersonation of the students' refined behaviour and joined him. Together we strode the Great Hall, consuming wine and canapés from silver trays in our own private and comical discourse.

Stephanie seized my arm. I swirled to meet such condescending eyes and conspicuous embarrassment that I knew my night of fun was over. Shame and guilt washed over me. I knew I was humiliating her. Her words were as stern as the daggers that flew from her glare in a gruelling education on the rules I was to follow within the walls of the prestigious institution, around the polished and sophisticated genteel of the college—people I thought were educated beyond their intelligence; people that couldn't feel or comprehend the fight I faced every day. With hostile encouragement she tugged at my arm. I risked a glance over my shoulder and noticed Lee was in the same belligerent grip of his partner. His face told me everything as we were dragged apart, but the accoutre moat of dresses and suits that separated us didn't stop us pulling faces across the hall of Larnach Castle.

I found myself shuffling through the milling crowds in rejected disassociation when a more normal, friendly, and unassuming smile caught me in its light. 'Hi Ben!' It was Christine, the College Master's daughter. I couldn't help but think of the irony of the moment. I had met Christine once before when she was visiting Stephanie, in Christchurch. She had noticed Stephanie ignoring me. 'Are you okay, Ben?' she asked with eyes that warmed my heart. I found myself blurting my honest opinion of the night. Christine frowned. 'I think you deserve to be treated better.' *Be treated better.* The words stuck to me like glue. Maybe that was what I needed to demand from people, from life. I was a decent person.

Surely, I deserved to be treated like one? In a spontaneous moment of daring, Christine took hold of my arm, pushed up my cream jacket sleeve, unbuttoned my black shirt cuff and wrote her phone number on my forearm. With each stroke of her pen, I felt the weight of the institution lift from my shoulders. 'Call me!' She smiled, then slipped into the shifting crowds that were making for the exit and the buses to town.

I slept on the floor of Stephanie's room that night. I had forgotten about Christine's number on my arm until Stephanie saw it in the morning. She dragged me to the bathrooms and scrubbed my arm pink, then marched to Christine's room. I heard the thump of her fist against Christine's door from down the hall. I felt terrible. When she huffed back into her room, I told her it was over. What was the point in being together anyway if we couldn't see each other? It was the first time I had stood up to her; stood up for myself. She stared at me in a mix of wrath, bewilderment and disbelief. Strangely, when I finally tracked down Lee, I learnt he had also broken up with his partner. The both of us drove back to Christchurch single men.

I sat in the tattoo studio with Mike and broke down as I told him about the weekend. That was the first time that big, hard man sat beside me, wrapped his arm around me, and told me everything was going to be okay. 'Life doesn't always take from us,' he said, 'it gives as well'. The months that followed that weekend, in deep conversations sitting above the Tattoo Company, formed many of my ideas about life. I came to the conclusion that running away for a life of adventure was more interesting to me than three more years of study for a degree in a subject I might never use. I began to formulate a plan for my escape.

During those months, I found the courage to ask Mike about the stories behind his tattoos. His life, and his beliefs, were the ink that covered his body. Their themes were reserved for hard men, and they were needled into his skin before ink became fashionable. He wore them like armour, and they meant business. Some he wore for strength, others for protection. One or two carved deep memories into his body. I got to know those tattoos well: flames ran from his wrists up his forearms; blazing, indignant skeletons road Harley Davidsons towards the viewer on each shin; a fire horse reared up on his back in a startling powerful pose; scales covered his upper right thigh like armour, and Celtic knotwork banded and patched his arms in meaning and superstition. A ram's head with flames dancing off it guarded his chest, and a savage boar on his left bicep symbolised the strength in his left arm. A lizard climbed the length of his right torso. Angry, broken faces on his elbows and knees warned an opponent of what awaited them. I began to understand how much his own childhood had affected him. He carried the burden of those abused years in those motifs—those persecuted, formative years that affected every friendship and relationship he ever had. I saw the need to let go of things, move on and not look back. I understood, in the way that a young and inexperienced mind does, that I needed to be present and plan for a brighter future, and that sometimes we cannot find the answers we are looking for at home. It was Mike's belief in me, and his warning not to take his path, that gave me the strength and courage to take that first step into the unknown.

About this time, my mother left my stepfather and found a place for her and my sister to live. My mother seemed happier after breaking up with my stepfather—less fragile and more in control. I thought things might finally be moving on. After a while, she began a relationship with Mike. Ironically, she had introduced us the day we stood on the pavement outside his shop on Colombo Street, inspecting the damage to the front of my car. In his clumsy way, Mike tried to stitch back together the broken relationship between my mother and me. Because of the respect I had for Mike, and our friendship, I gave it a shot. Then my mother sent my sister up to Auckland to live with my father and moved to England to be with her own dying mother. With her on the other side of the world, Mike confided in me that she had tried to commit suicide before she left. He had found her unconscious in her bed, carried her from her bedroom to his car, and raced her with heart pounding anxiety to hospital where she had been put on life support.

My brother moved to Auckland for an engineering apprenticeship with Air New Zealand. Knowing he had found his feet and my sister was in a more stable and loving environment gave me the clarity of mind to leave Christchurch before it got the better of me.

* * *

I deflected. 'How about you, Wayne? Do you have any family?'

'I have a sister, and my parents are still alive and well. I don't have any children of my own. There was a young woman whom I loved very much once. She was from France. I went to live in Paris with her for a while, but it didn't work out. I love Australia, and I missed the wilderness in Paris.'

'There was a girl I thought I loved very much before I left New Zealand. I think of her often on the road.'

Wayne's gaze was piercing and full of comprehension. 'Sometimes we must let go of the life we have planned and accept the one that is waiting for us. Everything in its right place and its right time, Ben.'

'What did you mean about meeting the spirit at the Devil's Signpost the other day? And on Battleship Spur?' I asked.

'The Gorge, Ben, is more than just a marvellous construct of nature. It's a spiritual place. It's full of spirits. They can't hurt you if you don't let them, but they can play games and tricks on you. If you're not careful, they might even send you mad, like they did Cristy.'

'Who's Cristy?'

'She was a guide, like you, only she was Aboriginal, and she was taught the ways of the Gorge by Fred.'

'Who's Fred?'

'Fred is a local Aboriginal elder and guide. He is descended from the Bidjara and Barada people. It's his portrait on the bar wall at the Lodge. He is a major figurehead in the Gorge, and he has a profound understanding of the area's spirituality. You see, even the Gorge has a spirit of which everything else is made up. Fred visits a few times a year when he comes out to work as a park ranger during the school holidays, so you will meet him soon.'

'So, what happened to Cristy?' I was intrigued to learn more about the spiritual world because I had felt a strange presence on several occasions when I was out on my own exploring.

'Cristy was an ace guide and one courageous young person. She was separated from her infant baby and family to learn tour guiding in a remote place. She had to deal with culturally alien middle-class white people all day, despite having the shyness that all Aboriginal people seem to have to some degree. But everyone that worked in the Gorge and everyone she guided loved her. She was drop-dead gorgeous and had a smile to sink a battleship, but the stress got to her. She started meddling with the spirits. One night she snuck up to Boolimba Bluff and set fire to the place near the women's ritual site on top of the Bluff. She was given a stern talking to and confined to her quarters, but then she disappeared again. Everyone was mobilised to search for her before she set fire to the place again. It was black as coal that night, but she was eventually found and brought back to the park's centre. If you knew Cristy, she was the most beautiful, smiling, friendly, charming young woman. It was very painful to see her that night. She was possessed, doubled over, snarling and growling like a deranged animal and cursing everyone, even those who'd become very close to her, with the coarsest vulgarities and hurtful insults you haven't ever heard. She seemed literally demon possessed. There was nothing anyone could do with her. The chopper was called, and she ended up in the psychiatric hospital in Rockhampton.'

I was shocked. To think the Gorge was such a powerfully spiritual place, full of benevolent, and belligerent, spirits, and that I might be trudging carelessly over sacred sites without knowing better.

'Maybe I shouldn't have divulged so much about Cristy,' Wayne reflected, 'but you might like to ask Fred about her when you see him, if you think it's okay.'

'How will I know if it's okay?' I didn't want to offend an Aboriginal elder.

'You'll know.'

'Have you had any experiences with the spirits?' I asked.

'Of course! Anyone who spends enough time in here will meet them in one form or other.'

'What happened?'

'Well, what I'm about to tell you happened around the same time Fred was teaching Cristy. I was privileged to attend when Fred introduced

Cristy to the Gorge. An elder teaching a young Karringbal girl the ways of the tribe, and me, a gringo, sitting in on it. Quite an experience. We were sitting on a log near Baloon Cave, actually right under the occupation cave high in the cliff by the road. As Fred explained the spirits and the role of the Gorge in Aboriginal spirituality, Cristy was getting wide-eyed with fear. Fred stopped and turned to her and said quietly, *They're only spirits. They can't hurt you.* I heeded that advice later. Cristy, unfortunately, didn't. Then, one night I went for a stroll up the road after working late, just to unwind a bit. It was a warm, still night and I wandered up the jump-up just past the Lodge, almost to the Baloon Cave area, when the air got suddenly very cold and clammy. I really got the message: *Don't go any further, you're unwelcome.* So, I whispered, *okay, okay,* and turned to head back down. Just as I did, a tearing wind came out of nowhere and blasted my back with that cold, clammy air. I quickened my pace. It was one of those things you don't forget, but I accepted it as fair enough and gave it no more thought. Probably just an air pocket that had seeped out of a side gorge, anyway. Then one night sometime later while I was lying in my bed in my donga, a belligerent and malevolent spirit came in through the door. You think I'm nuts, but if it had happened to you, you'd know. It was as subtle as a freight train. I lay there thinking hard, remembering what Fred had said—they're only spirits, they can't hurt you. It was obviously trying to intimidate me. But my cultural context is Christian, not Aboriginal, so I remembered what I'd been taught in Sunday School. They reckoned Christ could kick the arse of any subordinate spirit. I said out loud to it, *In the name of Jesus Christ, the Son of God, piss off!* Then I rolled over with my back to it and waited. I could feel it leave the room.'

I shook involuntarily as a river of goose bumps tingled up my arms and into the base of my neck. I knew I would have to be more considerate, and careful, about where and when I went exploring by myself.

'I think you're ready to start guiding on your own now, Ben. I'll let Trish know when we get back to the Lodge.'

We left our perch on the rocks and began our decent. I had a lot to think about, not just about starting guiding on my own, but an entirely new appreciation and sense of the energy that resided in the Gorge.

CHAPTER TWENTY-TWO

A TAPESTRY IS FORMED

'There are moments when all anxiety and stated toil are becalmed in the infinite leisure and repose of nature.'

—*Henry David Thoreau*

I started taking guided walks up the Gorge on my own.

From time to time, I saw Claudia on the track. Occasionally, she would drop by the dongers to catch up with staff from the Wilderness Lodge. Finally, a social evening formed around the bar.

'Have you been up many of the side gorges?' I asked, my heart full of anxiety fused in unbounded joy.

'Just the usual ones on my guided walks. Why do you ask?'

Claudia was three years older than me, mysterious, intriguing, and full of what I mistook for self-possessed charm. She was the daughter of an Italian immigrant mother and Australian father. Her journey to the Gorge had begun in Adelaide, South Australia, where she had finished studying adventure tourism a year and a half earlier, before taking her first job as a nature guide. She loved Carnarvon Gorge as much as every other person that fell under its enchanting spell.

'Would you like to explore some of the other side gorges with me sometime?' I asked, quietly pleased she hadn't investigated the many ravines and chasms that made up Carnarvon Gorge.

'Did you have one in mind?' Scepticism lined the smooth river of her forehead in a questioning frown.

'Any one of them. You can choose. They must all be interesting.' She was curious by nature, an explorer, and I knew she wouldn't like me knowing the Gorge better than she did, but she wouldn't explore it on her own.

'Okay. I have this weekend free. Is it okay if I bring a friend?'

'Sure, the more the merrier,' I grumbled with an undertone of sarcasm.

We set out at dawn the following morning with Christine and Doug. Christine was a new park ranger at the Gorge: young, shy, tall and slender. She was unassuming and attractive. Her cultural heritage was Aboriginal, descended from the Bidjara tribe. She had a connection to this land that I could only dream of. Doug was one of the chefs at the Lodge: tall, dark-haired and burly. He was confident and companionable, and a few years older than me. His grandfather's aunt was Edith Cowan, the Australian social reformer who worked for the rights of women and children, and first Australian women to serve as a member of parliament. Doug proudly showed me her picture on the reverse of a $50 note.

At creek crossing 15, we left the main track and waded through several hundred metres of waist-high blad26 grass, past rough-barked apple trees, iron barks and bracken fern. We crossed an obscure creek and came to the left flank of the Gorge.

The gradient abruptly climbed into precipice sandstone. Spotted gums and sprays of yellow wattle flowers curled around ivory outcrops, pillars, arches and fenestrations. As we pushed up a craggy slope and made our way alongside a low cliff high above the main track, I discovered a small, shallow tunnel in the soft stone. Five vertebrae lay in the entrance of the cave—the base of a spine, or so I thought. I called to Claudia.

'Do you think this is an old burial tomb?' I asked, pointing to the vertebrae in the cave.

'I think the bones are too small for a person.'

'It could have been a young child, they look human,' I said.

Claudia looked at the bones, then at me. She suddenly seemed uneasy.

'Maybe. Either way, we should leave it untouched. It's inviting trouble to disturb anything up here.'

The Aboriginal tribes that used to frequent the Gorge sometimes buried their dead, wrapped in bark cylinders, in the naturally forming tunnels in the sandstone cliffs. Although I couldn't be certain, there was a good chance we had just stumbled across the remains of an ancient burial site.

I wasn't about to argue the point with Claudia. We pushed on, continuing our ascent past fascinating formations in the striped and grooved sandstone that gazed out over the Gorge like ancient, spiritual faces locked in the stone.

We stopped at a bluff marked on our maps as Parrabooya—meaning *red stone*. Far below us, Carnarvon Creek wound its way through the Gorge in a glistening silver thread like a magical snake. I would later learn the name of that snake—that giver of life and protector of the waters.

I dropped my pack on the ground, flopped my legs over the edge of the precipice and sat for a moment, floating in the sparkling morning light. Once again, I could feel the pulsing life of the Gorge, pushing waves of energy through its sinuous arteries like a beating heart. The temptation to jump was almost overwhelming. I was wondering about the avian spirits when Christine sat beside me.

'This view is spectacular,' I said. 'It doesn't seem to matter where in the Gorge you climb, the view is always stunning, and always different. Wayne was telling me about the Aboriginal spirits the other day when we climbed up to The Ranch. I was just thinking about them then. Have you ever met a spirit before?'

Christine hesitated, and for a moment I thought I had asked her a question I shouldn't have. 'I felt one once, in a small unnamed side gorge, past Big Bend. A stampede of goose bumps ran straight up my spine. I'm never going into that place again, and I don't like to talk about it.' Christine's eyes were wide with fear and anxiety at recalling the event.

'Wayne told me one came into his room one night.'

'That's crazy. I didn't know that. What happened?'

'He told me it was as subtle as a freight train. He was in bed when it happened and he said to it: *In the name of Jesus Christ, the Son of God, piss off.* He rolled over with his back to it and he said it left his room.'

'That makes me even more scared now. I don't like the spirits, and I don't want to do anything to upset them.'

'I don't want to upset them either. I've been exploring a lot of the Gorge, remote places away from the main areas. Hidden locations where nobody else goes. I have a feeling some of those sites were gathering places—sacred sites.'

I questioned Christine about her work as a park ranger. She maintained the park campgrounds and walking tracks. She'd recently been busy combating a noxious weed that was threatening to invade and choke up the creek. Baiting and trapping feral pigs she told me was a constant battle. Like all of us who lived inside the Gorge, Christine found it a captivating and enchanting place that was filled with an inexplicable energy.

While we hiked back to the Visitor Centre that afternoon, my body felt so light I could have hiked into heaven. I had the impression I was being lifted off the ground by unseen wings. I'd never experienced anything like it before, and I sensed the unmistakable energy was attributed in some way to the nature around me. It was as if it were trying to communicate with me. A euphoric smile arched my lips in a cupid's bow as I glided along the track on wings of awareness. They couldn't all be malevolent spirits in the Gorge, could they? There were definitely healing elements to this place.

'Did you have a good day?' Claudia asked.

'Really good. The lookout was amazing, and I'm intrigued about the bones we found. I want to see what else we can discover.'

'I enjoyed myself too, and I'd like to see more of the Gorge before I leave at the end of this year.'

'You're leaving?'

'Yes. I'm going back to Adelaide, then I might go down to Tasmania or overseas somewhere. I'm not sure yet.'

I didn't want her to leave. For some reason my brain was already projecting thoughts of us into the future, working as guides in the Gorge or other parts of Australia, travelling the wilderness of the world.

'Are you coming up to the park rangers' quarters tonight for a drink?' Annie asked me when I got back to the Wilderness Lodge. 'You should. Everyone is going to be there… come on, you know you want to.' Her grin spelt mischief.

'Everyone?' I was suspicious. I knew she was trying to convince me to do something she wanted whenever she subtly added *you know you want to* at the end of a sentence.

'Yeah, the staff from Takarakka, all the park rangers, and we can drive up in your car. Claudia will be there too.'

'Claudia?'

'I knew that would get your attention.'

A large fire encircled by smooth round creek boulders sat in a clearing below towering gums, casting dancing shadows into the forest. A dozen or so people sat or stood by the fire conversing in pairs and trios. It was my first time meeting a lot of new people. I wanted to give my best impression.

Annie introduced me to the head rangers, several new rangers and a few staff that had come up from Takarakka. I did my best to make light conversation, but there was only one person I really wanted to talk to.

Claudia was popular. I felt like I was wearing a sign on my head that said: *Hey, I like you.* Even after spending the day exploring the Gorge with her, I was tongue-tied and couldn't relax in her company. Annie decided to help me loosen up by encouraging me to have a drink. The bourbon and Coke seemed to work. I slowly grew more social with my new peers as the night deepened around the fire. With my confidence growing, I walked over and sat down beside Claudia. I didn't want to make it too obvious that I fancied her, so I talked about exploring another side gorge that we had passed earlier in the day.

A sharp knock on the door of my room woke me.

'You ready? Do you still want to go walking? We were meant to head off at dawn, remember?'

'Ahh, yeah sure, just a minute.' I fell out of bed, blurry-eyed, and rubbed my head. Walking? Where had the night gone?

I grabbed my pack and headed down to the Lodge with Claudia for breakfast, scratching my head. Walking…? I was still intoxicated. I packed lunch, jumped into Claudia's car, and we drove up to the Visitor Centre.

My head was pounding in time to my gait as we strolled up the main track. Claudia hadn't said more than a few words since we left the

A Tapestry Is Formed

Lodge. I could see she was annoyed about something. While I had the courage, I asked her what was bothering her.

'How much of last night do you remember?' Her reply stung.

I didn't want to hear any more. I knew I must have done something stupid, but I couldn't remember anything. I looked at the ground and rubbed my head. I was embarrassed. 'I did something, didn't I?'

'Okay, so you don't remember picking me up and falling on the ground with me?'

I was baffled. I thought she was going to say I tried to kiss her. But this? In front of all her friends and work colleagues? What the hell was I thinking? I was quiet for a moment while I thought of how to apologise.

'Were we dancing?'

Claudia looked at me like she was about to give me another headache.

'I'm really sorry, I don't remember doing that at all… I think one of those spirits must have got into me last night,' I added, in a daring attempt to lighten her mood.

'Yeah, an alcoholic one climbed down your throat, you mean? Well, it's okay. Some people thought it was pretty funny. Just not me.'

'I hope they understood I just had a bit too much to drink.'

'They understand. Everyone gets a get-out-of-jail-free card around here, so you're forgiven. Just don't try using spirits as an excuse again. It's disrespectful.' A small smile broke her petite features, and she looked down at the ground.

A wave of relief swept over me. 'So, you know I like you now. It seems I made that pretty obvious last night. How about you?'

'That's okay. I like you, but as a friend.'

I had to catch my heart before it landed on the track in front of me.

'It would be nice to have you as a friend too.' I took a deep breath of the crisp air and locked my heart back inside my ribcage. Perhaps with time it might evolve into something?

'Where are we going this morning?' I sheepishly asked.

'Kamoloo Gorge, remember?'

Claudia stopped and pulled a long slender stalk from a tussock of blady grass. 'Here, I'll show you something.' I guessed she wanted to try to make me feel better. 'Do you know how to make grass spears?'

'No.'

'The Aboriginal kids used to make them out of blady grass, to play with.'

Claudia took the stalky end and folded, twisted and goodness knows what else before my eyes, but in a moment, she held it out in front of her and fired it down the track. I was impressed to see it fly several metres.

'Sometimes I show it to people when I'm guiding. The kids like it.'

'That's really cool.' Claudia knew some neat things about the Gorge that I didn't, some things even Wayne didn't know.

Just before we got to the Art Gallery, we ducked down a steep grassy bank to Kamoloo Creek. Kamoloo was a local tribe name. We followed the creek up to where Kongaboola Creek—meaning *two waters*—converged with it. The sun was already radiating off the rock faces when we felt the first cool breeze on our cheeks come from somewhere up in Kamoloo Gorge. We followed the creek to a deep, clear water hole at the base of a huge boulder.

'I need a swim,' I said.

'The water's cold, you know that don't you?'

'Yes.' I was already tearing off my clothes, down to my boxers. I dived into the pool and came back up with a gasp.

'I told you.' Claudia sat above the pool on the rock with a bemused and dismissive expression. I began frolicking in the water.

'Come on, get in. It's actually quite nice once you get used to the temperature.'

'It'll have to get a lot hotter than this before I get in.' The sternness of her reply convinced me she wasn't amused with my antics.

I climbed out of the pool and up the rock in a shivering jiggle to join Claudia and warm up in the sun.

'Have you heard of Grahame Walsh?' Claudia asked.

'No.'

'He and his wife used to own the land that now makes up the Takarakka campgrounds. Grahame is the leading expert in the Bradshaw art of the Kimberley, in Australia's north-west. He's also written several books about the Indigenous peoples of the Queensland Sandstone Belt.

There is one you should read if you can find a copy, it's called *Carnarvon and Beyond*. You will find it useful being a guide here.'

'Thanks.' I could see why Claudia was so well liked in the Gorge.

'Don't mention it.'

Further up the Gorge, Claudia pointed out a large bush with small red berries. 'Wild raspberries, you should try them. They're actually quite good.' She was a real guide, nothing fancy, completely at ease in her environment. I loved it. I watched her small, delicate hands carefully select several raspberries. She plucked them from the bush and handed me a couple. 'Good things come in small packages.' Her cheeks dimpled in a comely smile. I wasn't sure if she was referring to the raspberries, or if she had sensed me admiring her hands? Perhaps she was used to enchanting guys with those petite paws? We ate the raspberries modestly, savouring the sweet and bitter blend of juice and pulp. We moved on, drank from the creek, climbed over rocks and fallen trees, and clambered along thin ledges and around rock pools, stopping now and then to admire the weird, the wonderful and the beautiful.

The sides of the Gorge receded into the plateau escarpments as we made our way to the upper reaches of the precipice sandstone.

'You mentioned the other day you are leaving at the end of the season?' I asked.

'Yes, I want to do guide work somewhere else. I have a friend who works down in Lamington National Park, in south-east Queensland. Or there's Tasmania. Sue from Parks and Wildlife is getting transferred down there. I'd like to see New Zealand too. It's like Australia, isn't it?'

'It's nothing like Australia,' I said, a little dumfounded by her naïvety. 'There are real mountains there, with snow and glaciers, and rivers and lakes that are crystal clear or sapphire-blue. It's colder, and the weather is very changeable.'

'But they still have gum trees, right?'

'There are some gum trees there, but they are introduced from Australia as far as I know. Beech forests cover large tracts of the wilderness there.'

'Why do you like it here so much then?'

'It's different, it doesn't remind me of home. I like the wildlife, we don't have as much fascinating wildlife in New Zealand, mostly just birds.

And I like the wide-open spaces and the warmer weather. I don't feel like I'm trapped here. Australia is a lovely place to get lost in. It's odd, but being lost here gives me a feeling of security, like I'm finding my way to something more important while letting go of everything else that isn't.'

Claudia was silent for a moment. 'You want to see all of Australia?'

'Yes. I was thinking of heading south when the season finishes here. It will be too hot up north and the wet season will begin soon. I was wondering if you'd be interested in travelling together?' I asked, with some real courage.

'Where were you thinking?'

'I want to get down to Tasmania for the summer, so any national parks on the way.'

'I'll have a think about it. If you are going south, I might join you for a while. There's a couple of national parks I'd like to visit on my way back to Adelaide. How long were you thinking?'

'As long as you like. I'm going to be on the road for a while yet.'

'Okay, I'll let you know closer to the time.'

I let my heart fill with a joy I knew could also break it.

CHAPTER TWENTY-THREE
NATURE'S TEACHINGS

'Some see nature all ridicule and deformity... and some scarce see nature at all. But to the eyes of the man of imagination, nature is imagination itself.'

—William Blake

Annie came into the staff kitchen clutching a large chocolate cake. *Happy 22nd Ben* was written on top in white icing. Several candles were dripping wax.

Wayne grinned at me while Doug shuffled in behind Annie. Glenis and Karen from housekeeping joined in to sing happy birthday. It felt strange, but the warmth of their faces enveloped me in arms of recognition and welcomeness as a friend and work colleague. I would have let the milestone slip into eternity with a quiet beer if Annie hadn't made it her business to organise the celebration. It seemed I had another new family in the Gorge.

'You have to make a wish before you blow out the candles,' Annie announced.

I drew in a deep breath, held it for a second, and made a wish before blowing.

'Hip hurrah, hip hurrah, hip hurrah!' my new family cheered.

'What did you wish for?' Annie narrowed her mischievous eyes.

Annie could talk the leg off an iron pot, and occasionally her inquisitive nature bordered on nosiness. While we performed a balancing act across a narrow log over Micky Creek she asked me the question again. 'Why are you travelling around Australia by yourself?' I jumped off and hopped across a line of stepping-stones ahead of her. The track zigzagged into a narrow chasm.

'I left New Zealand when I was 19. No one else I knew was interested in coming with me. First, I went to the Northern Territory for a year to work on a cattle station, then I lived on the Sunshine Coast for six months and learnt to surf. That's when I decided I needed to see the rest of Australia. I didn't have anyone else to do it with, and I wasn't going to wait for someone to show up. The opportunity may have passed me by otherwise.'

'That's young to leave home. Why did you leave? And why don't you go back?'

'I left home when I was a lot younger than that. I didn't have any reason to stay in New Zealand.' I didn't feel much like talking about it and Annie seemed to get the message.

'What was the cattle station like?'

'Hard. It changed me.'

'What do you mean it changed you? And why did you stay if it was so hard?'

'It helped me to see how good life really is—the opportunities that surround us every day. It opened my mind to the possibility that I could do anything I wanted to. Failure was never an option. I would have died out there before I ever went back to what I left behind.' Sometimes I reflected on my near-death encounters and grasped how close I had come to death. Those incidents affirmed, in a way no words could have done, the value of my life and the opportunities it represented.

'It sounds like there's more to that story.'

'You don't know how strong you are until being strong is the only option you have. But it takes wisdom to know your limits and courage to speak out. I learnt the hard way.'

'Well, I still think you're strange.'

I turned around and saw her gauging eyes shift into a teasing smile. I smiled back and laughed. I guess it was unusual that I hadn't been home in so long, but I was happier living this way. There was something in the nomadic way of life that seemed more natural to me than settling into a society. Every day my thoughts reached out into a world beyond myself, into a place where the universe freely conversed with me.

I scrambled up a huge, rounded sandstone boulder and between two narrow walls of stone to a notorious deep waterhole called the Plunge Pool.

'Are you going to jump in?' Annie asked.

I frowned at her and then laughed. 'Are you crazy? That water is stagnant. Who knows what's in the bottom of that pool? We should go and explore Warrumbah Gorge. I never get to go up there as far as I'd like when I do the Mickey Creek Walk with guests.'

We followed the creek back down through the forest then took the track to Warrumbah Gorge.

As I climbed over the first car-sized boulder, I turned back to Annie. 'This is the furthest I take my most agile guests.'

'I can see why,' Annie said, as she stretched her short legs into foot holds. She reached up, and I gave her a hand.

We carried on bouldering, scrambled across tree bridges over shallow rocky pools, and trudged beneath precarious rocks wedged between the chasm walls. A velvety green carpet of moss materialised on the sandstone like a leprechaun's tunnel, and led into shimmying over deep pools as dark as ink in the fissured earth.

'I'm shorter than you,' Annie protested, when she saw the slit of rock we had to navigate over the black water. 'There's no way I'm going through there.'

'You'll be alright Annie, just copy me.' I put my backpack on back-to-front then wedged myself between the two walls, pressing my back firmly against one wall with my feet against the other.

'If I fall in there, I'm going to kill you.' Annie was right, or course. Her legs could barely reach the opposite wall, but she followed me, imitating my uncoordinated spider-like movements through the chasm.

'I think I just saw something move in the water,' I shouted.

'What is it?' Annie screamed.

'I don't know, maybe it's a giant eel or something?'

In that moment, Annie panicked, lost her slight footing, slipped, and disappeared into the slit of dark water with a splash. I looked down in shock.

She suddenly reappeared, black as oil and gasped, 'Help!' I dropped into the water beside her, entirely unsure how I was going to rescue her. Fortunately, and to my very great surprise, my boots firmly hit the bottom. I grabbed hold of Annie, in her panic she hadn't realised the water was only waste deep, and lucky it was too because I don't know how we'd have escaped if it was any deeper.

'Stand up!' I shouted. 'Just stand up. You're fine.'

'What about the giant eel?'

I could barely keep a straight face, but my joke had backfired on me. 'I was joking about the eel.'

'You bastard,' she screamed, and a handful of the filthy water slapped my face. 'I hate you.'

I bent over in a fit of laughter. We both smelled putrid. After wading through the stagnant muck, we emptied our boots and wrung out our clothes.

'Looks like this is it for the day,' I said, disappointed at the five-metre-high boulder that lay in front of us further up the canyon.

'Can we go around it? I don't want to go back the way we came,' Annie pleaded.

I studied the sides of the chasm. Even for myself it would be difficult. 'It doesn't look like it. We might as well have lunch here, then we'll have to head back to the Lodge the way we came.'

I was musing over my situation with Annie while I quietly chewed on my sandwich. She had become a good friend, but a few times she had indicated that she wanted more than just friendship.

'Annie, I like having you as a friend, but you know I'm only looking for friendship, don't you?' I wasn't really sure how to approach the matter as we sat eating our lunch. Her friendship, although a little overbearing at times, really was important to me, and I didn't want to mess that up. After all, if it weren't for Annie, I wouldn't have been here now.

'I know. You like Claudia. But I think she just wants to be single at the moment. Sorry to break your hopes.'

'I know that, but it doesn't change how I feel.'

'Well, I like having you as a friend too.' She was no more willing to accept my request for friendship only, as I was ready to accept Claudia's.

That evening Claudia dropped by the dongers to pick up Annie and me for a drive. I had a feeling that Annie had organised the outing. We drove out to Bandana Station. Out there, laying on the warm bonnet of Claudia's car, we gazed up at the heavens and chatted about life. The whole universe seemed to radiate in the sky that night, and for the first time in my life I felt connected to it all. I would have lived the moment a thousand times again. It was such a beautiful time in my life. But in that moment, I could also sense there was a strange triangle of misguided passions and friendship.

I spent the next seven days guiding large groups of walkers. I didn't mind being busy. It kept me from thinking too much about Claudia and Annie.

The tranquil weeks that followed ushered in the happiest moments of my life in the gift of being. I was a giant filled with the faith that could move mountains. My life merged with nature and a sense of the eternal. I experienced a heightened sense of awareness, alertness & expectation. I was filled with a deep sense of peace as the rhythm of walking became meditation. I walked back through the days of my life, dissolving my attachments to the world and the emotional wounds of my youth. Memories of my childhood, things I didn't even know I remembered, filled random moments of the day as I strolled through the sandstone corridors of life. I contemplated some of the more profound events which had shaped and changed its course so dramatically. I realised that without them, I couldn't be where I now was. I had come to a turning point, a crossroads: I learnt not to cling to negative experiences that resulted from decisions I'd made while learning. I finally forgave myself for my human failings and accepted that everything I had done, I had done to the fullest of my ability as well as I could. That despite my best efforts, I was not able to make things work in the life I left behind—a truth that granted me peace with the shadows of my past.

I spent my free days exploring every side gorge in the Carnarvon Gorge section of the national park. I was sure that my recent insights into life were just the beginning of a much bigger journey to come. As the weeks passed, I discovered worlds within worlds: microcosms and microclimates, sacred natural places that harboured rare hidden plant life and animals that were seldom seen—water dragons and green tree snakes, rainbow skinks and long-necked tortoises. I discovered perennial springs, pockets of rainforest, places where hundreds of butterflies gathered and fluttered about fern and moss-covered walls like magical fairies dancing in silvery light. Places where figs and ferns tumbled over cyclopean masonry and deep crevices, where vine trees grew among white cedar and swamp mahogany and yellow stringybarks grew on the dryer ground above. I discovered perfectly carved ravines; corridors where creeks flowed wall to wall. Prehistoric formations spoke of their long existence and memory, as the historical canvas of the ranges was laid bare before me. I opened the shining gates to a realm I hadn't known existed when I first came to the Gorge, a realm of new energies, ideas and feelings that were interwoven with the landscape and the story of its creation.

There were times I wished I had climbing gear, and times I wished I had a climbing partner to explore the gorges further. When Claudia's days off coincided with my own, and she wasn't busy doing volunteer work for Parks and Wildlife, we would often explore together. But for me those rare moments were never enough. They only made my heart yearn to be close to her and reminded me of my deep loneliness.

The first fires exploded into existence in early summer from dry storms as the forked tongues of lightning tasted the dry land. The atmosphere in the Gorge morphed from paradise to apocalypse. The Moolayember section of the national park was a blazing inferno while the Parks and Wildlife rangers attempted to control the fires with back burning. By night the ominous, deep orange glow erupted like a volcano from the Moolayember Cliffs. By day, the silvery-yellow light bathed the white-walled ravines in a strange blend of calm and alarm. Smoke choked the air in the breathless pockets of the side gorges.

CHAPTER TWENTY-FOUR
WHO ARE YOU?

'Deep into that darkness peering, long I stood there, wondering, fearing, doubting, dreaming dreams no mortal ever dared to dream before.'
—*Edgar Allan Poe*

I woke up wondering what the dream I had just emerged from was all about.

I was sitting inside an amphitheatre of stone, at the centre of a circle of what appeared to be Aboriginal elders. 'Who are you?' asked one. 'Why are you here?' asked another. 'What do you want?' asked a third. They were silent for a moment then, finally, a central figure spoke, 'What are you searching for?'

I communicated with the elders, yet no sounds came from my mouth. The elders perceived and acknowledged what I was trying to tell them. They spoke among themselves, each in turn looking at me and remarking to the elder beside them. They nodded. It seemed an arrangement had been made, an agreement that I could stay. They seemed to understand where I had come from, that I was here to learn and that I had become as much a part of their land as the other creatures that dwelled within it. The elders each in turn stood up, moved from the circle, and disappeared into the wilderness like phantoms.

I found Wayne down at the lodge before he met his group of walkers that morning and recounted my dream.

'You need to be careful, Ben. Not everything is what it seems or appears to be here. Every day you spend in the Gorge you are walking through sacred land. Many of the formations around the park hold great significance to the local Aboriginal people. They are the work of their ancestors during the creation period of the Dreaming. Ancestral heroes are said to reside at some of the features. Such mythological and spiritual beliefs are values from a time when people's holistic overview of their role in the timeless phase of the Dreaming held a respect difficult to comprehend by standards of today's society. The ceremonies that once took place here you couldn't begin to imagine. Now you're exploring these sacred places that most white men have never been to. Take care and tread with respect. The elders are watching you. I need to take this group up to Moss Gardens now, and I see you have a full day walk on, but we can talk some more later. By the way, you might see Fred on the track today.'

'Fred? He is in the Gorge?'

'He'll be here for a couple of weeks over the school holidays, it's a busy time. Lots of noisy children.'

I gathered my group of walkers and we joined Wayne and his group in the minibus for the ride up to the Visitor Centre. Wayne offered my group to join his as far as Moss Gardens. I appreciated the offer; I needed some time to gather my thoughts for the day.

About halfway between Wards Canyon and the Art Gallery, I noticed a tall, well-built man with greying hair on the track ahead of me. He was wearing blue jeans and a khaki park ranger shirt. As I got closer, I could see he was Aboriginal. The man was talking to a small group of people on the track. When I got close enough, I recognised him from his painting. I'd found Fred.

Fred was pointing to a large white myrtle shrub near the creek and had just stripped a handful of leaves off a low branch. 'This one is soap bush. If I rub these leaves into a ball here in my hands they will lather up, see. Then I can have a wash in the creek.'

Fred saw me. 'You must be Ben. Wayne said I might see you up the Gorge today.' His voice was warm and friendly, yet I felt insignificant in his presence. I was honoured that he had acknowledged my arrival. In my excitement I held out my hand, forgetting that it wasn't customary to shake hands with an Aboriginal elder.

'Nice to meet you, Fred.'

Fred politely ignored the gesture. I awkwardly lowered my arm, and his expression softened into a smile. 'It's nice to meet you too, Ben. Are you going up to the Art Gallery?'

'We're on our way there now.'

'That's good, I am going up there to do an interpretive talk now. You can follow us if you like.'

Fred bent down, plucked a fresh shoot of blady grass and started chewing on its sugary base. I later discovered that Fred routinely spent whole days in the Gorge without food. He said there was plenty available if he got hungry.

As we passed a small stand of cabbage tree palms, Fred pointed them out. 'See where the cockatoos have been eating the centre. That's heart of palm. You can boil it up and eat it. The women used the fronds to make food baskets.'

Down by the creek Fred pulled a leaf from a sandpaper fig and held it up for everyone to see. 'See this one? This one we used to make the boomerang and other tools that needed a smooth edge. Here, you feel that. It's rough.' Fred passed the leaf to a guest.

As the leaf was passed around, I watched the guests react to Fred's style. He really knew how to interact with people; he discovered the Gorge *with* them. The group was engaged and respectful of his time. He was a born teacher: calm, confident, trustworthy.

Further on, he found a grass tree and detailed its myriad uses. He explained how the women used the leaves to make dillybags and how they would get the nectar out of the flowers. 'The flowers are very sweet, the seeds were used for making a kind of bread and the long stalk when it is dead for spear shafts.'

Fred stopped at a large macrozamia beside the track—the ancient cycad which only grows a foot a century.

'See those nuts there?' Fred pointed to the top of the cycad. 'You can eat them, but they are very poisonous, full of carcinogens actually, so you have to know how to treat them first.'

'How do you treat them, Fred?' I asked for my group.

'First of all, you have to bake them in the fire, then you have to grind them up into a flour and then you have to leave it in the creek to leach out all the toxins. Then you can make a bread out of it.'

'That's a long process.'

'Yes, it is, but we were not in a hurry like folk these days.' Fred's humour was welcomed by the group in a chortle of laughter and comments.

We came to a pair of yellow and pink hibiscus in flower. The flowers themselves only lasted a day. They would open in the morning when I was on my way up the Gorge and be closing in the afternoon when I was on my way back.

Fred pulled a flower off one of the shrubs and showed everyone. 'You can eat this one too.' He popped the flower into his mouth and started munching on it with an expression of evaluating its flavour.

'Can I try, Fred?' I hadn't eaten a hibiscus flower, and I was always keen to experience more of the Gorge so I could share it with my walkers.

'Go ahead.'

I selected a juicy looking flower and plucked it from the bush. After chomping and grinding it to a pulp, a rich, slightly bittersweet flavour filled my mouth.

Fred observed my nodding approval. Satisfied, he continued. 'We used the sap for coughs and colds and the bark for fishing lines and nets. We also used the kurrajong bark for nets and containers but I can't see one here. There is one back at the Visitor Centre, though, if any of you want to see. It has large green leaves, and it has a sign under it, so you know.'

'This is a good one.' Fred walked over to a large shrub with glossy, elliptical sea-green leaves and tiny bright orange berries. He plucked a handful. 'See this berry? Be careful of this one. It's a quinine berry. Very poisonous. We used to give it to the women. It works like the contraceptive; stops the women from having the baby and causes miscarriage but makes them very sick.'

'How did your ancestors work out what they could eat and what they couldn't?' asked one of my guests.

'We tested the plants on our elderly who were sick or dying, so if they die it doesn't matter, maybe they get better, then we had a new medicine or knew if it is safe to eat or not. If it didn't work one way, we tried preparing it another until we got it right. Sometimes you just can't eat some things.'

The rate at which Fred could pick out so many useful plants was extraordinary. He spoke of the Gorge as if it were a plentiful garden. Like the clouds that block the sun's rays on an overcast day, my perception of the natural environment had been veiled until I met Fred. With the veil lifted, I saw the Gorge as a nurturing garden. I wondered how many more layers there were that I could not perceive, not just in this special place, but in life. If only guides like Fred were easier to find.

I admired the knowledge the Aboriginal people had gathered through the ages. Australia was one of the most inhospitable continents on earth. Through trial and error, the Aboriginal people had etched a living out of the landscape while preserving its natural beauty, following its seasonal cycles, moving nomadically when they needed to, and living in harmony with nature. They had developed customs, religions and sacred ceremonies that wove the spiritual world around the landscape. Their way of living with the land had changed very little for millennia until the first Europeans arrived—a forgotten world on a distant island continent.

There was already a considerable crowd gathered at the Art Gallery when we arrived—mostly retirees from what appeared to be a tour group and several families with young children.

'Well, I better start my interpretive talk now. It was nice to meet all of you.' Fred beamed an unassuming smile at us and made his way to a high point where the crowd would best be able to see him.

The crowd converged along the boardwalk when they saw Fred but was noisy and didn't seem that interested in the national park. Then Fred spoke in his soft voice. I was amazed at how quickly the crowd went quiet. With only a few words, he held them all. I listened with my tour group while Fred spoke about four tribes that had occupied the region for nearly 20,000 years. The tribes used the Gorge as a sort of passageway through the ranges and for sacred rituals and ceremonies, rather than a place to live. The Bidjara and the Karringbal had the closest connection to the Gorge area, but other tribes in the Carnarvon's were the Kongabula at the head of the Dawson to the east, the Kaira around Springsure to the north, and the Nguri to the south. They were hunter-gatherers and warriors who made clubs, stone axes, boomerangs and spears. They used bones and stones for points and made wooden shields. They made bark huts to shelter in, and constructed wells and dams for water reserves, bathing and fishing. In winter, they wore possum skin rugs to keep warm.

For ceremonies they had a bullroarer. This warning device was a small flat oval-shaped piece of wood with pointy ends that is tied to a piece of string. When another tribe was in someone else's territory, it was waved in a circle above the head. When it was used during the initiation of young boys, it was waved in a circle beside the body, creating a different sound to the former and warning women and children to stay away. Message sticks were used at ceremonies, and also passed onto other tribes as an interpreter or rite of passage stick to travel through their territory for trading purposes. They were marked with different notches to symbolise their meaning.

These semi-nomadic people used firestick farming to manage the land. Burning off large areas encouraged grazing animals to return in larger numbers to feed on the new growth, in particular kangaroos which could feed many people.

Fred spoke briefly about the brutal history of the Gorge: the fights that had erupted between the first Europeans and the Aboriginal tribes. Early expeditions had resulted in little conflict or hostility with the local tribes, but when glowing accounts of the country eventually reached squatters, they started taking up land around the edges of the highlands, and problems arose. Australia had been an undisturbed island continent for so long that the Aboriginal culture was not accustomed to the common cold or flu, which tolled heavily on Aboriginal lives. Diseases like smallpox, tuberculosis, measles and syphilis dwindled tribal numbers dramatically. Alcohol and opium also contributed to the demise of their culture.

As their numbers declined through the mid-1800s, the local tribes joined forces to wage war with the early settlers. They kept the settlers at bay for 20 years, ambushing them on the few reliable water sources in the region. At last, however, they were forced to succumb to the ways of the new invaders.

The land, which was considered sacred, was taken with no payment or agreement for its use. Their language was suppressed, and children were separated from their parents and moved onto reservations. They became known as the Stolen Generations, and their removal caused the development of future tribal elders to be impaired. Their traditional ways on the land, which had been passed on from generation to generation for millennia, were suddenly broken. To a culture that relied on word of mouth to pass on learning and knowledge, the effects were devastating.

Unfortunately, little is known of their rituals as they were so completely dispossessed, dispersed, degraded and destroyed. Fred himself grew up in a reservation called Woorabinda.

'I bet you want to know what all these pictures mean,' Fred said.

Pointing out a long, curving orange line running several metres along the length of the wall he explained, 'This one is called Mundagurra—the Rainbow Serpent. He is the protector of the permanency of waters.' There was an atmosphere of hushed reverence among the crowd. I thought about Carnarvon Creek and how it looked like a serpent snaking its way through the Gorge—I came to know it as Mundagurra.

Fred pointed to one of the stencil hand paintings with a missing finger and explained how it was a cultural depiction of a family. No more than three children per family were allowed. The mother and the father were the thumb and forefinger, the other three fingers the children. When a finger or thumb was missing this represented the individual that had died. The question I had about missing fingers had now been answered.

He explained how boomerang tips were used for stencil art to re-create the impression of emu footprints. He spoke about the engravings of genitals. Most common was the women's vulva—a sign of fertility.

I waited until the crowd had finished questioning and thanking Fred.

'It would be nice to speak with you about the Gorge sometime, Fred. I've been getting to know the place quite intimately. I had a dream last night and Wayne thought I should tell you about it.'

Fred's deep brown eyes spoke of generations of a people whose culture was deeply interwoven in a spiritual land. 'Wayne mentioned you've been exploring the Gorge. We'll talk more later, when we can be alone.'

CHAPTER TWENTY-FIVE
SPEAKING WITH AN ELDER

'The clearest way into the universe is through a forest wilderness.'
— *John Muir*

'In my culture, every young man must go on a journey; be initiated by the elders of the tribe before he is considered a man. This used to involve many different rites of passage, ceremonies and tests. It's a shame that much of it has been lost.'

Fred performed Aboriginal dance on special occasions. He also conducted tool and weapon-making demonstrations and was skilled at wood carving and finishing. During his talks at the Art Gallery, I'd heard Fred mention some of the initiations. Such rites of passage were initiated by the men of the tribe and involved a cycle of secret ceremonies and sacred rituals that could take place over many weeks, sometimes in seclusion and sometimes around the rest of the tribe. Young boys were taught the tribe's traditional songs and dances which contained the history and religion of their tribe. Some rituals included scarification, and finally the boys were circumcised. When they got older, more learning followed. The women of the tribe took the young girls through their own initiation rites.

I shared with Fred all I had come to know about the Gorge and the feelings it evoked in me. While we sat talking in Angiopteris Ravine, listening to the calming sound of water falling into the Freezing Chamber, I told Fred how I thought of the Gorge as a healing and spiritual place, a sort of teacher.

'The Gorge is many things to many different people all at once. It's a supporter of life and there are many spirits that live in here too,' Fred said.

At length I told him about my dream.

'A strange dream for someone like you to have, Ben.' By *someone like you* I assumed he meant a white man. 'What you have described to me sounds like the Amphitheatre. You have never been to the Amphitheatre because a rockfall has closed the track in there for some months now. Yet, there you were, sitting in it in your dream. Most white people don't find themselves surrounded by Aboriginal people in their dreams either, at least not without good reason. What's more interesting, and what you may not realise, is that the Amphitheatre was a sacred men's place, a place of initiation.'

'What do you think it means?'

'I don't know exactly, maybe an agreement has been made that you may pass through this gateway into the next world. I guess you must be on a journey of some sort that I don't know about, and for reasons I do not understand, but I think it must be important. The spiritual connection with Country: land, waterways, the nature spirits and other subtle energies that you have discovered in here is little understood by most people. If you look deep enough into nature you may, in time, find that you are looking right back at yourself. To glimpse one's own true nature is a kind of homegoing. Just don't go poking around too much, Ben, you might find something you don't want to find.'

I had a feeling I had already glimpsed what Fred was describing. I thought about the girl Wayne had mentioned the day we went up to the Ranch. 'Wayne told me about an Aboriginal girl who was guiding here, who you were teaching, who got too involved with the spirits.'

Fred sighed. 'Yes, Cristy. I was teaching her the spirituality of the Gorge. She was a lovely girl, but the stress got to her. She started doing some things she shouldn't have. She was trying to get the spirits' attention. She got their attention alright, just not in a good way. If you knew her, she was the most beautiful, smiley, friendly, charming young woman. It was painful to see her lose her way.'

Just then a cold draft funnelled down through the chasm from the Freezing Chamber. I felt the hairs on the back of my neck stand up as

I recalled Wayne's experience. Fred looked up but remained quiet. He seemed to acknowledge the gust. I didn't ask any further about Cristy.

'Keep an eye out for any signs that the Gorge is trying to communicate with you, Ben. You will know where you can go, and where you can't. Some people call it common sense, some intuition. There is more wisdom and knowledge within these old sandstone ranges than you can imagine. I'm sure you'll find what you're searching for out there. Just remember, all that is or was or ever will be is right here in this moment. Where will you go when the season finishes here?'

'South. I'm unsure where at the moment.'

'The worst thing you can do is not make a decision about what you want. You are still young, Ben, and throwing yourself at life like the fast-flowing river throws itself against the rocks as it makes its way through the mountains, reluctant to slow down in its excitement to get somewhere. Eventually, however, the river reaches the plains where its path broadens and its waters slow, as your own life will with your years. There will always be calm pools to rest in, eddies and rapids to tackle along the way through the journey of life; times when you are in the flow and times when you are not. Like the water, you must let yourself be guided. Take the path of least resistance. This will bring you the most joy in your life. And remember, there is no rush. One day you will carry your memories out to sea with you.'

Speaking with Fred helped me to see that most of the people I met had a message for me and that I had one to share with them. His wisdom made a mockery of my youth as I struggled to comprehend the depth of his words, but I understood the importance of what he was trying to tell me. How would I learn to flow my own natural course through life? Where did my path of least resistance lay? I wondered how different my life would have been if I'd had wise elders to guide me into adulthood.

'Before you leave the Gorge, Ben, take a walk up to Battleship Spur and stay there a night. If you're ready, the nature spirits will share with you a story that might help you on your journey.'

I sat above Wards Canyon, thinking about my conversation with Fred. Below, the sound of water falling into the Freezing Chamber echoed from deep inside the chasm. Every element was filled with life. It was as if the rocks and trees were breathing, and the water was the lifeblood pulsing through the landscape. Hiding under every unturned leaf and stone, in every stream and tucked away in every canyon, an inexplicable energy resided.

I wondered how one could look at something as exquisite as the Earth's ecology and do something that would risk the balance of this system? I realised I was a part of a society with unprecedented leisure time, affluence and mobility. But industrialism needed to consider its effects upon the Earth—upon human life, and upon the environment.

My escape from the industrial paradigm had allowed me to tap into the timeless and magical realm of nature. I felt a part of myself moving away from material survival; relinquishing my need for control over my situation and security, as I awoke to a new world—a world that felt more real somehow as my entire perceptual and conceptual framework was reformed. I was learning to consciously incorporate a wise and compassionate guidance into my life through a new awareness of spirit and the interconnectedness of all things. I wondered about coincidence and the mysterious processes that underlay the human experience. I realised I needed to decide what way I was to learn as I moved forward, through doubt and fear, or through wisdom.

I walked to the edge of the escarpment, sat upon the warm sandstone ledge and gazed over the landscape, lost in the deep contemplation that had become an ever-increasing part of my life. Haze hung like a grey mist from the fires that continued to smoulder and burn in the Moolayember section of the park. Some days were worse than others, blotting out the sun and stifling the air as the season shifted gears into summer heat. Station owners were burning firebreaks where their properties bordered the park, to prevent further outbreaks and to protect their land and livestock.

I counted on my fingers the side gorges I had explored: Kooraminya Gorge, Hellhole Gorge with its enchanting deep emerald Fairy Pools, Wagooroo, Kongaboola, Kamoodangie, Kamoloo, Warrumbah. Each of them flowed into Carnarvon Gorge—each a separate life support system and world in its own right. Every branch was an evolutionary possibility on the road of life. I realised we all forge our own path in life in search of our dreams. I realised that all paths, like the many branches of the Gorge, eventually come together and merge into one, taking us back to where we began. Our longing for life is a torrent rushing with might to the sea, carrying the secrets of the hillside and the songs of the forest with us. All our journeys, unique like the many side gorges I had visited, are one and the same. Each of us harbours the same fears and anxieties, hopes and desires along the way. We all have the same basic wants and needs. In the end, life leads us to where it wants us to go, to where we need to be.

CHAPTER TWENTY-SIX

AWAKENING

'In every walk with nature one receives far more than he seeks.'

— *John Muir*

I met Claudia at the Visitor Centre early in the morning. We shouldered our packs, tightened our boot laces and picked up our heels. Our destination was Big Bend. From there we would further explore the Gorge using Big Bend as our base camp. We'd planned to visit Battleship Spur but Claudia had confused her days. Our two-night mission had become one. I was disappointed.

There was only one major side gorge I hadn't explored. It was Nabooloo Gorge—Nabooloo means *little baby*. Nabooloo Gorge was a kilometre and a half further up from Big Bend. I'd found some interesting, and useful, information on the side gorge in a book called *Exploring Queensland's Central Highlands* that Wayne had lent me. With childish excitement, I described it to Claudia.

The loud 'cooee' of recently arrived koels followed us up the main track. The koels were visiting from New Guinea and other distant islands as part of their summer feeding grounds. They were known as the storm birds from their sharp replies to thunder from the brooding summer storms. The past few days had already seen several storms pass over the ranges in deluges of rain, thunder and lightning. Jade lances shot from earth and tree in response, spearing the landscape in virgin greens in a quickening transformation of the dry, blackened and charred checkerboard of the park. The thought of getting caught in a torrential downpour while we were exploring sat in the back of my mind. I didn't like the idea of being stuck in a side gorge during a flash flood—a very real possibility at this time of year.

About halfway to Big Bend I stopped Claudia and pointed out a prominent stone feature a hundred metres off the main track. Below it, a sheltered face of bright sandstone crouched under a small overhang of rock. The feature had caught my attention while guiding groups on full day walks, but I had only stopped to scrutinise it more closely with binoculars once, spotting out-of-place colouring upon the walls.

We each shot a glance up and down the track to ensure no one was coming, then ducked into a jungle of kangaroo and blady grass that lined the track. As the terrain sloped gently upward to the base of the towering cliffs, the grass thinned into a small clearing.

I watched Claudia. Astonishment seized her in its hypnotic grasp. Her gaze shifted from the rock paintings to me. Pride lifted me off the ground. The rock art was detailed and incredibly unique; unlike anything I had seen anywhere else in the Gorge. Prominent stencil paintings covered the base of the cliff: a pair of baby's feet, hands, arms and boomerangs frozen in vivid red and orange ochres. The faint outline of a small body, a child, was stencilled on the wall. No one had ever mentioned anything about this site to either of us.

'This find is incredible,' Claudia said, her eyes still wide with disbelief.

'I didn't realise there was so much art here,' I replied, thrilled that I'd succeeded in impressing her.

We studied several engravings as we walked up and down the cliff face in search of artefacts and other signs of habitation that may have been left and forgotten.

After several minutes, careful not to disturb anything, we thanked the spirits for allowing us to visit and left the hidden site.

An hour later, we dropped our packs at Big Bend and made camp. After a light meal, we carried on into unknown territory.

I spotted the telltale signs of a dry creek bed stemming into Carnarvon Creek from the right flank of the Gorge. 'This must be it,' I said to Claudia.

'Are you sure?'

'Trust me, I know what to look for now.'

We followed the creek bed through an entanglement of undergrowth and found a remarkable ravine. It was deep, narrow, and lined with moss, ferns and fig trees that clung to heavily shelved walls. The walls undulated from their base, climbing in vertical wavelets. Some areas looked like moon craters. Soft light filtered down, emphasising its steep sides and the peculiar shapes. I was at once taken by a feeling of caution. An entirely new and unfamiliar energy resided in here, unlike anything I had encountered in any of the other side gorges. It felt as if someone or something were watching us as we walked, like an unseen force guarded this unique chasm with brooding jealousy.

The air grew clammy the further we pushed on, nothing unusual for a side gorge. I stopped to examine the bones of a dead wallaby that lay in the middle of the path, contemplating its fall from the dizzying heights above. The flesh had rotted away, leaving the bones in a perfectly preserved state of structure, like the skeleton of a ship. I thought of the many creatures I had found and rescued in Warrumbah Gorge during my days guiding: snakes, lizards, gliders—they all got stuck in there. If they survived the fall from above, but didn't find a way out, they usually succumbed to the inhospitable cold and lack of food. I wondered how many hundreds, maybe thousands or even tens of thousands of animals had lost their lives at the bottoms of the numerous ravines that made up the sandstone belt. Archaeological excavations might unearth unknown species. Perhaps the remains of dinosaurs were buried at the bottom of some of these gorges. The strange feeling that we were being watched started to tie knots in my stomach.

The walls squeezed together then bulged into a small amphitheatre, about the size of a bedroom, and an enormous boulder that blocked our path in an impassable jump-up. Wet season rains had carved out a deep pit in the canyon floor beneath the boulder. An old tree trunk sagged heavily over one side. I turned to Claudia.

'There's no way I can get up there,' she said, reading my thoughts.

I pushed on the sagging trunk. I knew I'd be a fool to doubt what I felt in my stomach, especially after speaking with Fred. 'I have a feeling that this one is best left alone, anyway. Let's make our way back out and see what we can find further up.'

We walked out of the side gorge and into a furnace of heat. An hour later we arrived at The Island—a colossal stand of sandstone nearly a hundred metres high that sat in the middle of the dry creek bed. Although it was normally dry this far up the Gorge at this time of year, water still flowed underground, and it pooled in deep ponds around the base of The Island. A variety of waterfowl paddled, dived and nibbled on reeds.

'Do you believe in God?' Claudia's question baffled me. We'd never discussed religion. I wondered where she was going with her question and chose my words carefully.

'I believe there are things at work in this world and in our lives that I can't well explain. Sometimes I choose to call that God.'

'Like what?'

'Like karma, serendipity, coincidence, intuition, signs that tell us where to go and what to do; messengers that help point us in the right direction if we are lost; two people separated by a great distance thinking of each other, or a shared memory at the same time. The wise, enlightened voice that pops into your head from out of nowhere and shares insights into life beyond the peripheries of human contemplation and comprehension. Perhaps it's our own innate powers to sense things out; the power of our subconscious mind in creating what we want in our lives, but it's almost miraculous the way some events play out—the way universal intelligence seems to connect all things like a huge web of receptors. It makes the brain cower under the incomprehensible, unfathomable, bewildering mystery of it all.'

'Why do you believe in that?'

'I've seen it at work. Every day little things happen that tell me I'm on the right path, that I am creating my life experiences. Don't you believe in something?'

'I don't know, I guess there is something, but I don't know what it is.'

'You know you can make anything happen in your life, don't you?' I told her with conviction.

'Maybe.'

I knew she was unsure where life was going for her, and I understood her anxiety. I was familiar with the drifting uncertainty of life, about where the future was taking me, even when I knew what I wanted. It could be very confusing and unsettling, but I had learnt to trust in life and accept change as a necessary part of it.

'Sometimes you just have to let life take care of life,' I said.

'What do you mean?'

'You must allow room for change, good or otherwise. If you cling and resist at that point, it means you are refusing to let go. If you don't go with the flow, you will suffer. Dissolution is needed for new growth to happen. One cannot exist without the other. I never had a plan when I came to Australia, just an idea that I wanted something more from life. When I had the courage to let everything go, many things happened that aided me on my quest. Accepting the flow of life has been more beautiful and natural than anything I have previously known. Believing that what you are about is valuable, is important, is taking you somewhere, and has some greater meaning and purpose than you can perceive is the hard part—continuing to believe in yourself, when everything says turn back.'

'So, you don't think if everything is telling you to turn back that you should?'

'I guess it depends on the situation, but I think most often it is life challenging us, to see if we are ready to move onto the next chapter. You always feel it most when you are about to cross a new threshold. If you don't do it, if you listen to that voice and stay where you are, then you never grow. That voice is fear. Fear can keep you safe, but it can also cripple you.'

'Well, if you really believe you can make anything happen, I want you to prove it.'

'Okay, tell me how, and I will.'

'I bet you can't find a koala.'

'That seems a bit trivial, but it's a deal. I bet I can.'

The chances of finding a koala in the Gorge were slim to none, and Claudia knew this. They preferred the high-country forests, where they were out of sight. I searched high and low, keeping my eyes peeled on the treetops.

It was uncanny the way that koala appeared. It was like the universe wanted to help me prove a point. No more than an hour had passed when I spotted one in a tree overhanging the creek bed. I could hardly believe it myself. It was the only koala I had ever seen in the Gorge.

'See, there, I told you! You just have to start looking and things will appear. Still don't believe me?' I pointed at the koala.

Claudia rolled her eyes and shook her head. 'What are you talking about, there's no koala there.'

'What? Are you kidding? Look, it's right there, see?' I pointed again.

It was almost like she couldn't see it because she didn't really want to see it. Finally, her eyes found the shy, motionless creature.

'I guess it's hard to find something if you don't know exactly what you're looking for,' I said.

'You got lucky.'

I wondered if I might meet more people like Claudia on my journey, people unaware of the light my own conscious had awakened to. Would I still be able to connect with them, or would I become an outsider? Were there others like me? How much of the picture was I still missing? I wasn't so sure just then; wasn't sure if what I was learning was spiritual or human. Either way, the two seemed to be connected somehow.

It was getting late in the afternoon when we turned back from The Island.

'Why are you always so happy?' Claudia asked irritably, as we made our way back to Big Bend. 'Life is easy for you, isn't it? I mean, you don't really take anything seriously, do you?'

I was surprised and slightly offended by her presumptuousness. Maybe she was just tired. It had been a long, hot day.

I took a deep breath. 'I'm light-hearted and content. I don't think there's anything wrong with that. As for being happy, well, I wasn't always this happy. I only discovered how good life really is after spending a year in the desert, on a cattle station. It's amazing what a desert and hard work can teach you about life.'

'You were a jackaroo? I didn't realise that.' Her tone shifted completely.

'I love the outdoors, and I take my experiences here seriously. My life hasn't always been easy,' I said.

Whoosh! A flock of rainbow lorikeets cutting the crisp mountain air just above our heads hurtled down the Gorge like missiles. Claudia ducked and threw her hands over her head.

'Just a flock of lorikeets,' I reassured her. 'You need to lighten up a bit. Life's great,' I continued, 'I mean, what's there not to be happy about? I know life can be confusing sometimes, unfair, painful, devastating even, but it's these times that we learn the most about ourselves. We're privileged to be in such a beautiful place and time. Life's an exciting journey.' I was burning with passion, but she didn't really seem to understand. 'Sometimes you just have to let go, be open, and let life show you the way. If you don't, you may end up a long way down a road you never meant to travel. Forget about your goals and ambitions for a while. Take it easy on yourself. Just breathe and appreciate all that you have, here and now.'

'Do you really think that will work?'

'I know it will work.'

I dropped a six-pack of Coopers Pale Ale in the creek at Big Bend—Claudia's favourite beer. I stripped down to my boxer shorts and jumped in the icy waters for a swim in the deep pool that sat under the smooth curving undercut of the cliff. Sweat washed away in an oily slick upon the surface. Claudia sat by the creek, cooling her swollen feet. I splashed her between gulping back mouthfuls of water and diving to the bottom of the pool to see what I could discover. Above the pool, welcome swallows ducked and dived through the air, weaving and whirling, chasing after insects. We had the campsite to ourselves.

Evening was heralded by chirping crickets calling from the forest. Soon the warm, humid night was alive in a high-pitched chorus, mingled with the verse of owls and gliders.

Claudia prepared dinner while I sat by the creek in the fading light. I wondered about spending the night in her tent, squashed up beside her.

'Wook wook, wook wook' a barking owl called nearby. Other rustlings and calls filled the gaps between our tired conversation before we retired to Claudia's small tent. The certainties about life that I had confidently shared through the course of the day crumbled into uncertainty around my pending departure. I didn't want to leave the Gorge. We shuffled into our sleeping bags and got comfortable. Just before Claudia turned out her flashlight, I found myself holding her gaze. Should I lean in and kiss her? Her eyes seemed to enquire, imply and wait. I hesitated. How could I after she had made it so clear that she wasn't interested in more than friendship? Besides, we had enjoyed a beautiful day together. Was it worth risking that? The moment passed. I smiled at her, rolled over and tried to go to sleep, confused as all hell and silently cursing myself for not taking a chance. I heard Claudia turn away from me as I tossed and turned in pent up passion. I had missed my moment.

'Good morning.' I woke Claudia and unzipped the tent. A cool draft of fresh air forced its way into the warmth of our cocoon. She rolled over and buried her head in her pillow. 'I'll get up soon,' she murmured.

After breakfast we packed up camp and started making our way back. It was odd to be starting the day at Big Bend, almost like my stay had come full circle. When I walked out this time, I wouldn't be coming back.

I hesitated at the turn off to Boowinda Gorge. 'I'm going up to Battleship Spur for the night.'

'What? Why? Aren't you leaving tomorrow?'

'I'm sorry, I forgot to mention it yesterday, I have one last thing I need to do before I leave.'

'Well, come on then, what is it? Why the big secret?'

'I can't tell you now, because I don't really know what it is myself. But I'll tell you when I see you next.'

Claudia rolled her eyes at me. 'Well, I'll see you back at the park's headquarters before you leave so we can arrange when to meet in Lamington National Park. Good luck.'

'You never know your luck in the bush.' I smiled at her.

'Is that one of your sayings, is it?'

'I guess you could say that. I learnt it on the station.'

'I have one of my own, I guess. It's *I see what other people don't see*. It's been fun exploring with you, Ben. Thank you.'

I shot her a smile and said goodbye.

Following Fred's instructions, I headed up Boowinda Gorge, climbing high into the ranges. It was a blistering hot and humid day. I didn't know what I would find or what to expect from spending another night on my own in the high country.

I made Battleship Spur late in the afternoon. After setting up camp for the night I sat at the lookout and gazed out over the national park. Memories of my first days flooded my mind.

The wilderness, I realised, gave humanity its sanity. Here, I had discovered a flow to life that I hadn't known before, a flow that was undisturbed by outside influences. In the morning, I would be leaving it all.

While I gazed over the Gorge, I fell into a trance. The air swirled around me, the view before me became dreamlike, and a profound energy enveloped me. I transcended time and space for a moment of eternity. In that instant, I half expected something to materialise before my eyes—a flash of light, a warp in time and matter, or a vision of some sort. I sensed a veil would drop, the illusion would crack and fall away, and the truth about life would finally be revealed as I was ferried across the oceans of existence. Then it passed. The air around me settled from its electrified state into a lake of calm. A profound silence settled like an invisible mist over the land. That wild, empty wilderness continued to inexorably mould and mix itself within me.

My awareness had awoken, as if from a dream. My mind was reborn to a new world of thought—a magical world beyond the physical and material, a world rich in intelligence that was beyond words. Within the silence of my own being I found enlightenment. Life was full of unlimited potential and possibility. I felt an overwhelming desire to share the ideas and energy that was spilling from my being.

After six months in the Gorge, surrounded by the myriad wonders of the natural world, walking had become meditation. Exploring the many sandstone corridors into other worlds had allowed me the time to tap into the universal mind, unbounded, undifferentiated. My inner world was untamed, wild and free, unrefined by culture, rules, or logic. Every moment sparkled with eternity. Every leaf, tree, flower and rock had meaning to me. The whole landscape, and every intimate formation within it, was a work of art. I revered all living things. My indigenous mind lived at will in its natural home in a sensual world beyond time; climbing, swimming, rock hopping, listening to nature. I could have melted into the earth or a tree and flown away as a bird. Watching a single leaf fall to a creek and float away on its current was like watching the journey of life and death in a single moment. I watched nature repeat its cycle around me: a life lived, a story told, a time passed. I recognised my own mortality as the impermanence of all things made itself known to me. I realised that nothing ever dies; that form merely changes form; life roles into life. I finally understood the mysterious, interminable significance of it all—the great synthesis of nature that is life—that the wilderness was the only way to the true self.

That night I dreamed I was walking down an enchanting riverbed surrounded by trees and ferns. Nearly out of sight, I perceived stone walls bordering the river. It was like many of the side gorges I had visited. As I neared an open area, I felt a gentle breeze. The further I walked into the space the stronger the breeze grew, like it was trying to push me back, until it became a strong wind. I fought against it to continue. Then, suddenly, I left the ground and flew forward. I faltered in the air as uneven pressures threw my flight off balance. I landed. No sooner had my feet touched the ground than I took off again, this time moving up and forward before losing the sensation again. I jerked awake, my arms fighting against the sides of my sleeping bag as I tried to open them like wings. I was breathing hard, my heart pounding in my chest, and my hands shaking. What did it mean? I wondered. What significance did this dream have to my journey?

I became aware of my tent fly flapping against the side of the tent in a stiff breeze, then the faint sound of a voice. The forest seemed to be calling to me, pleading with me, 'come,' it said in the witch's voice of a million leaves rasping together, 'join us, jump!' I thought of Fred and what he had said about the nature spirits sharing a story with me if I was ready. I wasn't about to leap off Battleship Spur and try to fly back down the Gorge just because I had had a flying dream; I grasped that there might be some obstacles ahead of me which might throw me off course. I thought of my childhood dream companion, Giant Benjamin, and his ability to fly. Perhaps it was time for me to learn how.

I got out of my sleeping bag and groped for the zip to the door. Unsure of what I would find, I crawled outside. Like a displeased spirit, a stiff, cool breeze shook me awake with invisible hands. A cold, silvery light outlined gnarled and crooked shapes dancing in the wind around me. I breathed a sigh—just trees. I gazed into the sky—crisp and clear. Millions of distant stars painted the heavens in sign language. There was a majesty that existed in nature that would never be equalled by anything man made.

I fastened the flapping fly, climbed back into my sleeping bag and stared into the darkness. As I drifted back to sleep, I wondered about the road ahead and what it would bring.

I awoke to a symphony of bird song and a sunrise that welcomed the next chapter of the road. I stopped at the park headquarters to see Claudia, arrange our rendezvous, and share my profound experience. Ever the sceptic, she didn't believe the story of my night up there.

It was too late to think about getting on the road when I got back to the Lodge, so I spent the afternoon packing and preparing the Falcon to leave the following morning. I sat on my balcony for the last time that evening and watched a dollar bird swoop and dive through the air before landing in a nearby river sheoak and letting out a harsh 'krak-kak-kak'. The quiet, rhythmic babble of Carnarvon Creek sung the delicate wisdom of ages over the rocks below me. I now understood that the dry eucalypt forest before me was a refuge for wildlife and the magic of Aboriginal culture. I contemplated my good fortune to have found such a beautiful place and time. I had never imagined finding anything so deeply spiritual when I set out on my journey; anything so real and revealing about the truth of life.

In the morning I said goodbye to my Lodge family one by one.

'Take care, mate,' Rob said, as he gripped my hand and gave it a vigorous shake. 'I'm heading back to the Kimberley. That's where you should be going next, trust me, if you enjoyed this, you're gonna love it up there.'

'Maybe I'll see you over there.' Rob wasn't the first person to mention the Kimberley to me, and for nearly as long as I had been in Australia, I'd had the feeling that I was destined to make it there some day.

Tears streamed down Annie's face. 'You'll keep in touch, won't you?'

'Sure,' I said. I didn't know what to say, but I knew I wouldn't be looking back once I left. I couldn't. I would miss the place too much.

'You've been a great friend, Ben. I can't express how grateful I am to have met such a down-to-earth, unique person like you. And thank you for all the long talks. Listening and taking in everything you said to me night after night has opened my eyes and given me a whole new outlook on life. I hope the next road you travel leads to many more great times and fond memories. I hope you find what you're searching for.' Annie let out a sob.

I embraced Annie. I knew none of this might have been possible if she hadn't spoken to me at the bar that first night at the Lodge. She was one of fate's accomplices. I would never forget that. I wanted to tell her how much she meant to me but sharing what was in my heart didn't come easily to me then. I lacked empathy, I clung to freedom, and I offered my heart to all the wrong people.

I stood back. 'Have you seen Wayne this morning? I wanted to see him before I left.'

'I think he had an early walk on, so he might have left already.'

Just then, Wayne came jogging up to my car. 'I'm glad I found you, Ben. I wanted to leave you with something to think about on the road. I thought it would make sense to you.' Wayne puffed out the words. 'Okay, here it is. All things are in process rising and returning. Plants come to blossom, but only to return to the root. Returning to the root is like seeking tranquillity. Seeking tranquillity is like moving towards destiny. To move toward destiny is like eternity. To know eternity is enlightenment. Knowing eternity makes one comprehensive. Comprehension makes one broad-minded. Breadth of vision brings nobility. Nobility is like heaven. Well, that's it. I hope you found a slice of heaven here, and I hope you find what you're looking for out there. Once you are awake, you shall remain awake. Just remember there are times of dormancy, times when we must look within for the answers on our journeys through life. Godspeed, Ben. I'm glad our paths crossed. Till we meet again.' Wayne shook my hand then turned and wandered off up the track to the Lodge. Would I ever see that charming old sage again?

'What was that all about?' Annie frowned confusion at me.

'Just a few discoveries I made in the Gorge.'

'Okay? Are you going to say goodbye to Claudia?'

'I'll see her in a few days. We're visiting a national park in south-east Queensland.'

I could see Annie in my rear-view mirror, waving, until she was out of sight. Just before I turned off the dirt road onto the highway, I took one last look back at the Gorge. Would I ever find anything as wonderful as that place? At any rate, it had given me another part of what I was looking for.

The roads were long, hot and drowsy that day. The bitumen disappeared into a mirage of uncertainty ahead of the Falcon. I pulled off the road to rest. The engine was baking. I got out and lay in the grass under the shade of a spindly bush on the side of the road while it cooled. Not one person who knew me from back home had any idea that I was out here. I was alone and unknown. I closed my eyes and quickly fell into a deep slumber.

The vision that appeared before me was one I will never forget. Like a revelation, I glimpsed a simple, yet humbling truth about human existence. In that moment, I found a pure and unattested place where the self is no longer the self but rather a single part of an energy with every conceivable element in it. I felt an overwhelming peace in the understanding of the revelation of being. I felt the majesty of cosmic law, without illusions, purged of hope and fear. I let go and was freed, a universally guided pilgrim.

I gradually became aware of my surroundings: the heat of the afternoon sun, a gentle breeze rustling the grass, and the weight of reality settling back on my shoulders. In that moment, I knew that, though everything had changed, nothing had really changed. I was living an ordinary human life with ordinary human responsibilities, but I had been freed, allowed to see the greater vision of life. Now I wanted to ensure my life was useful. I wondered if I would ever experience anything more precious and beautiful on my journey than this single moment of understanding alone?

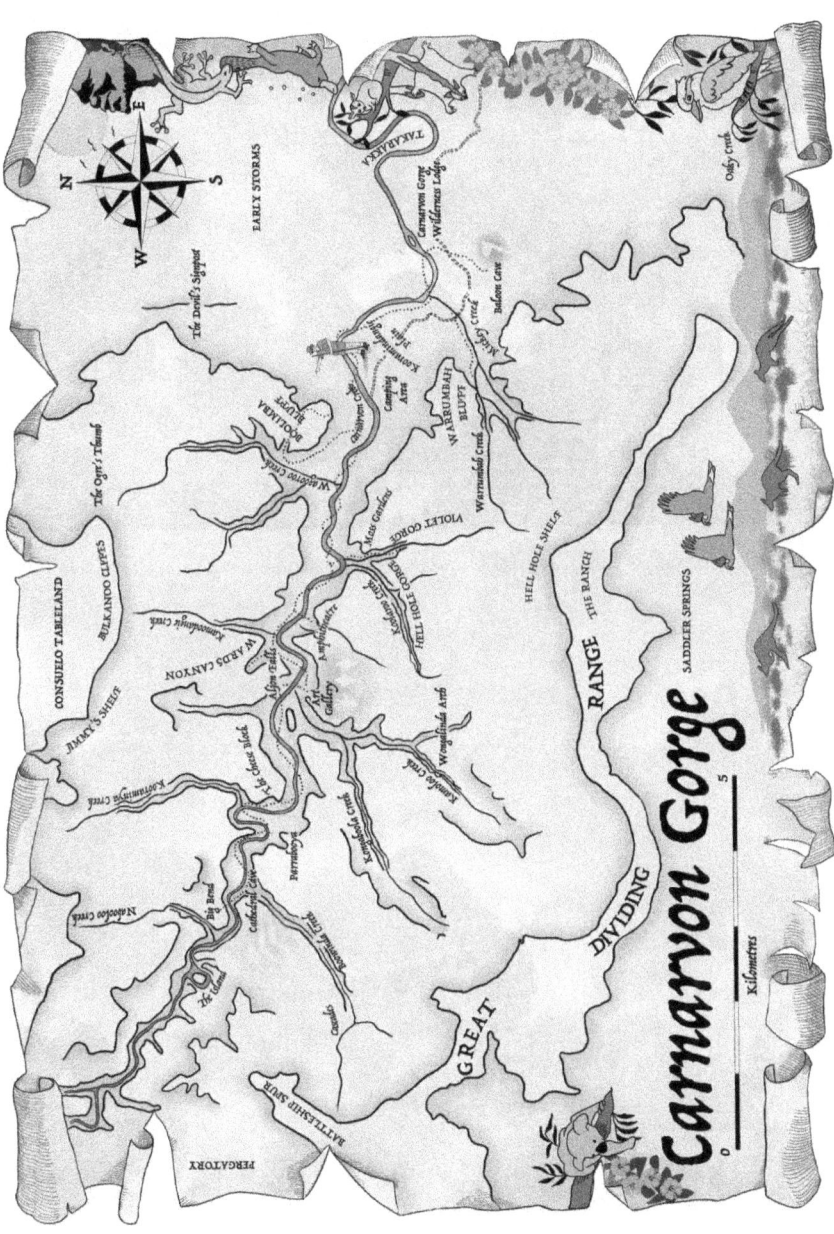

My first sunset in Carnarvon Gorge, on the Goombangie Cliffs, above Baloon Cave.

View from Battleship Spur, looking east over Carnarvon Gorge.

Wayne and me at Moss Gardens.

Describing the macrozamia to a group.

View from Clematis Ridge at sunrise, looking south.

Releasing a green tree snake that I rescued from Warrumbah Gorge.

Releasing a greater glider that I rescued from Warrumbah Gorge.

View from southern flank of Clematis ridge, sunrise walks were on the northern flank. Gorge entrance is near bottom right corner of photo at the break in the ridge.

The A-Frame, where the Lodge welcome, introduction to the Gorge and guided walk talks were held.

Lace monitor (tree goanna).

The Devil's Signpost.

View from The Ranch, looking north-east over the Gorge.

View from Parrabooya with Christine (foreground) and Claudia (background), my first day exploring with Claudia.

Exploring Kamoloo Gorge with Claudia.

Rainbow skink.

Kooraminya Gorge.

Hellhole Gorge—Fairy Pools.

Wagooroo Gorge, western branch.   Wagooroo Gorge, eastern branch end.

Wagooroo Gorge, western branch end.

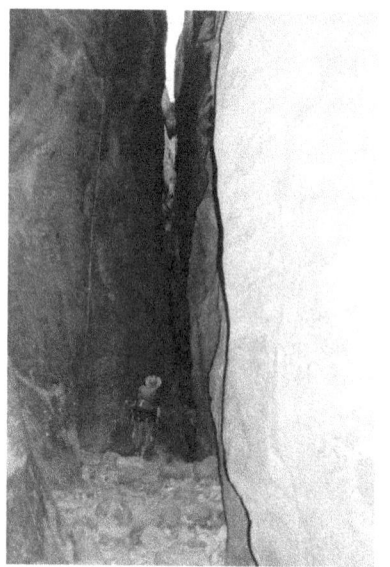
Warrumbah Gorge.

Kongaboola Gorge.

Variegated fairywren.

Fred giving a talk at the Art Gallery.

Fred performing Aboriginal Dance.

View from above Wards Canyon.

Exploring Nabooloo Gorge with Claudia.

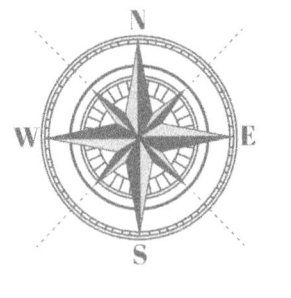

PART THREE

CHAPTER TWENTY-SEVEN
MARYBOROUGH TO BENDIGO

'Not until we are lost do we begin to understand ourselves.'
—Henry David Thoreau

It was still hot and humid when I made it to Maryborough late in the evening. I wound down the window and drove slowly through town. The air was thick and sticky. It was quiet, and I suddenly felt lonely.

I pulled over at Queens Park and peeled myself from my sweat-soaked seat. I wasn't sure where I was going to stay for the night, so I decided to go for a walk through the park. I was soon surprised to find myself surrounded by over five hectares of landscaped gardens and huge trees that created a magnificent night-time oasis.

Eventually, I found myself at the end of a long, narrow wooden jetty on the Mary River. I sat down, hung my legs over the end, and gazed searchingly up and down the river. Several small, old wooden boats sat peacefully, moored along the river's edge. I lay back and stared at the sky. Heavy cloud hung in an oppressive blanket. I took a deep breath and tried to relax while exotic noises filled the sultry evening around me: croaking frogs and screeching flying foxes. The majority of the continent still lay out there, an undiscovered mystery.

I sat back up and peered into the dark watery world below my feet. Like a pearl emerging from the depths, the full moon appeared from behind parting clouds and stared back up at me. I suddenly remembered I had to get to the Kimberley and the pearling industry that spanned that remote coast.

After spending a week with Claudia in the Gold Coast Hinterland, I struck south on my own. Claudia was driving back to Adelaide. I might see her down in Tasmania later in the year if I was lucky. I thought about our last few days together in the park while the kilometres passed beneath the Falcon, drawing us apart. Our tents were nearly washed away by hailstones the size of golf balls as south-east Queensland was hit by record storms. The torrential downpours had also brought out thousands of leeches, making the park a miserable, wet place to be and cutting our time together. But we had shared a few days of spectacular weather when we first arrived, days walking and talking that I would never forget.

Almost miraculously, the weather had abated the evening before we parted ways. We walked to see a nearby glow worm display. Gazing up at the glow worms under an overhanging rock was like looking at the entire cosmos. I was reminded of the bigger picture in life again. Below the glow worms a stream trickled over stones, orchestrating the flow of time ever present in our short physical lives while the glow worm cosmos twinkled through eternity. Droplets of water fell through the wet foliage above our heads, and a choir of frogs croaked up a chorus. In the end, we had shared one last magical moment together. I said goodbye to Claudia during a break in the weather the following morning. In a way, I was envious that I too wasn't heading back home to see folk I knew. I didn't have a home. We hugged and wished each other well. I felt a thread unravelling inside. Nothing but uncertainty lay on the road ahead, and I knew it would take every ounce of courage I had to stay true to what I believed in.

Kilometres of flooded paddocks lined the road south. Oddly, much of the land surrounding the flooded areas looked like it hadn't seen rain in months.

I made New South Wales and clearer weather. Sydney sucked me into a maze of highways, byways and one-way roads then spat me out. The cold glass and steel suspicious eyes of the city reminded me of my time away from civilisation. I felt like Winston Smith from George Orwell's *Nineteen Eighty-four*—uncomfortable, disconnected and out of place after spending so much time in the wilderness. What was there for someone like me in a place like this?

I felt my chest relax when I finally made it clear of the industrial complex. I carried on, spurring the Falcon south through Parramatta, then Penrith and finally up into the Blue Mountains where I felt like I could really breathe again. I pushed on, through the country towns of Lithgow, Oberon and Goulburn.

From Canberra I ran down the dark kilometres to Cooma and then took a dogleg west to Jindabyne. From Jindabyne I pushed up to Thredbo and into the Snowy Mountains.

The township of Corryong sprung up from out of nowhere as I crossed the border into Victoria. More small towns flew by: Wodonga, Violet Town, Murchison and Rushworth. Finally, after three days driving, I hit the Midland Highway and reached the large gold mining town of Bendigo.

I hadn't seen my brother since before I left New Zealand. It was hard to believe two and a half years had passed so quickly. He was employed as a diesel fitter in a gold mine. He was still at work when I arrived.

'You've changed, Ben,' Sam said, after we finished hugging. I was delighted to see my brother. It lifted the burden of loneliness from my shoulders, and I relaxed.

We both grinned broadly at each other and laughed. He still looked like the brother I had left in New Zealand, a curly haired gentle giant, but something was different.

'A lot has happened since I saw you last. I don't know where to begin,' I said.

'Perhaps we should start with a beer?' he offered.

I described the outback, and how living out there had changed my view of the world, and life in general. I told him about the joy I had found living on the Sunshine Coast, surfing, and painted a picture of my most recent journey in Carnarvon Gorge, and Claudia.

'You seem happy, like you've sorted some stuff out in your life, Ben.'

'I've worked through a lot of things. I'm happy with life. But I need to finish this journey around Australia before I settle again. How about you?'

'Me? Well, you know I moved over here to be with Krystina?'

'No?'

'Well, I did, about six months ago. We're going good; thinking about heading up to Queensland to live ourselves. You'll be able to meet her. I'll give her a call; we should all go out for dinner.'

I had never met Krystina, but I knew my brother must have thought she was special to have moved countries to be with her.

Over dinner, Sam fawned over Krystina. I could see he was head over heels in love with her. Krystina was striking, extroverted and young. It humoured me to see him giggle around her and dote on her, and it dragged from the dark closet of my heart the feelings I once had for Stephanie. Those memories, like dreams, thrived in the dark, surviving in the deep waters of my mind like shipwrecks on the seabed. I wondered what she was doing now. It had been nearly two years since I had spoken to her.

It wasn't without regret that I left that warm moment of possibility.

'Take care of yourself, Ben. I hope it isn't so long before we see you again, and I hope you find what you're looking for out there. Maybe next time I see you we'll be in Queensland.'

I embraced my brother in a bear hug. Then, with all the composure I could keep, I stood back and looked into his eyes. 'You too. Krystina seems like a nice girl. I'm happy for you. Take care. I'll be in touch.'

I didn't know then it would be another two and a half years before I saw him again.

CHAPTER TWENTY-EIGHT
SOLITUDE

'There are days when solitude is a heady wine that intoxicates you with freedom, others when it is a bitter tonic, and still others when it is a poison that makes you beat your head against the wall.'
—*Sidonie Gabrielle Colette*

Days soon became weeks, and weeks turned into months as I drifted across the continent—Tasmania, Victoria, South Australia. Often, I didn't know where I would end up next or even where I would sleep for the night. I spent my days and nights alone. I lived in solitude, longing to let go, to drift free of things, to accumulate less, depend on less. I fell from the lofty highs of cosmic insights and realisations, of growing self-awareness and glimpses of enlightenment, into a haunting abyss of loneliness. I became separated from a universe I had known as conscious, connected, intelligent and compassionate. I got lost in the inexorably dark depths of my psyche.

My world was reduced to mere personal issues that seemed incomprehensible and insurmountable. I created meaningless mountains in my mind as the very issues I had been churning through, many of which I thought I had dealt with for good, resurfaced in a fierce battle within. Depression crept up on me, hidden in the linings of thought. Those thoughts circled like vultures: What am I doing? Why have I been gone so long? When will I go back? Am I running from my problems? Why am I spending so much time on my own? Is this a necessary part of the journey? That world spilled over into my dreams, dreams of being chased by demons. Always running, always hiding, only ever one step ahead. They hid in the shadows, prowled, stalked and hunted me in the small dark hours of the night. I felt like a fugitive, running from my past, carrying with me the tremendous weight of my invisible suffering.

I thought until I tore every idea, belief, reality and truth to pieces. I separated myself from a common bond that bound every human being. I became lost, out of touch and disconnected. I ranted and raved in seclusion as I floated between worlds, searching for a new truth.

I drove the highways and byways of life, hiked through the mountains of my past, walked through fertile valleys to discover amazing waterfalls of joy and swam in the icy-cold rivers of my innermost fears. I fished highland lakes and rivers and remembered my father whom I so missed; a father I didn't know how to get close to or connect with. I watched the seasons change in myself as the surrounding landscape became golden and red with autumn then naked with winter as I crossed the inner deserts of my psyche. I walked down countless beaches while contemplating life, searching for the light I had lost.

Some days I felt an oppressive emptiness, like I was the only person left on the planet. With growing realisation, I could feel myself becoming weary of the undulating moments of life on the road as the pangs of my old life called me back. I was tired and felt strange and lost in a faraway place.

Often, I considered reconnecting with humanity, but I soon realised it was possible to be surrounded by people and still be lonely. I needed a friend, someone real to talk to, not another stranger that knew nothing about me. I missed Carnarvon Gorge and the Sunshine Coast. I thought intensely on what I had left behind in New Zealand: my family, old friends, and Stephanie. Missing the people I loved was a kind of grieving for me. Some days, and some nights, that grieving choked me. Every place felt empty of meaning, identity and love. Trapped in my mind, in my own adventure, the road became a bitter tonic. A part of me wanted to run and hide; to shelter from the storm of uncertainty I'd created; to be around familiar things and people. I craved a home and a plan but doubted it would fix the way I felt. Something was happening inside me. A change was taking place. Painful growth. Between clinging and letting go, I felt a terrific struggle. I dragged with me the stale shreds of that former life. I was no longer that old person, and not yet the new. I would never be going back to what I left behind. I had lost that life; it didn't exist anymore. That home was no longer home.

I observed humanity as I passed silently through scenes and lives, contemplating my place within it all. I watched holidaymakers joyfully exploring the countryside with their families. Young couples and old alike. I felt a growing desire to fall back into harmony with the unseen order of things. I desperately wanted to belong somewhere, to something, to someone. I had a longing to become part of a community, to find a home. To have a purpose. But a voice inside me said I needed to keep going, to trust and have faith. To keep believing that what I was about was valuable, important. That life was taking me somewhere and had some greater meaning and purpose than I could perceive. It said the agony of breaking through personal limitations is the agony of spiritual growth, and that I must understand that much of my pain was self-chosen, that it was the bitter potion by which the physician within me was healing my sick self. Trust the physician, it said, and drink his remedy in silence and tranquillity as you explore the world beyond this moment.

I felt like I was chasing a mirage as I plunged into the desert of my being, searching the interior for answers, for memories of my rebirth in that vast, empty void.

I knew the desert country well enough: how to navigate that inner being. But the way in which the empty void of the outback hit me in South Australia, straight after I left Port Augusta, was quite unlike anything I had expected. I was sucked into the emptiness with startling abruptness, the baking bitumen of the Stuart Highway blurring into a haze of uncertainty. I suddenly felt anxious about the road ahead, and what I might learn about the physician inside of myself.

Blistering kilometres of barren, scrub-covered wastelands crawled past my windows. It was late in the afternoon when I pulled up at a rest area for the night and rolled out my swag under the stars.

I made Coober Pedy early the following morning. It was so hot in Coober Pedy that many of the town's residents lived underground in *dugouts*, giving the place its name. Coober Pedy is an Aboriginal word meaning *white man's hole*. I wondered what kind of hole I was in now.

I wandered around the town, admiring opal jewellery and ornaments. Before white men plundered this place, opals lay on the ground everywhere. I pressed on. Traffic was scarce on the long, straight highway north. Now and then a road train came thundering out of the mirage ahead like a spaceship arriving from another planet. I gripped the wheel as the Falcon was shoved aside like a Matchbox toy by the wake that followed them. I crossed the border to the Northern Territory and took a detour to visit Uluru and Kata Tjuta.

I made Erldunda Roadhouse late in the evening, forced off the road for the night by kangaroos and camels. I was 1300 kilometres from Adelaide.

The MacDonnell Ranges rose from the flat desert like a petrified tidal wave. I crossed the Todd River—a waterless swathe of sand and coolabah trees twisting through the ranges. I drove into Alice Springs. Alice hadn't changed much since its early days as a relay town for the overland telegraph line from Adelaide to Darwin, linking the more civilised southern end of the continent to its remote and wild north. The old telegraph house, where a man once tapped out a message to his wife before dying of spear wounds, still stood on the outskirts of town.

Tennant Creek materialised out of the desert. I recalled my last campdraft here, and Rod's commentary: 'Ben O'Neill, on Arcadia, from Walhallow. Ben is New Zealand's best campdrafter. You're in the wrong field, mate, these aren't sheep, baa baa baa....' Hardened stockmen scrutinised my composure and ability, my country's pride was now riding on a good run. Then something happened that even I was surprised by. After successfully getting a beast out of the camp, I headed out around the course. Rod's now more respectful commentary faded into the background as I pulled back hard on Arcadia's reins to stop her overstepping the beast; manoeuvring outside the beast, now inside, keeping just off its tail as I guided it successfully around the course. It was a good run.

A round of applause went up from the small crowd of seasoned outback souls watching through the white rails of the arena and from the shelter of the bar. I was stoked. Even Cameron congratulated me when he saw me.

After a minute Rod came back over the microphone with my score. 'Ben and Arcadia score 74 points in the Jackaroo draft. Nice ride there.

Next up we have Andrew from Brunette Downs.' It was Brains, and he won third place by one point.

I wondered how Cameron was going on Walhallow and considered driving that way to Darwin. Perhaps he needed a jackaroo or a borerunner? After fuelling up, I got back on the endless, empty highway and watched as the rolling Tablelands cast a familiar golden ocean of grass around me. It was getting late when I made Daly Waters. I pulled in and rolled out my swag for another night under the stars.

I arrived in Mataranka early the following morning—famous for its emerald thermal pools. Then the outback town of Katherine, and Nitmiluk National Park—home to the spectacular Katherine Gorge. As I kayaked the deep river, which carves its path through steep red cliffs lined with pockets of ancient rock art and waterfalls, I recalled a story my friend Andy from the station had told me two years earlier. He'd just arrived in the Northern Territory to look for work on a cattle station. After spending a few days in Katherine he'd found his way to a truly magical place called Low Levels on the Katherine River at Katherine Gorge. It was a hot humid day and despite the signs warning of freshwater crocodiles, he dived in. After enjoying a refreshing swim, he decided to explore further down river and found a road leading to a dam where he met a couple of Aboriginal kids swimming in the river. Another boy was washing his motorbike.

There was a sign there too—this one warning of saltwater crocodiles. Andy had heard of how they could get in there on the wet season flood waters and that wet season had been a good one, so he asked the kids about swimming there. They said it was fine. Andy jumped in and splashed around in the rapids with the kids. After a fantastic time, Andy made his way out of there safely and, a few days later, turned up at Walhallow.

Some weeks later he was reading a newspaper out on the station when he came across an article about a young boy who had been taken by a saltwater crocodile at Low Levels. The boy had been taken while washing his motorbike. That gave young Andy a scare: to think how carefree he had been yet in such imminent danger. I was reminded of the unforgiving nature of the country I was back in—the untamed Top End.

I made camp at Edith Falls, situated in the northern half of Nitmiluk National Park, and unwound the tight coil of my mind while exploring a short loop track around a small lake and falls. At the top of the falls, I found a deep rock pool and dived in without having to worry about crocodiles. While I floated on my back gazing at the evening sky, I thought about Darwin.

CHAPTER TWENTY-NINE

DARWIN

*'A man who dares to waste one hour of time
has not discovered the value of life.'*
—*Charles Darwin*

Travellers from all over the world coloured the tropical streets of the territory's capital with foreign accents and exotic faces. I wasted no time looking for a place to stay, then went in search of Paspaley Pearls. I was sure that was the name Denis had given me.

I found the Paspaley building in the centre of town. I opened the shop door and stepped into a showroom of pearls: earrings, necklaces, bracelets and rings filled glass display cabinets in opulent lines and elaborate designs. Several pictures of white boats in turquoise waters backdropped by rust-red rocks hung on the shop walls. In others, figures worked on smaller boats, hauling up lines carrying nets full of shells. They were the pearl farms. A picture of a diver hand-collecting wild shell off the seabed caught my imagination.

'Can I help you?' An attractive young lady wearing a pearl necklace appeared beside me.

'I'd like to work for Paspaley Pearls,' I said.

A delicate, confused frown formed across her brow. 'On the pearl farms?' she finally asked.

'I guess so,' I replied, I hadn't really thought about it.

'You need to go through Extraman to get work on the pearl farms. That's the labour hire company. We don't do any hiring here.'

I wrote the name and phone number down.

I secured an interview with the labour hire company the following week. After passing a standard fitness for work medical, I answered questions about my aptitude for the job and watched a video about working on the pearl farms. It involved flying in and out of the remotest parts of Australia: the Top End and Western Australia's Kimberley coast.

'Can you fly out tomorrow?' asked the receptionist.

I was dumbfounded. 'Sure.'

'Great, I'll let them know. You'll be going to the Osborn Islands. The plane leaves at 8am.'

I walked out of the building, fist pumped and yelled.

After putting my car and belongings in storage the following morning, I leapt into the taxi.

'Airport please,' I demanded impatiently, as I glanced at the time.

Twenty minutes later the taxi pulled up outside the Pearl Aviation terminal. I jogged inside the building and found half a dozen people waiting in a small room with a security guard and a baggage scanner.

More people trickled in. They knew each other and talked in small groups and circles. I stood to one side.

A chiselled islander with high cheekbones and long dreadlocks strode confidently through the door. He walked over and stood beside me. With a single, sweeping gaze, his deep, dark-brown eyes sized me up. He nodded then looked away. I decided to introduce myself.

'Hi, I'm Ben.' I offered my hand.

In a powerful voice that resonated from the base drum of his chest, he returned my introduction. 'Danny.'

Danny grabbed hold of my hand, gave it a single bone crushing shake then looked away again. I noticed his left forearm was twisted and mangled, the fingers gnarled, wizened and curled like a claw. The arm seemed shrivelled from lack of proper function.

The security guard called our flight and opened a door before scanning our bags. We crossed the tarmac to the waiting Pearl Aviation Metroliner, then sweated and complained as we shuffled into the stifling cabin like sardines into a tin. We taxied onto the runway and lifted into the air. From my seat, I stared down at the sunburnt rock, spinifex and eucalypts that covered the vast expanse of northern Australia.

Before long, we were ejected onto the baking tarmac at Truscott Airbase, on the Anjo Peninsula in Western Australia, to await our connecting flight to the Osborn Islands.

Like a scene out of an old James Bond movie, a sparkling white 1950's Grumman G-73T Mallard landed before us. The side door popped opened, and a white collared pilot lowered the boarding steps. I jostled for a window seat while the co-pilot handed out earplugs.

The Osborn Islands soon appeared below: towering rocks studded a huge bay that ran off into a reddish glow in the unseen distance. The white crescents of beaches clashed with tumbled masses of brownish-orange rock and the aquarium-blue water of the Timor Sea. A small white ship named *Vivienne* sat in the bay surrounded by countless rows of black buoys that reached out to sea. Small barges made their way along the rows, hauling up the precious cargo that hung from the lines—pearls.

The closest specs of civilisation lay to the west, at Vansittart Bay, another Paspaley pearl farm, and Kalumburu, a small Aboriginal community. Beyond the coast, the wildness reached for thousands of inhospitable kilometres inland.

A foaming jet of water shot past my window as the undercarriage skimmed across the warm sea. The Mallard slowed and came to a stop near *Vivienne*. Like a postcard, my window framed the scene outside as the plane gently rocked from side to side. I removed my earplugs, unbuckled my belt, and scrambled for my luggage. The co-pilot climbed from the cockpit into the cabin and unlocked the side door. A dazzling, glittering reflection of sunlight and water spilled and splintered into the cabin. I shielded my eyes from the blinding glare.

I caught sight of a long, narrow, blue and white dory approaching the plane with a dozen occupants. The boat pulled alongside and everyone on board the plane formed a chain. Boxes of stores and luggage were passed out to the boat. Then we swapped places with the outbound crew. A few g'days, banter about work and see-you-in-two-weeks comments animated the exchange. The changeover was fast and efficient. The dory pulled away and began making its way towards *Vivienne*. The flying boat started its engines, skimmed out of the bay, into the air, and disappeared.

On board *Vivienne*, I was inducted to the boat and the farm. The induction covered mustering areas in case of emergency, locations of emergency and lifesaving apparatus, chain of command and work obligations. I was shown my cabin, what areas of the boat were off limits and informed about the farm's health and safety procedures. The procedures covered working on the water and living in a remote and isolated location with respect to the availability of medical help. Using sun protection, keeping hydrated and the more immediately life-threatening dangers: crocodiles, sharks and jellyfish.

I settled in and acquainted myself to the people I would be living and working with for the next two weeks. They were a motley bunch, aged between 19 and 51, mainly from Western Australia and the Northern Territory. Their mix of backgrounds and characters encapsulated the Top End. Ozzy, *Vivienne's* captain, was an old prawn trawler skipper; Kelta, the farm manager, was of Malaysian decent and an ex-pearl diver; Beard was an ex-bikie with a foot of facial hair and a skin of rough tattoos, who mumbled so badly I often had to ask him to repeat himself. I imagined him as a pirate. There were a couple of old trawlermen that looked like leather, smelled like fish and were as abrasive as 80 grit sandpaper; a few seasoned pearl farmers; a couple of engineers that referred to themselves as *Ginger Bears*; and several lads around my own age from mixed backgrounds. The women included Camille, a tall slender girl with long wavy jet-black hair and brown eyes, who told me Chopper Read was her cousin; her friend, Katie, a comely blonde of average height with light blue eyes and head-turning breasts; a short butch girl I later found out was a lesbian; our old cook; and a girl that the men informed me liked to hook up with the new guys so I should watch out, unless I was interested.

I sat on the bow of *Vivienne*, gazing over wildness. Before me was one of the world's most spectacular and dangerous coastlines, a place where vast areas of land and sea are still marked as uncharted on maps and sea charts. The coast was a treacherous labyrinth of islands, hidden reefs and huge tides, paradisal white sandy beaches and mangrove lined inlets infested with crocodiles. It was home to the largest pearl farms in the world. Beyond the coast lay over 420,000 square kilometres of virtually untouched, pristine wilderness—a wilderness that was formed when the world began, about two and a half billion years ago.

This landscape is a complex maze of ancient red sandstone valleys and sheer cliffs with tumbled masses of colossal boulders at their base. Scattered among the uninhabited loneliness, arid bushland and patches of remnant rainforest cling to life in the deep grooves and valleys along invisible watercourses. Tucked away, concealed for thousands of years in remote caves and under large stone overhangs, rock art records forgotten stories, weaving myths, legends and magic around the landscape.

The sun dipped beyond that wild horizon, the sky morphed into fire and the silhouettes of the Kimberley landscape arched off her majestic glowing cliffs. The gold medallion of the full moon rose from the indigo sea of twilight. The outback became insignificant in that moment, on that coast. I lay down on the warm deck and gazed into the infinity of space, and fell into the black net of night that bulged and overflowed with its glittering haul.

CHAPTER THIRTY
THE OSBORN ISLANDS

'There is pleasure in the pathless woods, there is rapture in the lonely shore, there is society where none intrudes, by the deep sea, and music in its roar; I love not Man the less, but Nature more.'

— Lord Byron

The crew mess bustled in bushy hair and sleepy eyes, in slurps and burps and breakfast time quirks. I shovelled down my cooked breakfast and cereal and prepared my lunch for the day.

Outside the sea lay calm as a pond, not a breath of wind stirred in the bay. It was still dark and comfortably cool. The shell cleaners piled into the two dories that were tied alongside *Vivienne* and, crew by crew, were dropped at the small aluminium barges that sat at their moorings. The barges were known as ABs—purpose-built machines that had evolved on the pearl grounds over many years of trial and experimentation. Efficiency, ergonomics and environment were the architects of their design.

I jumped into AB 38 with Danny and Steve—a sharp-looking, dark-haired, keen-eyed school leaver from Victoria. Danny was the boat foreman and one of the farm foremen.

Danny opened the hatch to the engine bay of the AB and performed several routine pre-start checks, before cranking the loud diesel engine to life. Other ABs responded with mechanical growls that echoed across the bay. Steve called me to the bow of the vessel where a pile of lines, buoys, plastic net panels and a gaff were stowed. He pointed to the boat's bridle and explained how to untie us from our mooring. While Steve fidgeted with the knot, the line sparkled like a magical thread sending bioluminescent ripples through the dark matter of the sea in a miniature expanding universe. He then showed me how to stow the bridle.

As we got underway, I watched the other crews leaving their moorings, scattering across the bay to different parts of the farm in the pale blue of dawn. Steve and I donned long white plastic aprons and pulled on our boots and gloves.

We motored up to one of the buoyed lines of shell and Steve hurled a grapple. It splashed on the opposite side of the line and he hauled until he hooked the line, then took a couple of turns on a winch and began winding in the bow. As he did, Danny brought the barge alongside the line with a series of thrusts from the jet drive. Then, the three of us lifted the line and placed it on two large winches on the starboard side of the barge. Danny put the engine in neutral, then started the panel cleaning machine and increased the engine's revs to power the water pump. He turned the winches on and adjusted their speed to a slow crawl ahead.

As the AB began moving along the line, Steve hauled panels of shells from the water and slid them into the cleaning machine. A series of high-pressure nozzles inside the machine obliterated any soft growth. Steve also cleaned and inspected the lines, buoys and knots.

By way of a conveyor belt, the first panel of cleaned shell inched its way out the other end of the cleaning machine and onto a table between Danny and me. Danny then demonstrated the process of shell cleaning or *chipping*. With a tool shaped like a blunt chisel, we began vigorously knocking off any barnacles, oysters and limpets that had attached themselves to the shells and scraping worms and sponge growth from the hinges and byssus.

I was exhausted and disillusioned by the end of the day. Pearl farming was nothing more than fast-paced factory work on the water—a 'process worker in paradise,' Steve had said.

While I showered, I gazed at the ebullient sea and the wild, rusty red landscape beyond it through the porthole. *Vivienne* rolled in lazy oscillations. My right wrist was aching from hours of shell chipping. A small lump from an overworked muscle or tendon had formed. 'All quite normal,' Danny told me. I would have to suffer like everybody else until I got used to the repetitive nature of the work. I could barely hold onto the chipper by the end of the week.

As the days merged, the spell of pearling life was cast upon me in fiery sunrises and sunsets, in leaping fish and soaring eagles, and in the camaraderie of the shell cleaning crews that shared the remote isolation of our small floating home.

'We'll call you the saltwater cowboy,' Danny bluntly stated, as he eyed my old Akubra while we lunched. 'Why do you have a cowboy hat?'

'I was a jackaroo on a cattle station in the Northern Territory.'

'A real cowboy hey? Well, we don't need any spurs to ride these waves cowboy,' Danny boomed.

'How about them bare-backed mermaids?' I asked.

Steve and Danny laughed.

'Why did you want to come to sea then?' Danny asked.

'I've been wanting to experience life at sea ever since I read stories about it while I was working on the station. It seemed like an adventure.'

'Well, you made it brus. I love the sea. Wouldn't be anywhere else.' Danny looked like he was a part of that coast—wild, dangerous and unpredictable.

'They call us *farmies*,' Steve said. 'Some of these guys like to call themselves *marine growth removalist technicians*. Nothing as cool as a cowboy, though.'

Steve had finished up at high school and come north to work and save money on the pearl farms. He was impatient for his Canadian girlfriend, Alex, whom he met in Geelong, to join him.

'I heard there's another vessel-based pearl farm near here?' I asked.

'You heard right,' Danny said. 'It's called Vansittart Bay. We call those farmies the *Fancytarts*.'

'Why?'

'Because they stay on a big fancy boat!' Danny laughed.

Working with Danny and Steve brought amusement and a fresh perspective to my days. Danny was light-hearted, and his contagious laughter shook my own chest with that lightness. Yet his friendly nature didn't mask the secrets hidden in his dark eyes—a curious mix of survival, courage and ethnic struggles that spoke of a battler. Danny was a proud man. He'd moved to Cairns, from the Thursday Islands, above the tip of Cape York in Queensland, to find work. His childhood had been rough, torn and disjointed. After living and working in Cairns for several years, where he had a daughter named Roxy, he continued on to Darwin for work and discovered the pearling industry. He had a tattoo of his daughter's name on his left pectoral muscle that he proudly showed me. 'Like the surf brand brus.' I'd heard of it.

Through the afternoon wash and hiss of the cleaning machine, I watched Danny inspect a dead pearl shell. He tore the pocket open and removed the shell from the panel, then delicately extracted the pearl from within the soft milky folds of the oyster's decaying flesh. He held it up to the light and stared at it for a moment, as if to read his future. The pearl had a story of its own to tell, a story that had started down at Eighty Mile beach, in Western Australia, two years earlier.

'You ever seen a pearl before?' Danny asked me while he examined its surface.

'Not straight out of an oyster.'

Danny passed me the pearl. 'This is a good one, don't drop it.'

The pearl was the size of a blueberry, perfectly spherical. All the colours of the rainbow seemed to radiate from its creamy white lustre. As I gazed at it, I wondered at its story. For a moment, I caught my reflection in its lustrous glow, and I knew the pearling adventure was for me.

'Don't stand in the bite of the rope,' Danny boomed, as he pointed to my foot and the coil of line around it. 'It's dangerous.'

We were doing anchor work which involved setting new lines of buoys, pulling out old lines and re-setting their anchors so they could be loaded with fresh stock later in the season. The lines were under a tremendous load, flinching and twitching with tension. One wrong move and they could take one of us to the bottom in an instant, break a limb or even sever it. I quickly moved my foot before shackling the end of the line to the anchor.

'I was standing in the bite of a rope and when the anchor was let go, I went down with it.' Danny recounted a story of how he wasn't paying enough attention one day while he was doing anchor work on another farm. 'I thought I was going to die, I shot to the bottom so quickly, my ears were screaming with pain. Then my lungs began to convulse, and I fought with every muscle in my body to keep my mouth closed. I had to wait until the anchor set and enough tension came off the line before I could free myself. There was a strange calm in that moment, as I became acutely conscious of my pounding heart and my blood pumping through my body. I was lucky my foot slipped out of my boot, otherwise I wouldn't be here today. I clawed my way to the surface and took the biggest gasp of air when I made it. That gasp gave me my life back.'

I never put my foot in the coil of a line again.

The following afternoon Danny asked me to come with him to Middle Osborn Island. 'We're going to clean up the beach, brus, just you and me.'

Danny wildly shook his dreadlocks to the club beat blasting from his portable stereo as we sped across the bay to the island. He turned to me, laughed an ecstatic mouthful of white teeth, and his smiling cheeks rose like two coconuts off his pronounced cheekbones. For a big, booming islander, he had a surprisingly high-pitched laugh—a laugh I guessed he only shared with those he saw as friends.

We dropped the anchor 20 metres off the beach, in water deep enough that the boat wouldn't get marooned when the tide went out.

The tides of the Kimberley are the third largest in the world. The 12-metre difference during a spring tide is enough to catch even an experienced mariner out. Those great tides churn the milky ocean of immortal life and feed the pearl oysters their rich flow of nutrients.

Before we jumped over the side and made the swim ashore, we scanned the shoreline for crocodiles. I noticed a metre and a half shovelnose ray swimming close to the beach and pointed it out to Danny.

'That one's okay, it won't bother us,' Danny said.

We both peered over the side for sharks. Everything was clear. I pulled off my shirt, stood on the gunwale and poised to jump in. I was about to dive when a three-metre hammerhead shark swam under the boat in a swift hunting movement.

'Shark!' I yelled.

In a single bound Danny leapt to the side of the boat and peered into the water. Beneath us, the leviathan swam in graceful ease, speed and efficiency through the water.

'Whoo! That's a big one! That one isn't okay, brus. We should wait a minute,' Danny said.

My eyes followed the shark until it disappeared. 'Do sharks that size usually come so close to the shore?' I asked, in disconcerted syllables.

'Sometimes.' Danny's countenance had taken on the same serious demeanour as when I first met him at the airport. I later came to know that gripping expression as his deep-in-thought stare. After a minute he said, 'I'll drop you off at the shore, then bring the boat back out and swim in by myself.'

'You'll swim by yourself?'

'Yeah, we don't both need to swim, brus.'

Danny nudged the bow onto the beach and I jumped ashore, then he anchored the boat and dived over the side. Within a few powerful strokes he surged from the water like Aquaman and strode up the beach. He untied his dreadlocks, and they fell to the small of his back. He bent forward and encouraged the amaranth ropes to untangle with the claw combs of his hands then, with a Rasta's toss of his head, he threw back those great dreadlocks, flexed the coffee-bronze of his muscles and laughed at me. He was wild and free in ways I would never be, and he belonged in that country as much as the rocks and waves and sky.

The broken shell beach dipped deep into the milky sea. Dark grey-black boulders the size of cars and tangles of native bush crowded either end. The foreshore rose steeply from the water's edge into bush-clad slopes that ended in sharp rust-coloured buttresses far above us.

We got to work clearing the shoreline of pearling paraphernalia that had accumulated: lugging old coils of line down to the shoreline to be taken away, and heaving anchors, chain and buoys up to higher ground and out of reach of the tremendous tides.

Before we flew out, we gave the AB a full wash down. The engineers inspected the vessels of the crews that were flying out, servicing and repairing them as necessary for the crews that were flying in. We refuelled our AB then took it out to a mooring and waited to be collected. Steve was excited to get back to town. His girlfriend Alex was flying in. Danny was looking forward to relaxing and catching up with his brother for a beer. His brother worked on another pearl farm. I had Darwin to explore.

The Mallard swooped in and collected us in the early afternoon. With an odd sort of nostalgic sentiment, I peered out the window at the glassy sea and rows of buoys running to the distant horizon. I watched as *Vivienne* became a spec in the wilderness before disappearing from sight altogether. Two weeks of life as a pearl farmer had come to an end. Two weeks in one of the greatest wilderness areas left on Earth. I didn't know if I'd be coming back; if I'd ever again see the coarse, comely and curious characters I'd lived and worked alongside. Everyone got a trial first swing but not everyone got offered a permanent position. Some people were sent off to other farms, some weren't invited back, and others chose not to come back.

Foreign faces and open smiles swept me through the streets of Darwin in a river of tempting scents and sweaty aromas. I met humid stares and scrutinising glares. Air-conditioned bars with misting fans and cold beer attracted jostling crowds to seated shade and outdoor dining. I set about exploring the many clubs, pubs and bars on Mitchell Street—Darwin's main drag of watering holes.

The Mindil Beach Sunset Market, which attracted large crowds, ran twice a week. As I picked my way through the bustling crowds, I noticed the influence of Asia in the faces and culture of the Top End. Thai, Sri Lankan, Indian, Chinese, Malaysian, Brazilian, Greek, and Portuguese cuisine, and barbecued wild meats like crocodile, kangaroo and water buffalo wafted through the sultry air like gastronomic fishing lines, hooking passers-by. Colourful arts and crafts vendors peddled their wares: handmade jewellery, natural remedies, artistic creations and unique fashion statements. I saw fire twirlers and whip crackers. I watched buskers, bands and other talented performers as I weaved my way through throngs of people and palm lined boulevards of market stalls. I stopped to gaze at Jupiter and its moons through a telescope and thought of how insignificant Earth was.

I followed a path down to the beach and sat on the warm sand. Bongos, didgeridoos and guitars strummed, thrummed and beat the heavy air in ostinato thumps and exotic tunes. A lemon sunset over the Arafura Sea peeled into mango, then orange and passionfruit. Moonbeams climbed and danced through plumed palm fronds.

I caught up with Danny for a beer and to find out if I'd been hired.

'Congratulations,' Danny bellowed. 'You're coming back out to the Osborn Islands. You're an Osbornite now.'

I was a pearl farmer.

CHAPTER THIRTY-ONE

THE HARVEST

'The heart of man is very much like the sea, it has its storms, it has its tides and in its depths it has its pearls too.'
—*Vincent van Gogh*

The harvest is an exciting part of pearl culture, but the arduous and patient process starts two years before, off Eighty Mile beach, where divers handpick the wild *Pinctada maxima* oyster off the sea floor. The pearls of this, the largest shell in the Pinctada family, eclipse all others in size and quality.

During the harvest, the pearls are collected and graded. Five characteristics decide a pearl's value: shape, size, colour, lustre and complexion. Eventually, they find their way to jewellers and buyers all around the world.

Three boats, painted in Paspaley white with their names stamped in broad black letters across their bows, dropped their anchors in the bay. Among them was the farm supply vessel, *Christine*. *Christine* was the supply ship for all the Paspaley farms. It travelled more than 1000 nautical miles on its supply run, from Broome in north-west Western Australia to the Cobourg Peninsula, north-east of Darwin. The other vessels were *Clare 2* and *Delumba*, both dive boats.

The crew on *Vivienne* were mustered in the mess to receive their working orders. A buzz of excitement over crew allocation and job delegation tore through the meeting in playful banter, reluctant obligations and serious instructions. Many of the crew were seeing their first pearl harvest, others were old hands, welcoming the variety of work and splash of new faces over the coming weeks. Even Beard, who never appeared to get excited about anything, let a pirate's smile part his lips. 'Arrgh!'

A barge-sized pontoon was tied to the stern of *Vivienne*. There, two crew worked with a deafening, messy, high-powered panel cleaning machine that obliterated fouling. Several other crew members worked, repairing damaged panels, bundling them into small piles and stacking them on wooden pallets.

The ABs deployed like water boatmen out over the bay—some a bit like the whirligig beetles I had seen in Carnarvon Gorge—going around in confused circles under the gold-drop sun of a new day.

I hauled panels of shell aboard and untied them from the lines with dextrous strength and agility, before passing them down our small process line.

'Can you do that a bit faster, Ben?' Steve grunted sarcastically.

Danny cast his eye often in my direction, like a teacher watching over his protégé. 'I trained him,' he spruiked, when he heard Steve's comment. He jabbed his thumb into his chest and laughed. 'I trained him!' Danny echoed his claim for credit loud enough so Katie, Camille and Beard could hear. Danny nodded his respect at me. We had become good friends.

'Okay you lot, listen to me,' Danny boomed. Everyone stood to the best of their attention as the AB rocked, rolled and gyrated on the chop and churn of the windswept bay. 'Pull open the pockets that hold the shells and tip them onto these tables here.' The cleaning machine had been removed and extra chipping tables now sat in the middle of the AB. 'Then put the shells into these black wire crates and stack the crates down the side here so they can be collected. Understand?' Danny pointed to the port side of the AB and received obedient nods.

A jet boat called *Aqua Pig* periodically collected our prized haul and took it back to the main harvest vessel, *Clare 2*, to be processed. On board *Clare 2* the crews worked just as manically in the operations room and on a large pontoon tied along its starboard side. Four large shell tanks full of crates of shells were being opened by shell openers. They sweated in sanguine torment as they worked furiously in the stiflingly humid tanks to keep up with the shell technicians, gently prizing open thousands of oysters and inserting a small wedge in the open mouth.

The opened shells were then sent back up to the operations room in the crates where the pearl was extracted and a new nucleus put in its place. The nucleus, or *irritant* that was put in the oyster was a small bead of American pig-toe mussel shell—a freshwater clam from the Mississippi River that was the least rejected irritant. The pearl formed as the oyster coated the nucleus in nacre to protect itself. Finally, after a patient wait of two years, a gem was extracted.

Technicians wearing white gowns and wielding specialist stainless steel instruments whirled in a Shinju Matsuri dance of dextrous elegance and cunning precision, extracting pearls and implanting beads with expert proficiency. Unworthy oysters were sent to the pontoon while the worthy were slipped back into panels and whisked out to the lines by *put-back* crew.

Out on the pontoon, a dozen crew members worked at their own radical pace, culling old oysters and any shells the technicians decided weren't up to pearl producing standards for another harvest. Containers of shells popped out of the vessel down a conveyer to two long tables on the pontoon where any pearls that lay hidden within the lotus folds of their flesh were collected. Next, the meat and guts were removed into buckets. The bivalves were then split at the hinge into two separate halves, sent down the tables to be cleaned and graded then packed in neat concentric spirals in 44-gallon drums for export as mother of pearl.

The meat from the culled oysters was separated from the guts at the guts table by more busy hands. Occasionally, a cultured pearl slipped past the shell cullers. Here it was collected, but the best part of sorting the guts from the meat, I discovered, was finding a keshi pearl, in this case a *cultured keshi*, which came in a melange of shapes, sizes and colours.

Naturally seeded pearls—keshi pearls—are a rare sight, but cultured keshi pearls often turned up in oysters with cultured pearls. Keshi pearls are formed when a small piece of grit, like sand, shell or coral naturally gets into the oyster. If the oyster is unable to expel the irritant, it coats it in nacre.

The pearl meat was washed, weighed, bagged and boxed then frozen to await the Mallard when it next flew in. Tens of thousands of shells underwent the same efficient process.

That evening the crew of *Vivienne* committed gluttony. Ear-shaped scallops of pearl meat were chewed, savoured and swallowed in sweet aphrodisiac mouthfuls of batter, coconut cream and sweet chilli sauce. Sated, I lumbered out of the mess and onto the back deck holding my belly. I gazed around for a moment. The lights of the other vessels shone across the bay, reflecting off the heaving, breathing bosom of the Timor Sea like giant glowing sea snakes. Thousands of baitfish teemed in boiling balls under *Vivienne's* lights. Barracuda, trevally and queenfish stealthily hunted the shifting, shimmering mosaics, launching sporadic attacks on the shoals, shredding the dancing schools into glittering silver ribbons and explosions of red. I watched dozens of bright purple jellyfish float aimlessly about, their large bowl-sized bodies moving in pulsing monospasms through the water.

From out of nowhere, a dolphin shot through the water like a torpedo chasing the larger fish in a bioluminescent glow like a dolphin-shaped Milky Way. Many of the older guys on the boat called the Kimberley *God's country*. I could now see why Rob, back at the Gorge, had said the same. It seemed that anyone with any knowledge of the Kimberley referred to it this way.

I climbed the steps to the second deck then scaled the small ladder that led to the top deck. I lay down on the warm steel and stared at the countless stars that blinked and flashed in glittering handfuls of diamonds cast across the ocean of night. Now and then, a meteorite blazed through the heavens like a distant cosmic firework. A satellite glided slowly through silky black space.

I was two weeks into a five-week swing in the islands. Sometimes a five-weeker would come up at the last minute. This usually happened when someone failed to turn up for the plane in Darwin, usually because of an overindulgent week off. The next plane wouldn't be flying in for another week. In order to keep the crews on their normal rosters another crew member would have to stay behind and cover the week the person wasn't there, then carry on with their usual two-week swing. Sometimes they just needed extra hands, like during harvest time.

The days ebbed and flowed. I was assigned a dory and my own crew to untie droppers from the lines that had been relieved of their precious loads. Halfway through the harvest all the vessels moved from the northeast side of Middle Osborn Island to the south-west side of the island. A pearlers party was held on Middle Osborn to celebrate the halfway point and all the crews' hard work.

I could see the glow of lambent flames dance in the quiet dusk of evening. Smoke and glowing embers rose into the cosmos. Shouting, laughing and singing echoed across the bay.

'Are you coming over to have a look?' Steve asked me. 'They're drinking, so I don't think I'll stay long.'

'Sure.'

Steve was down-to-earth, matter-of-fact, and his maturity often surprised me. We puttered over to the island with Katie, Camille and Beard in a small tender, leaving a blazing trail of planktonic prop wash in our wake. The buoys that marked the lines bobbed up and down like glowing orbs in the water, sending Saturn rings into sea-space. I gazed up at the stars often—meteorites rained from the fathomless night like teardrops falling from the mourning dress of night. A meteor shower perhaps? The night was crystal clear. The Kimberley moved, tugged and raptured the matter of my being. Trying to comprehend that monumental wilderness was the beginning of my understanding of my own insignificance.

The beach was still 50 meters away when Steve killed the outboard and pulled up the leg. We glided through the water and stopped on the slippery suck of the tidal mudflat.

'Looks like that's as close as we're going to get,' Steve said. It was the middle of a spring tide.

I waved a torch beam along the shoreline for the fool's gold eye shine of crocodiles. Then we disembarked the small boat and hauled it several metres further up the mudflat. With a squelch the anchor sunk into the mud.

'Can't stay long. I'm not waiting for anyone. If you're not back in half an hour you can come back with another boat later. I'm not swimming for this one when the tide comes in,' Steve said.

I grabbed a radio, and we began making our way across the mudflat. I wondered how long a stonefish could survive out of the water. Stonefish are the most venomous fish in the world and are happy to lie in shallow rock pools and on mudflats. Standing on one brought pain that made you want to kill yourself, if the venom didn't.

The light of the fire revealed the progress of the party; pearlers old and new talked, jested and flirted in growing familiarity. Some were backpackers, here only for the harvest, others were farmies, and a handful were experienced pearl divers. The crews indulged and mingled but I felt distant. I thought about joining them for a drink. I looked at Steve.

'I don't like drinking,' Steve said, as he watched the drunks of the party. 'It always makes people do things they later regret. Do you drink?'

'Occasionally. Are you okay?'

'You've done some interesting stuff, Ben. How long have you been travelling for?'

'I left New Zealand three years ago now.'

'You don't miss home?'

'I haven't really thought about it for a while.'

'I'm…' Steve began, then hesitated.

'You seem a little pensive tonight,' I prompted.

'I'm… having some trouble with Alex, she's being really hard to deal with at the moment. I like her but it's doing my head in being stuck on the boat with her. I guess she feels the same.'

I recalled what it felt like to be in love, and New Zealand came gushing back into my heart in an overwhelming torrent of memories. I didn't know when I would go back. I took a deep breath. 'I was in love with a girl once. We met when we were in high school, like you and Alex. She left for university in another city, and I stayed behind in Christchurch. It wasn't until we had that time apart that I realised there was a lot I hadn't seen and done with my life that I wanted to, and I couldn't see how I was ever going to if I stayed with her—or anyone for that matter—so I left. I still think about her sometimes, and I guess I never thought I'd be gone this long. Perhaps you guys just need a little space?'

'Yeah, maybe. We're planning a trip to Canada, that's why we're out here working, but I think it's getting too much living on top of each other. Sometimes I think I'd just like to travel on my own.'

'I've spent a lot of time of my own, Steve, and I often think it would be more fun sharing the things I have seen and done with someone else. But I would have missed out on a lot of other necessary growth and incredible experiences if I were with someone. There's always a compromise I guess, a sort of trade-off for whatever you decide to do in life. You just never know if you're getting a good deal or not. That's life's little secret.'

'Any advice you can give me?' Steve asked.

'My life circumstances are different to yours, but I would say don't take things too seriously, just enjoy every moment for what it is because every moment sparkles with the magic of possibility. That possibility is life; life is like a heartbeat—sometimes it's erratic, sometimes it's in harmony, always it beats to the rhythm of your own dreams and desires. I had a lot of insecurities when I was younger; a lot of things I had to work out. I thought I could work through those things by seeing and experiencing life around different people and in different places, and by learning what other people's ideas were on life and living. I wanted to be a man of the world. I needed to be on my own to do that. There have been times when I've felt terribly lonely on the road, yet I often needed to be alone. I'm still travelling down that road now. In a way, I have become like the wind—with always somewhere to go but with nowhere to be. I've learnt that it is up to us to find meaning and purpose in our lives; life is both half what we create and half what is our fate. I believe that for every opportunity missed there is an equal and opposite opportunity waiting to be explored. I think our awareness of life is like the universe: constantly changing, an ever-expanding horizon reaching into the unknown. You must ask questions about your life: where are you going, what are you doing with it, why are you here? The universe, your higher self, will provide the answers you need, in a way you can understand. You may not always be capable of hearing those answers, and they may not always come in ways you'd expect, but they will come. You should honour that guidance. I didn't realise how much I would change; how much my view of life would change. It's hard to imagine how much our experiences will alter our perception and attitude towards life, other people, and the world around us. Sometimes I wonder how different my life would have ended up if I hadn't altered its course so dramatically—if

I hadn't made the decisions I had and followed them through with the sacrifice and courage I did. The essence of the freedom I have discovered is all intertwined with possibility, but freedom is a dangerous friend to have if you are not a wise traveller. It's a paradox. In that freedom lies everything and nothing all at once. That is where the creator is born. It's also where insanity hides. Of course, we will surely know tomorrow what we should do today. You have a lot to look forward too, Steve, even if it doesn't work out.'

Speaking with Steve made me feel like my loneliness was given some nobility and purpose as I did my best to express my impression of life to him. Sharing those perceptions was the only real gift I had that might help him on his journey.

'It sounds to me like you are taking the steps which will gain you mastery of your destiny, Ben. Thanks for your insights.'

'We can only try.'

'I think we'll go back down to Geelong after this swing. We'll have nearly enough money, and we can work down there until we go. That way we'll have more space to do our own thing and be around our friends.'

'I'll be sorry to see you go, Steve. I haven't been to Canada, but I'd like to get there some day. I know you'll enjoy travelling.'

I wandered over to the fire and pulled a huge black-lipped oyster from the flames. The oysters grew in large clusters on the colossal black boulders that lay strewn along the coast. For a moment I lost myself in the flicker and glow of light, and a thousand memories of my life on the road leading up to this moment flashed before my eyes. I walked back to Steve.

'We should get back to the boat, I don't want to get stuck here,' Steve said.

'What about the others?' I asked.

Steve glanced at Katie and Camille. Both girls were being hit on by pearl divers. Beard was necking back a beer and staring into the flames of the fire. 'Looks like they're staying,'

We traced our steps back over the mudflat and located the boat. Water was already swirling around it. I scanned the waterline with the torch for eye shine before we pushed the boat far enough from the shore to put the outboard down and start the engine. With a last shove, we left the shore and jumped inside the tender.

'Safe,' Steve said.

I watched as *Vivienne* and the other harvest vessels became small white specks in the bay. After five weeks in the Kimberley, I'd lost track of time. What was five weeks in the span of two and half billion years? Like Walhallow, and like Carnarvon Gorge, I'd fallen back into nature's paradigm. Time passed in cycles of the moon and tides and the change in seasons. What mattered was the present. I thought about the economic tides I was flying back to: the fleeting hours, minutes and seconds of the days, weeks, months and years that were ebbing away in a constant rush toward an uncertain future.

People, traffic, noise, the stink of the concrete jungle. It was suffocating. I sat down at the bar with Danny, and he ordered us a couple of bourbons.

'This is how we get over the shock of coming back to this reality brus.' We clinked our glasses together and tipped them back.

'Another one?'

'Sure.'

Danny ordered two more bourbons. 'What did you think of the harvest then?'

'I enjoyed it, and I learnt a lot about pearling.'

'It's interesting, but it's nice to get back into the normal routine too. We have more time to do other stuff then, like fishing. Do you like fishing, brus?'

'Sure.'

'Good, when we go back out, I'll take you to some good spots I know. There's also some rock paintings I want to show you.'

'Rock paintings?'

'Yes, old Aboriginal rock art. I will take you to a special place, but just don't tell anyone about it.'

I was intrigued, I hadn't set foot upon the mainland in the Kimberley. To see ancient rock paintings that few people have, or would ever see, would be truly amazing.

I holed up at the Barramundi Lodge for the week. A package of mail Biruta had been hoarding for me arrived at the Darwin Post Office. Among the bank statements, junk mail and other newsletters was a letter from Claudia with several photos and a short note: *Hope your travels are going well, if you would like any more photos let me know and I'll send them, Claudia.* I sat on the end of my bed gazing at a photo of us in Lamington National Park, sitting on a rock by a waterfall, and fell into the image and the tumble and splash of water. The depth of that period had shifted my heart and mind into a more awakened state. The months of solitude that followed had wounded my soul. I looked at the postmark on the letter: *Tasmania, 24 November 2004.* She had made it to Tasmania as she had mentioned she might, and she was there when I was. I cursed myself for not getting in touch with her when I was down there. I wished I had called her instead of stubbornly waiting for her to call me. It burned my heart intensely. Experience was a brutal teacher.

I pulled on my jeans and a shirt and dragged my heels around the clubs, pubs and bars, through bourbons and beers and bloated stares. A face stood out in the crowd like a ray of light. I'd seen her before, and I'd felt an irresistible urge to say hello, but my courage had failed me. I decided tonight was the night to change that story. I walked over to her.

'Hi, how's your night going?' I gave her my best smile. I didn't have anything clever to say, no lyrical parlay to impress her with. 'My name's Ben.'

Her eyes spoke to me first, then her voice. From them flowed the openness of her heart in a single word: 'Jennifer.' Her name wrapped around me like cotton wool. 'My night's going well, how about yours?'

Jennifer was half Filipino, half Australian. Her long, straight, jet-black hair cascaded over her shoulders and ran down her back like a waterfall at night. She was a full head and shoulders shorter than I was, delicately proportioned but athletic. As she held my gaze, I fell under the spell of her large, seductive, fathomless almond eyes. A naïve innocence and thirst for life I hadn't seen before blazed from those eyes, and they radiated a love and integrity I craved.

For a Top End girl, Jennifer articulated in clever phrases and well-thought sentences. She had friends and admirers that passed, stopped and stared. She belonged in Darwin. I envied her belonging; the warmth and acceptance she drew from those around her.

'From New Zealand?' she asked. 'What have you been doing here?' I watched her lips shape the words and wondered what they would be like to kiss.

'I don't really know where to start,' I said. 'But I guess it began with an unexpected friend and an idea.'

Her curiosity fell into the ocean of my experience, and we dived into long conversation about our pasts, significant life events, and plans for the future. Her honesty spoke directly to my heart, but I remained vague about my reasons for leaving New Zealand, outside of travel.

Fate had cast us together that night, in fiery questions, enquiries and epiphanies. And fate had other plans too; things it wished me to see in myself. For the moment, I allowed myself to be drawn into her life; into the warmth of her heart, and the humid life of the city as her eyes pierced my soul.

CHAPTER THIRTY-TWO
KIMBERLEY DREAMING

*'Ten thousand stars were in the sky, ten thousand on the sea.
For every rippling, dancing wave that leaped upon the air, had
caught a star in its embrace and held it trembling there.'*

— *Joshua Slocum*

The dory sent a bow wave curling along the shore in front of the crocodile. Motionless, the reptile watched as we sped past. He was at the top of the food chain out here, the most cunning and skilled of predators that ever lived. Sixty million years of survival was evidence of this.

Above the crocodile, olive-green entanglements clung to ancient mahogany and charcoal-black escarpments. I watched a white-breasted sea eagle soar high above us, its upswept wing tips catching the thermals off the island.

Aeons had passed. Civilisations had come and gone, religions born, man had flown to the moon and landed rovers on Mars and yet, this place had remained silent, remote and wild. It would still be here long after human civilisation was gone.

'I'll show you those rock paintings after work today,' Danny said.

I wondered if the crocodile had triggered a memory.

That afternoon we took the dory and made our way across the bay to a small, steep beach on the mainland.

'This way.'

I followed Danny up the coarse sand beach strewn with broken, bleached shells and coral. Just above the high-water mark, a shallow cave, more of an overhang, hid among giant boulders.

'This is a sacred place. We must treat it with respect.'

We ducked inside the shade of the cave. Danny sat down and pointed at the wall, and then at the ceiling of the cave. I squatted beside him to better take in the rock paintings.

Finely detailed stick-like figures painted in brown and yellow ochre danced on the wall of the cave. They were Bradshaw paintings.

Bradshaw, or *Gwion Gwion*, paintings are an incredibly sophisticated style of rock art that predates most of the rock paintings around Australia. It is thought that they may date back more than 25,000 years. The style is completely different to traditional Aboriginal rock art, and there is some speculation as to who left these paintings scattered through the north-west Kimberley region.

Above our heads, on the cave's ceiling, an orange crocodile outlined in dark red ochre curled into a crescent. The crocodile was from a completely different period. Perhaps it was Wanjina, which would make it only 3000 years old. At two completely different periods, perhaps separated by thousands of years, sentient beings had sat here in the shade and thought about what they were doing; people with the power of perception and understanding, who wondered at the lightening and the eternal silence of this lonely coast. People whose lives were closely connected to nature. What did the landscape look like then? It is said that the sea has risen to cover many of the old habitations, art sites and the land bridge that once connected Australia to Asia. Were the Osborn Islands once inland mountains? Was this beach once the top of a range with lush valleys below?

'Sometimes I feel an unseen presence intensely in this place; some kind of energy,' I said to Danny. 'It feels like I'm on the verge of some great discovery, like some profound secret of life is about to be shared with me, but then it doesn't seem to come. It can't break through the invisible veil that separates me from it; my form from its formlessness. I've felt it before in another place I worked, in Queensland, in a park called Carnarvon Gorge in the Great Dividing Range.'

'It sounds like the Dreamtime,' Danny said. 'It's hard to separate the ethereal from the physical sometimes. Out here they're always mixing. Your thoughts become intertwined in the landscape; the landscape intertwined in your soul. In the end, who knows what's real and what's not? Does it really matter?'

I wondered what lay hidden in the rocky landscape beyond the cave as I studied the scene: huge boulders balanced on fine points like spinning tops surrounded by spinifex and straggly eucalypts. The scene reeked of Australia's vast and intriguing interior. I considered how long the land must have remained undisturbed for everything else to erode around the chiselled boulders. Were the ancient inhabitants of the land still walking the red rocky crags through sweet native scents upon another plain, waiting to share their secrets with those who had ears to listen? Or, was Danny right? Had I been spending so much time on a lone path in the wilderness, in the world, that I had mixed reality with the dream world? Sometimes it was hard to tell. I glimpsed an awakening of the universal mind that led me to my soul as I contemplated the very essence of life. Had I been here before? 'Of course I had,' said a voice, 'for I am in everything, everywhere, always.' From this earth my memories came and to it they shall return.

'Come, there is another place I want to show you.'

Danny drove the dory into a small inlet further around the bay. 'This place is called the Block of Flats, maybe you will find some of your answers here.'

As the sun dipped below a line of hazy, smoke covered ranges in the distance, I followed Danny through an extensive network of sandstone caves, caverns and overhangs. The ceilings of the caves stood on pillars of rock that resembled melted candles. A prolific display of Wandjina and Bradshaw rock paintings covered the walls, ceilings and overhanging rocks in rusty-reds, orange, white, yellow and brown ochres. Kangaroos jumped across the walls, six-fingered hands splayed out from tall skinny figures, fish leapt off the ceiling, a large white and red speckled stingray swam through the sandstone with a giant yellow turtle. A horned monster with seven fingers on its right hand, eight on its left and five toes on each foot had me musing about the artist's intentions. There were more six-fingered figures, their hair standing on end in six upright points with circles at the ends. Others held spears, and yet more figures were very strange: fat bodies and skinny legs met abnormally long, skinny claw like toes—four on each foot with one little stub for a fifth. Their arms were the same: long and skinny with similar shaped claw-like fingers on each, gnarled and pointed. I thought of Danny's gnarled hand and fingers, and I wondered if he was a reincarnation of those spiritual figures.

I followed an orange rainbow serpent over an undulating wall. A reddish-brown striped and banded crocodile stalked its prey. Then, an almost life-sized figure in brown ochre—a man with eleven bulbs coming from his head; on each hand six fingers and on each foot six toes. Between his legs hung his exaggerated organ. His nose and eyes were dark brown and thick stripes ran through his entire body. The figure lay, resting upon his right arm. His left arm was bent over, the hand intersecting the side of his head. Paintings overlapped paintings. What did all this mean? Was this some kind of sacred site, a place of initiation? Of significant ceremonial importance?

'We should get back to the boat, it's getting late, and we don't want to get caught out by the tide,' Danny said.

'What happened to your hand?' I asked Danny, as we made our way back to the dory.

Danny was quiet for a moment. I felt uneasy, I wasn't sure if he minded me asking him, but I thought I knew him well enough now.

'A crocodile nearly got me, but I managed to escape his jaws.'

'You were attacked by a crocodile?' I was shocked

'*Nudding jah*—just kidding.' Danny laughed at his gory joke. 'One night, when I was much younger, I was walking home minding my own business when I was mugged by a man. I was walking beside a sea wall when it happened. When I tried to fight him off, we both fell off the wall and onto the rocks below. I put my hand out to break my fall. I broke some ribs and shattered the bones in my hand and wrist. I have never been able to use my hand properly since then.'

'What happened to the mugger?'

'He hit his head and nearly died. I didn't know that then, so I just ran away, frightened for my life.'

I was glad to see the Mallard when it flew in; I couldn't wait to catch up with Jennifer. I was hungry for another look into her eyes.

We met for dinner that evening. 'You look gorgeous,' I stammered. Her beauty was intoxicating.

Jennifer was dressed in a black tube dress that gave itself willingly to the curves of her seductive figure and the sultry evening of the Top End. She wore high-heeled platform shoes to match, which elevated her petite stature. A subtle amount of makeup accentuated her cheekbones, nose, lips and eyes. Her long, silky black hair spoke of the night. She was the most beautiful women I knew in Darwin, and the effort she had made especially for me had an effect—I felt like the most important man in the city. Yet, once again, it was her almond eyes that I found myself falling into, and her sweet honest smile that held a truth I wanted to know; a truth that I feared. Our conversation strolled through the cosmos, and I found myself falling for her intellectually. We began to relax around each other in the passion of our laughing and playing. I never tired of her company as we delighted in exploring each other, physically and spiritually. She was a poem, a painting, the coals of a fire, a night of stars and a moody river, the ocean in a storm and flat calm, a wilderness of desire. Yet I knew that there were dark depths to her that would never be plumbed, not by me, not by anyone, not even by herself.

We waded through the crowds at the Mindil Beach Markets, tasting culinary delights and admiring local arts and crafts. I found a cowboy hat, threw it on my head and gave her my best cowboy smile. 'What do you think?' I winked.

Her lips parted with a teasing smile. In a motion of endearment, she grabbed hold of my shirt, pulled me close and kissed me delicately. 'Let's go down to the beach,' she whispered.

The sand, the sky, the ocean, all became lost; absorbed within the moment between us on the beach. We were both full of desire for each other. I expected her to be wild with passion, and on the second night she was, but that first night she was slow and gentle, almost dreamy as the touch of our fingers carried the memory of our night beyond innocence. We looked at each other with new eyes, made love again, and I laughed and roared like a lion. Then we were suddenly hungry.

My head was a buzz with thoughts when I dropped Jennifer home. She made me want to stay in town, to finish pearling and work locally so that we could establish a proper relationship. I lost control of my feelings for her; I was impatient to fill the empty space in my heart. I wanted that life so much it scared me.

Between trips at sea I tried to centre myself in nature. I visited Litchfield and camped in Kakadu. I swam in huge pools beneath wild waterfalls surrounded by jungle, hiked over plateaus and through mazes of rock paintings. I cast my eyes over wetlands and wildlife that stirred my imagination, but whenever I was away, my heart yearned for Darwin and for Jennifer, caught in a web of memories and mystery as the months rotated.

We met under the enormous old fig tree in the city mall, where we always met before I flew back out to work. There, on the grass, under an umbrella of tree-of-life branches we discussed my pending departure. I didn't want to go back out to work in the morning. Two weeks would feel like an eternity, as it always had since our lives had become entwined. The soft touch of her lips tied my life to hers. I pulled her close in a spoon of warmth and a tsunami of emotion hit my shores. I didn't want to let her go. And maybe I shouldn't have.

Jennifer pulled away and gazed into my eyes for a long moment, right into my soul, searching for an answer to her own question, and for the first time she saw what had been hiding there all along.

'Someone hurt you, didn't they?' Her discerning, delicate frown framed her question in the lie-detecting instruments of a polygraph.

'What do you mean?' I pulled back, her words cutting like daggers.

Her perception, her intuition, the crash of change in emotional subject, caught me off guard. I looked away. I knew exactly what she meant.

'I can tell by the way you look at me. You don't trust me. You're scared of getting close. You're running from something, perhaps yourself. Or searching for something you think you lost. But you don't realise you never lost it, it has always been with you, you just have to remember it. It's in here.' She gently placed her hand against my chest.

I fell quiet and fought to stop the dams of my eyes from bursting. Like an old wound reopening, her words awakened the fear and loneliness that still swam in those deep waters behind my eyes, in my heart. I was too afraid to get too close, to let anyone inside, in case they hurt me, in case they were taken from me. I hadn't told her about my past. Somehow, she had sensed it.

I felt a distance flare up between us as I closed off. I was exposed raw, my beating wounded heart longing to be assuaged.

'It's okay, Ben, you don't have to tell me about it.'

I tried to pull my thoughts from the blow that had just shattered my dreams. I lifted my head and saw compassion in her eyes, but I couldn't accept it. It made me feel weak, flawed and unworthy. It smashed the pedestal of my achievements from beneath me. My pride quivered and reality yanked me from my adventure so violently that the script I had so artfully written over my insecurities ended in a blotch of black ink that smothered my mind in darkness. It forced me to look inside again and ask the question that had been waiting there to be asked all these years—was I able to love and accept and trust *myself*? Was I okay with who *I* was, here and now, or was I still running from the ghosts of my past? A part of me wanted her to hug me, to tell me that everything was going to be okay, to breathe fire and break the ice that had formed between us, and a part of me wanted to lash out in my defence. I wanted to tear the mask from my face and the ghosts of my past from my psyche. But I could no more banish that fiendish fear and lurking loneliness from my thoughts than I could my own shadow from myself. It followed me everywhere, no matter where I went or what I did. I still didn't have an answer to it.

We parted ways at the fig tree. My smile was fake and hers left a question.

The Islands brought some relief—from the crowds and from the emotion of Darwin. I found solace in my work routine and in the wild Kimberley landscape. But Jennifer burst into my thoughts more than I could tolerate. I wondered about our last night together and our awkward conversation. If only I could jump on a telephone and call her, explain to her, and ease my anxiety. Thoughts swarmed like locusts, devouring the presence of my being.

Then, one afternoon, I felt strangely content and at peace with myself and the world. I had been pulling droppers off the buoyed lines with my own crew all morning. We stopped for lunch, just the three of us on our floating island; not another vessel in sight. A light breeze whistling almost inaudibly through the green shade-cloth awning cooled our sun-drenched bodies. The sea thirstily licked the sides of the barge in a metallic slosh that lulled me into a sense of calm, security and detachment. I lay back on a pile of lines and slipped into a dreamy slumber under the warm azure sky. Images spun, tumbled and churned into a wash of years across Australia: rustic scenes and wild adventures, deserts and highlands, and my life at sea. People, places and pearls.

CHAPTER THRITY-THREE

A TURN OF TIDES

'For every thing you have missed, you have gained something else, and for every thing you gain, you lose something.'
—Ralph Waldo Emerson

I found a small, quiet beach surrounded by tropical native bush just below Bicentennial Park in Darwin. Yachts sailed wistfully by on the lazy tropical breeze. I sat down on a rock under a shady, broad-leafed tree where the gentle cheer of wavelets lapping at the rocky shoreline filled the silence. Hermit crabs crawled around my feet leaving patterns in the sand like Aboriginal paintings. I tried to lose my thoughts in the seascape as I watched the tide slowly flood and the sun draw the evening curtain to the horizon.

I had been trying to get hold of Jennifer since landing back in Darwin. I was due to fly out in two days. My phone finally chimed. It was Jennifer. I paused before opening the message. I already knew I didn't want to read it, but I had to. I sunk beneath the waves of my fear when I finally did. I deliberated over my reply; disappointed she hadn't the decency to speak to me in person and questioning her reason for ending our relationship. In the end it was pearling or Jennifer, the journey or the comforts of home, and the risks that would come with that choice. With a broken heart, I chose the adventure.

Jennifer was right, of course. Getting close to people scared the hell out of me. It seemed that whenever I did, I rejected it, like an inbuilt defence mechanism. I was only just learning how deep those waters of mistrust flowed. If it wasn't my heart I was trying to protect, it was my freedom. Or so I told myself. Often, life just seemed to have other plans.

Perhaps I was missing something? Making meaningful connections was important to me. What I struggled with was accepting them. Trusting them. Keeping them. Getting close, familiar, implied being vulnerable. Love eluded me, and yet it was the one thing missing from my life that I needed most. Not just the love of a women, but the love of my family and friends. What I was really searching for was that love, and I was searching in all the wrong places. I had a sudden desire to be someplace familiar, surrounded by old faces I knew and whom knew me. *'It won't be easy, but nothing worthwhile doing is.'* Mike's advice popped into my brain like a bolt of lightning. I wondered how Mike was getting on, and whether he'd made it to Australia.

I continued to sit on my rock until well after sunset. The tide ebbed into darkness.

I walked through the Mindil Beach Markets, looking for comfort in the company of crowds. I felt like I didn't want to be anywhere: not Australia, not in the Osborn Islands and definitely not in Darwin. While I waited in line to get some food at a stall, I overheard a conversation. 'Love is like a bird, you reckon? Mate, love is more like a boomerang, and they can bloody hurt when they return too… You let a bird go free and it'll never return…' I felt even more dejected, like life was tormenting me. I tried to pull myself together and focus on the road ahead.

I was surprised when my phone rang. 'Is this Ben?' a burly voice asked. 'I need you to come down to the Duck Pond in the morning and help get *Delumba* ready to go to the Osborn Islands.'

I didn't know it then, but that phone call was the beginning of my journey to Broome and the life that had been waiting there for me all along.

The following morning, I was in Frances Bay Mooring Basin searching for *Delumba*. The basin was known locally as the *Duck Pond*. Bearded, tattooed, tanned fishermen sweated as they tugged on lines where they worked in the rigging, mending nets that hung from booms. Down on deck other men worked at painting, grinding, welding, loading and unloading gear. Some of them were selling their catch, mostly containers of prawns. Several boats were up on a slipway being repaired and painted. The stench of old fish lingered in the air.

I met captain Ron—a big, burly, unshaven man. He thrust out his chest yet still his spectacular beer-belly asserted its authority. Captain Ron was in charge of taking *Delumba* to the Osborn Islands. *Delumba* was one of the pearling fleet's dive boats, an old 24-metre converted prawn trawler. *Delumba* had been at the Osborn Islands during harvest, and now it was being sent back to be used as a crew vessel because *Vivienne* was due back in Darwin for refit.

After a short induction to the boat, I began loading food supplies and large cargo bags full of lines onto *Delumba*; generally readying her for putting to sea. I finished the day hosing and scrubbing the boat down while sweat poured from every pore in my body caused by the foreboding heat, exacerbated by a late night on the town.

Delumba departed Darwin the following morning at 5:00 am. After passing through the lock at Francis Bay Mooring Basin we stopped to refuel at Fisherman's Wharf. I watched the sky morph into a treasure chest of rubies and gold as we left the harbour and reached out to sea.

The coast gradually receded far to the south into the Joseph Bonaparte Gulf, a giant wedge of sea driving inland between the Northern Territory and Western Australia. I soon found myself surrounded by deep, heaving blues as *Delumba* stretched her sea legs out over the Timor Sea. Flying fish leapt from the water and flew past the boat before spearing themselves back into the ocean.

Later in the day, Captain Ron taught me how to use some of the navigational equipment in the wheelhouse. I learnt to plot *Delumba's* position on a chart, marking our progress by radar and GPS.

It was nearly midnight the following evening when *Delumba* made the Osborn Islands. I gazed at the mainland from the main deck of the boat. The wild, unforgiving coast was ablaze with bush fires from recent dry storms. To starboard, out across the dark sea, the reflection of a sickle moon shimmered off a seemingly endless stretch of water that peeled away over the horizon to the islands of Indonesia.

Ron bellowed down the opening that led from the mess to the large cabin below where *Delumba's* crew slept. 'Wakey wakey, hands off snakey!' A few of the men muttered under their breaths but got up.

After weighing anchor and moving to the other side of the bay, where *Vivienne* and *Marilynne* were anchored, several of the crew on *Vivienne* moved across to *Delumba* and the remaining crew to *Marilynne*, another dive boat which, at 33 metres, was quite a lot larger than *Delumba*. It took the whole day to move everything from *Vivienne* onto *Marilynne*, and just before sunset *Vivienne* departed for Darwin.

After being chopped and changed on several ABs for a week, I was officially given my own AB and crew for shell cleaning. At the end of that first official day in charge of my own boat, I sat with the other foreman, discussing work, tallying the day's lines cleaned and pearls retrieved. I glanced around at the men and women I worked with. I saw through the windows of their faces' contentment, courage, and compassion. I also saw a choice. In that moment I could have stayed, worked my way up to farm manager and had my life in Darwin, but that dream, that contentment, had withered with Jennifer, and in its place the call to move hummed in the background of my thoughts.

I had progressed to the position of boat foreman faster than anyone else on the farm. I knew I had Danny to thank for putting a good word in for me. The news I knew I had to give him—that I was leaving the farm—weighed heavily upon me.

The humidity soared as dry storms and showers became more frequent. Despite the heat I had experienced in the outback, I had never been subjected to such unbearably humid conditions. A constant, mild dehydration and unquenchable thirst lingered through steamy days as the irritating hours crawled by in tortuous calms. To add to the torture was the unavoidable fact that we were working on the water but not allowed to swim in it. Some days, however, the temptation to jump over the side was greater than the fear of being eaten by a shark or crocodile, or being stung by an Irukandji or a box jellyfish.

'I'm going to leave,' I finally told Danny while we sat on the large pontoon attached to the stern of *Marilynne*, watching a distant storm pass by.

'I thought you were going to move on, brus. I could feel it. You still have to finish this journey you're on.'

I watched the sun dip behind Middle Osborn Island as humongous storm clouds billowed into shifting mountains of fire in the sky.

'I feel like I could stay here, but something is telling me it's time to move again.'

'That's your intuition. You should listen to it if that's what it's telling you.'

Thousands of baitfish teemed under the pontoon's lights as tawny nurse sharks twisted and turned into yin and yang amongst them. Bush fires burned along the eastern edge of the bay, outlining the rugged coastline with an ominous reddish-yellow glow. Great, formless smoke clouds hung above the glow in a heavy blanket. I felt liberated in a timeless land for a timeless moment. I found it hard to consider ever living in a city again. It seemed unnatural. It seemed like not living.

'It's a beautiful time of year out here.'

'Yeah, it's beautiful alright, and a time of great change and transformation,' Danny said, as he lent across the table like a voodoo man about to practice his black magic on me. He glanced from side to side, to make sure nobody else was nearby. 'How much do you know about pearls then, brus?' His dark brown eyes stared into my soul and made me feel uneasy.

'Only what I've learnt out here, from you,' I said.

To me, pearling was an entrancing romance in which adventure was the only sure thing. Maybe I would become a pearl diver and make my fortune? The day I had seen my first pearl, I knew there was something in this adventure business after all.

'Then you don't know they possess special powers?'

'What kind of powers are you talking about?' The hairs on the back of my neck stood to attention as the storm clouds flickered and flashed with lightening. The dull, distant beating rumble of thunder punched the air like a bass drum.

'According to many myths and legends, pearl shells are fertilised by storms and thunderbolts from the heavens.'

I wondered about the storm that was passing now and the pearls that might come from it. There was another storm coming—my journey to Broome needed to happen before it got too wet to cross the top of Australia.

'The power of pearls is recognised all over the world,' Danny continued, 'through a symbolism shared among all civilisations right back to the Neolithic agrarian communities. It's said that pearls ward off demons, evil spells, disease and poverty. They can bring prosperity and ensure good harvests. The pearl is also considered a symbol of fertility and of the cycles of life; of wisdom gained through experience, divine presence and the journey of the soul or the spirit toward perfection. You have a journey to finish, brus. Don't drift aimlessly in the oceans of life like a ship with no rudder or sails and no captain. You need to find yourself a pearl.'

I thought about what Danny had to say. Maybe he was right? Maybe a pearl was what I was looking for? But not just any pearl. I needed a pearl that would help me find my way home, wherever that may be.

Cargo loads of shell began making their way from Eighty Mile Beach to the pearl farms along the Kimberley coast and the Top End. This part of the season was known as *put-back*. The wild shell fished off Eighty Mile Beach, and from around the Lacepede Islands, earlier in the season had been seeded by technicians and then tended by divers for several months. It was destined to spend the next two years on the farms before seeing the first harvest.

Paspaley 3 and *Paspaley 4* delivered cargo load after cargo load of shell. *Paspaley 3* was a large, sleek, fibreglass boat that looked more like a superyacht than a working vessel. *Paspaley 4* was purpose built for the industry, the main operations vessel, and a virtual floating laboratory. At 51 metres and over 1200 tonnes, and carrying a crew of up to 50, she was the pride of the fleet.

A few days before I flew out, a boat called *Odin 2* arrived at the islands. *Odin 2* was replacing *Delumba*, which was going back up to Darwin for refit. I moved aboard *Odin 2* and made myself at home in the cosy confines of her single, eight-bunk cabin in the bow. That was when I met Sam, a strapping young Kiwi bloke with dark-brown hair and blue eyes. Sam had just finished the turning season on *Odin 2* down off Eighty Mile Beach. Turning involved diving the lines of wild caught shell after the technicians had seeded them. Next year he would be diving for pearl shell.

'Finishing up in Darwin when we get there,' Sam said in a thick Kiwi accent I hadn't heard in years. 'Then I'm going home for a couple of months. It's ideal.'

'You're a pearl diver?'

'Yep, am now. Just got a line so I'll be diving for shell next year. That's where the money's at, bro. You have to get over to Broome if you want to dive, though.' Sam seemed excited about coming back the following year to dive for pearl shell.

I told Sam about my plans to head west before the wet season cut me off from Broome. We chatted about New Zealand too. Sam was from Whakatāne in the Bay of Plenty, in the North Island. He had been working in Broome for the last two years, farm diving and, more recently, working as a decky-spare on the dive boats as well as turning. I couldn't help but think that it was a little more than coincidence that we had met.

'You want to try and get a job as a decky-spare, that way you'll be next in line for a line, bro. Do you dive?'

'I haven't got my diving certificate yet; I've been meaning to get it for a while.' I was ashamed to admit it.

'Oh, bro, you have to get that first, then just start calling all the skippers and ask them if they have any jobs going. That's the way I did it.'

That evening *Delumba* departed for Darwin. 'See you in Broome, Benny.' Sam nodded from the aft deck as they got under way. I watched *Delumba* head out of the islands and into the open sea. Life as a pearl diver seemed *ideal* as Sam had put it. Now I could see a new direction in my life at sea, and it made me happy.

Before I flew out, I spoke to the manager about taking an extra week off in town. I wanted to get my open water dive ticket. I also enquired about getting a transfer to a pearl farm called Kuri Bay, which was serviced from Broome, so I had work lined up when I got there. Suddenly, I couldn't wait to get across to the Port of Pearls.

I completed my open water dive course at Cullen Bay Dive Centre. Unfortunately, the marina gates were not operational at the time, so we never got out to the dive site to complete my actual open water dives. The green, murky, warm water of the marina remained my only diving experience.

Before I flew back out to the Osborn Islands, I unexpectedly bumped into Danny. Fate, it seemed, had thrown us together one last time to say goodbye. We made our way to a nearby bar for a beer. I watched bubbles of nostalgia rise from the bottom of my glass as we reminisced about the times we'd enjoyed over the past six months. 'Don't forget to find that pearl,' Danny reminded me as we left the bar. He grabbed me, hugged me like a bear and patted my back. 'Take care of yourself out there, brus.' He turned and walked away.

When I arrived at the Osborn Islands, I learnt from the farm manager that my transfer to Kuri Bay had successfully gone through. I had to get over to Broome.

CHAPTER THIRTY-FOUR

KURI BAY

'The sea is everything. It covers seven tenths of the terrestrial globe. Its breath is pure and healthy. It is an immense desert, where man is never lonely, for he feels life stirring on all sides.'

— Jules Verne

It was the middle of a sweltering hot afternoon in December when I arrived in Broome. I drove through Chinatown, Broome's town centre, and up and down its two deserted main streets, past corrugated iron shops offering food, services or pearls, an outdoor theatre, a couple of pubs and a grocery store. Red dust stained the buildings.

I pulled up beside Male Oval Park and stared for a moment: several Aborigines roamed about in a nomadic way; some lay under the shade of trees. Where was everyone? Why people had told me Broome was better than Darwin, I couldn't quite understand at that moment. I had just arrived on one of the most isolated coastlines in the world, at an outpost surrounded by the Indian Ocean and a desert, the latter which I had just crossed.

I got out of the Falcon and wandered among the buildings of the Japanese sector. Sheba Lane had a notorious reputation in Broome's pioneering days. It was the red-light district where Chinese, Europeans, Japanese, Malays, Dyaks, Siagons, Filipinos and Javanese had piled into opium dens, brothels and mahjong palaces after months at sea searching the shell beds. Consuming alcohol in the steamy nights of the north-west led to swearing and bickering that often erupted into violent clashes in the dusty streets. Tales of murder, rape, theft, brutality and treachery in which pearl shell mattered more than human life existed side by side with stories of courage, honesty and pioneering vision. Jonny Chi Lane was now lined with art shops, cafés and second-hand bookshops.

I walked further down the road, where the lower-level indentured labourers, Thursday Islanders, Koepangers and Manilamen, would have been penned up in tents and shacks, hand-processing thousands of pearl shells, and repairing the luggers lined up on the shores of the mangrove-lined Dampier Creek. Over 400 of them operated in Broome's heyday.

On the fringe of the town the lowest and poorest of all, the displaced Aborigines, would have lived in their humpies, exploited and abused by their white masters, treated like slaves.

My clothes were sweat-drenched. I walked back to the Falcon and drove on in search of air-conditioned accommodation, eventually finding Kimberley Klub, a backpacker hostel near town. I secured a bunk in a four-dorm room for the next two nights. I needed to organise somewhere to store my car before I flew out to Kuri Bay.

I soon found that trying to get anything done in Broome took time, especially at this time of year. This place ran on *Broome Time*. After a futile hour of searching for available storage, I finally landed a unit through First National Realty. The pretty, young receptionist seemed to understand my dilemma as I informed her I was heading out to work in a couple of days.

'How much?' I asked again.

'$400,' she said. '$200 for bond and $200 for the first month's rent.'

I could only spare $200 full stop. I still had to feed myself for the next two days. I explained my situation further and asked if I could make bond when I returned. She looked at me as if to weigh my character. 'I'll see what I can do.'

The girl left her desk and walked into an office. I anxiously waited. She soon returned with a handful of papers.

'Sign here, here and here, and come and see me when you get back. Promise?'

'I promise.' I later found out her boyfriend also worked for Paspaley Pearls, as a pearl diver.

With the help of a small local map of Broome, I navigated my way down curious streets: past corrugated iron houses with red dirt yards, bungalows on stilts with large verandas enclosed in trellis and shade cloth. The dwellings looked flimsy and temporary, almost ramshackle, thrown together as if any day they may be blown away in a cyclone. Boabs and mango trees sprouted from roundabouts and street corners. Red dust stained the roads, paths and tin buildings. Broome hadn't received the deluge of wet season rains that Darwin and the east Kimberley were experiencing. I found the storage facility, located my unit, emptied the Falcon and made my way out to Cable Beach.

I had never seen a picture of Broome or Cable Beach. It was a surprise when I saw it for the first time. From the top of the sand dunes, I could best appreciate the view. To my right a great swathe of white sand arched away into the distance. To my left, and still several kilometres distant, Gantheaume Point protruded into the turquois ocean in slabs of red rock. A lighthouse stood to warn vessels of the potential fate that awaited them if they strayed too close to shore. I took off my shoes and let out a hoot as I ran down the dunes. I had the entire beach to myself. Sand and saltwater swirled around my feet in a welcome ceremony. I had finally made it to the other side of the continent, to the Indian Ocean.

The Mallard just cleared the jagged ridge before descending quickly. A small settlement appeared below: a dozen long, narrow buildings perched on the sides of a wide lush gully. We flew down the gully and between two steep, rocky headlands that reached out into Brecknock Harbour like two long fingers. With a spray of foam, the Mallard skated over caledon water and turned to come back up the bay.

A small tender pulled alongside the plane and the passengers followed the stores onto the boat. A few minutes later we docked alongside a long, narrow floating jetty and disembarked.

I met the farm manager and was shown to my new room, one of four in a building that overlooked the bay. Louvres and fly screens covered the window openings. A broad veranda ran the length of the building, which lent itself to the bay scenery and the tropical climate.

'We get our power from generators, and our water comes from a perennial spring over in the next gully; best water you've ever tasted. You'll hear a siren in the morning when it's time to go. You wouldn't believe it but some people can actually sleep through it. There're also a few dingoes around here, so you might hear them howling some mornings. They live at the top of the gully, in a den near the ridgeline.' The farm manager pointed to a large building below my living quarters. 'You can get something to eat in the mess down there, and then get ready to head out. I'll see you later.'

I dropped my gear in my room and walked down to get some food.

The mess resembled a large school hall. Fly screens with propped storm covers ran down one side of the building to let the humid air breathe. At the end of the building, a balcony overlooked the bay. From here, it was easy to admire the sloping headlands that jutted out from Kuri Bay into the larger Brecknock Harbour. In the distance, the steep, rusty cliffs of Augustus Island marked the resting place of *Otama Maru* and the site of the first pearl culturing operation to be established in Australia. Above the doors that accessed the balcony, a colourful scene was painted across the gable: a pair of jumping dolphins, a white flying boat swooping into the bay, ABs steaming out under fluffy white clouds and the lush green headlands that sheltered the bay stretching out to its entrance. Kuri Bay was written near the top centre. It was a happy scene.

The first pearl farm to be established in Australia was at Kuri Bay. Thirteen men including carpenters, engineers and technicians took a three-week voyage from Yokkaichi in Japan to Broome, sailing over on a 50-ton wooden pearling vessel named *Otama Maru*. On board was the equipment they believed they would need to establish a pearl culturing operation on Augustus Island, the Kimberley's largest island. The men arrived at a virtually uninhabited region and set up camp where they saw fit, living under canvas and sleeping on stretchers. They had minimal shelter from the wet season storms and little knowledge of the region. *Otama Maru* became the farm's lifeline, supplying needs and correspondence via Broome. The challenges of the huge tides soon forced the crew into the more sheltered waters of Kuri Bay.

Kuri Bay is named after Mr Sakumitsu Kuribayashi of Nippo Pearl. Mr Kuribayashi provided technical and marketing expertise during the establishment of the farm, where the first successfully cultured South Sea pearls were grown. Kuri Bay lies 420 kilometres to the north-east of Broome.

The sharp chirping of crickets filled the humid evening as I sat on my balcony watching a distant storm flicker and flash. Two men climbed the stairs to the balcony. They paused to introduce themselves.

'Everyone calls me Fox,' said one of the men, 'I'm the caretaker. Been out here longer than anyone else. They'll have to carry me out of here before I leave. So, what did you want to come out here for?' Fox's shock of silver hair and wrinkled face gave away his years. I guessed he was about 65, but he had vigour and appeared as hard as old nails.

'I want to get a job pearl diving, so I had to come over to Broome. I was at the Osborn Islands before this.'

'Nice up there. Anywhere in the Kimberley is nice really. It's *God's country*. So, pearl diving. You have a death wish or something? What would you want to go and do that for?'

'It sounds interesting.'

'Interesting? It's interesting alright, just look at all the pearl diver graves in Broome. Sharks, the bends, faulty equipment. Them's just some of the things they used to die from. Nowadays it's just the jellyfish you have to watch out for... and the sharks... and the bends. Still sound interesting?'

I was dumbfounded. I didn't know how to reply to his discouraging remarks. 'I heard it pays well,' I said. 'Well, there is that. Just don't do it for too long otherwise your bones will turn to chalk—bone necrosis they call it. Too much nitrogen starves the body tissues of oxygen. Your joints will go first. Well, I'm in charge of a few things around here, been here so long I'm part of the landscape so, if you need anything, let me know and I'll see what I can do.'

He made it sound like we were in a prison, and if I thought of anything I might need smuggled in, I could count on him. 'Okay, thanks.'

'This other fella here is Mick,' Fox said. Mick was reserved, but he had been grinning at me the whole time Fox was speaking. He raised his eyebrows and nodded. 'Hey, mate.' The two men walked down to their rooms. I sat back and questioned my motives for becoming a pearl diver while frogs chanted a croaking melody for the coming rains. The heat and humidity were stifling. I could hardly believe it was nearly the end of the year. I'd had enough of pearl farming, I knew that much. If

I didn't get a job as a diver, I would hit the road again, make my way down to Perth and see where life took me from there.

I spent the next three months cleaning shell at Kuri Bay. The Kimberley proved to be both torturous and spectacular over the wet season. On several occasions we prepared for cyclones—we were living on the most cyclone-prone coast in the world. Out on the ABs we lashed down the cleaning machines and tables, took in the awnings and stowed and secured panels, lines and buoys. The ABs were then moored in sheltered alcoves of the mainland on cyclone dedicated moorings.

Life-sapping hot, humid days persisted between the most tremendous storms I'd ever seen in my life. The farm was frequently hit by line squalls. It was easy to spot a line squall approaching. At the storm front, huge gunmetal-grey clouds rolled and tumbled in a biblical wave from the heavens. Behind the roll cloud, inside the cumulonimbus that followed, lightning bolts kilometres long cut the atmosphere to shreds as they looped and crossed the sky before colliding into the earth and sea. Thunder split the air and pealed across eternity, announcing its arrival. A blast of cold air was driven before the storm and the temperature plummeted. Within minutes the cooling breeze became a gale that sent the calm ocean into a sea of galloping white horses. Whiteout followed with torrential downpours bursting from the clouds and driving at us like millions of needles. To prevent the ABs from being driven uncontrollably to sea, or dashed upon the rocks, we tied off to the lines of shell we were cleaning. Then we hunkered down and weathered the storm, wedging our bodies between the bulwark and the engine bay to prevent ourselves from being thrown into the sea as the barge was tossed madly about on the waves. Through scudding drifts of spray and foam, complete disorientation set in as we were battered into another world through a frenzy of churning, foaming waves, spraying across the deck in salty sheets. Enormous, angry, atom-splitting whip cracks and roars of thunder followed the cold, white flashes of lightning. Then, almost as suddenly as it came, the dark veil of rain and cloud that threatened to drown us dissipated and revealed a new world; a rugged coastline awash with waterfalls spouting from cliffs.

I watched the Kimberley morph into a tropical paradise of lush vegetation. The fresh water aided the tyrannical blooms of fireweed. I knew fireweed from the Osborn Islands, but the unforgiving quantities it grew in during the wet season were beyond expectation. Fireweed is a spindly brown weed that looks like clumps of old pine needles. The weed is covered in stingers that fire on contact then burn intensely as they leave their poison under your skin. Painful, itchy red welts covered the legs and arms of the sensitive, clumsy and unprotected. Neoprene sleeves helped protect the forearms of the crew member pulling panels out of the water, because it grew in proliferation on the droppers and panels. A few people delighted in throwing fireweed across the backs of their mate's legs.

Christmas was celebrated at Kuri Bay with a bountiful spread of food: turkey, ham, beef, crayfish, prawns, salads, roast vegetables, fruit and cakes. Everyone was given the day off to join in the feast. Every man and woman ate their fill, laughing and chatting in festive jests.

After lunch I made my Christmas phone calls from the loneliest telephone booth in the world. I gazed out over the Bay while I told my father about the progress of my travels, life in the Kimberley as a pearler, the wet season, and my plans for the future. It had been months since we had spoken.

'I'm envious of you. It sounds amazing what you're doing. I would love to have done something like that.'

My father's words spoke to my heart—he had been an avid diver and shell collector in his youth, and in sharing his own heart's youthful desires, he finally seemed to understand what I was out here trying to do with my life.

'How long will it be before we see you next?' He seemed eager to find out. I had no idea.

'I'm not sure, but when I've done what I'm over here to do I'll begin making my way back to the east coast.'

'Well, we're all looking forward to seeing you again. Take care out there, son. Have you spoken to your mother at all?'

'Not in a while, I don't know if she has a phone in England.'

I hung up, determined that next time I saw my father I would be a pearl diver.

I found Fox and Mick sitting on the balcony in deep discussion, but today the tone was more sombre and serious.

Mick and Fox were mates, and the balcony of our shared accommodation was the familiar ground on which they yarned, joked, politicised, discussed work and solved the world's problems. Sometimes they just sat there quietly, staring solemnly at the tropical storms with a beer and cigarette in hand, lost in memories of life and landscape.

'You should listen to this, Ben,' Mick called me over. 'Pull up a chair.' Mick was also from New Zealand. He'd left as a young man and spent time on cattle stations and, after that, a long time in the pearling industry. He was a bit rough around the edges, like any bloke who'd spent years in the wild country.

I grabbed a chair and got comfortable. Fox was on the point of sharing a story about crocodiles from when he worked as a police constable in the Kimberley. Fox was a retired senior constable of the Broome Regional Office. He'd spent 20 years as a policeman in the Kimberley. In that time, he had seen more than his share of grotesque, blood-curdling, hideous sights and heinous crimes. I guessed the crocodile that had been hanging around the end of our floating jetty at the time had triggered the memory. One evening, while I was fishing from the end of the jetty, I'd watched that crocodile stalk and hunt its prey. In a defiant show of superiority, it surfaced with a huge fish, threw its head back, and gulped it down before vanishing back underwater.

Fox continued when I sat down. 'It was in March of 1987 when I got the call. I didn't know it then, but it was going to become one of the most publicised crocodile attacks in the world. Shame really. She was such a pretty young thing.'

Mick and I sat silently as our wild surroundings wove into the story.

'It happened at King Cascades up the Prince Regent River. It's a lovely place but bloody dangerous. She was only 24 years old, a former model come over for the America's Cup, which was being held in Perth at the time. The bloody Yanks got the Cup off us too that year. Her name was Ginger Meadows. She'd managed to get herself onto a charter boat called *Lady G* helping out as crew after the Cup. *Lady G* was making its way back over to the east coast via the top of Australia. Sounded like a great adventure at the time, I guess. It was the day before her 25th birthday when they got to the Prince Regent River. They knew of the Cascades from brochures they had on board, so they jumped in one of *Lady G*'s tenders and headed up the river for a look. It's not a short way either, some 20 kilometres up that prehistoric looking place. When they got there the captain went exploring with the first mate and deckhand. Ginger and another girl decided to go for a swim beneath the falls. You'd have to be half mad if you saw that place, but I guess crocodile safety wasn't so well publicised back then.'

'They're going to have to start culling them again,' Mick said. 'Their numbers are getting up and they're moving further down the coast. They've seen a few around Broome lately.'

'There'll be another attack before they do anything about it,' Fox said. 'Anyway, the captain spotted the crocodile from the top of the falls and shouted to the girls. When they saw it coming towards them, they climbed onto a rock ledge below the falls, but they were still in waist deep water and unable to climb any higher. Unfortunately, Ginger panicked and tried to make a swim for the tender. The crocodile bolted for her, grabbed hold of her and took her under. Her friend, who was in hysterics by this stage, stayed on the ledge and she was safe. It's hard to know if the crocodile would have gone for them if they'd both stayed there. The first mate managed to get to the tender. He collected the other girl just as the crocodile surfaced with Ginger in its mouth. They raced towards the crocodile, but it dived. After that they didn't see them again.' Fox's grey eyes held me in a piercing stare before shifting his gaze out over the balcony. 'You just gotta be so damned careful up here,' he said. 'We got the message from Darwin that afternoon. I was put in charge of the investigation. The next morning we flew into St George Basin where *Lady G* was anchored, and I started to piece together the story of what happened. Then we had a body to find. It wasn't until the following day when two small boats arrived from Koolan Island that we got up to the Cascades to search for her. Everything seemed slow, but it is such a remote bloody area. We found her up there, but it wasn't a pretty sight. We eventually got the body back to Broome. In the meantime, her husband had flown over from America and was waiting there, he wanted to see the body. It was bloody sad I can tell you.'

I sat silently, thinking about what Ginger's husband would have seen, and what Fox would have said to him, and Ginger's parents. Little did I know that I would be swimming in the mouth of the Prince Regent River, in St George Basin, years later, disentangling a towline that had become wrapped around the propeller of a luxury charter boat I would be working on.

Crocodiles, sharks, jellyfish—the wild, isolated Australian coastline teased and taunted my imagination with its inherent dangers as I followed the rapid flowing creek up from the slipway. I pressed through lush tropical undergrowth and waded through the stream, climbing over rocks and small boulders. I had finally been given word that I had a job as a dump-offsider on one of the pearl diving boats. I had yet to find out exactly what a dump-offsider did, but I knew it involved diving and was the beginning of the road to becoming a pearl diver. The heavy fall of water echoed from a small gorge up ahead of me. I soon came upon a series of cascades where the gully steepened. I continued to climb. Near the top of the gully, the gorge levelled out into the surrounding ranges. My T-shirt was soaked in sweat when I climbed out onto a bright, rusty red escarpment and sat down. I gazed down the gully and out over the bay, all the way to Augustus Island—a picture of solitude, complete and undisturbed. Below me the water cascaded in a cheer down the rocky gully to the forest floor. Above, azure sky arched in speckled clouds of elation, liberation and reward, drifting slowly by like congratulatory banners. It pleased me, that sight, after so much grey and rain, and after so much waiting. Ninety-three millimetres had fallen the previous night. Fox took daily recordings of rainfall, temperature and wind speed and reported his findings to the Bureau of Meteorology. We were receiving some of the highest rainfall ever recorded in the area.

Flights out of Kuri Bay were looking unlikely as a low pressure system off the coast began to intensify. That night I packed for the possibility of an early departure. I needed to get back to Broome and get ready for the pearl shell fishing season. I had a pearl diving course to complete and pass, a pearl diver licence to apply for and a stack of dive gear to buy.

The plane didn't come. While I waited that morning to see if a later flight could be scheduled, the weather report came in. The system had developed into category 2 Tropical Cyclone Daryl. It was 200 kilometres north of Broome. Aircraft between Darwin and Broome were grounded for the next few days. All the crews that were due to fly out quickly became restless and irritable, me included. Some of them, like myself, had just finished a five-week swing. Some resolved their restlessness with drinking, others with exploring the nearby creeks while Cyclone Daryl moved off the coast.

It was an overcast morning and a light drizzle fell. 'I nearly forgot to give you this,' Fox said, as he handed me a pendant made of pearl shell carved in the shape of a Maori hook. 'It will keep you safe at sea. I think that's what it did for the Maori, you being from New Zealand and all. They tell me pearls offer protection too, as well as attract good luck and wealth. Don't ask me how, but this is as close as I can get you.'

I took the pendant, which was attached to a leather cord, and put it over my head so it hung around my neck. 'What do you think?' I asked Fox.

'Looked better on me, but I guess it'll do. Wear it when you're diving. Hopefully those sharks will leave you alone, and all the rest of that nasty stuff. And don't worry about those other divers, bunch of macho, cocky bastards. You're a good guy, Ben, don't go and mess that up.'

'Thanks Fox. I hope I see you around sometime.'

'You'll probably see me around. I'm not going anywhere. Well, you better catch your plane. There might not be another one for a while.'

I said goodbye to Mick and joined the other crews flying out.

CHAPTER THIRTY-FIVE
THE PORT OF PEARLS

'A ship in harbor is safe, but that is not what ships are built for.'
— John A. Shedd

Broome's past is a toilsome history filled with wild, romantic adventure, fortune seeking, hard work and, sadly, brutal management of the Indigenous population.

The story of Broome started with the discovery of the South Sea pearl oyster—*Pinctada maxima*—and the richest shell grounds in the world. Thousands soon flocked to the tiny, dusty, isolated outpost from all over the world in search of mother of pearl. It would become a part of Australian legend.

The settlement quickly became a town of considerable wealth derived from the pearling industry. Almost overnight Broome became the pearling capital of the world. In the coming decades pearling would become Western Australia's fifth largest export, supplying nearly 80 percent of the world's mother of pearl.

Long before, pearl shell had been used by the Aboriginal tribes of the Kimberley and Pilbara in rainmaking ceremonies, body coverings, ornamentation and a cure for illness. Pearl shell traded with neighbouring tribes travelled as far away as South Australia.

After the beaches were stripped bare, local Aborigines were forced by white masters to skin dive or dive *bare pelt* for the wild shell aboard what were effectively the first pearling vessels—simple row boats. Aboriginal divers were subjected to harsh racism and violence under miserable and unpaid conditions. This was the time the trade of blackbirding developed, taking Aborigines from their camps, often against their will, and putting them in shackles. They were then walked to the coast to work on the pearl grounds. Some were shot, others were taken to the Lacepede Islands, north of Broome, to await work.

By the mid-1880s, shell was becoming too deep to dive for without diving apparatus. So began the era of the hard hat or helmet divers. It was a new period in the evolution of the industry, which provided pearling with much of its mystique and wild romance, along with a tremendous loss of life.

The hard hat diver's equipment consisted of a rubberised canvas suit, domed copper helmet, leaden boots and metres of rubber hose. The diver was lowered to the seabed by his tenders and air was pumped down to him by manual pump. These new divers were of Asian descent and became the most important men aboard the luggers they fished from. Some of this air of importance still lives among the pearl divers of today.

Diving was a dangerous game. One in ten divers perished from the bends (diver's paralysis), others from beri beri—a result of thiamine deficiency easily cured by proper diet. Sharks were also a threat, and drowning was common. The bends remains a risk in pearl diving today.

Pearl luggers were small, offering cramped living conditions. Days were long, diet was slim, and crew were expected to stay out for weeks or even months at a time with their supplies replenished by fleet schooners. Other than the skipper, who was usually the only white man on the boat, there was a cook, tenders and shell openers. It was well known that most of the pearls found were stolen by crew, becoming snide pearls—a pearl from a dubious source—to be sold on the black market.

Above all, the Japanese gained a firm foothold in the fabled pearl diving industry. They became known as the most efficient divers, to the point where they threatened to take control of the entire industry. Over 900 of these pioneering pearl divers rest in the Japanese cemetery in Broome today. Their graves are marked by unusual, coloured beach rocks with Japanese symbols upon them.

Hard hat diving, despite being responsible for a tremendous number of deaths, continued until the introduction of modern diving apparatus at the beginning of the 1970s. This revolutionised pearl diving, making it far more efficient. It coincided with Australian divers gradually taking over the industry from the Japanese. Steel vessels displaced the wooden pearling luggers as a modern era of proficiency was ushered in. Even so, pearl diving remains a frontier industry that pushes the limits of diving.

Doctor Harpreet Singh was of Indian descent. He had a bushy black beard, beady brown eyes and wore a turban. He poked and prodded me, then made me stand with one leg in front of the other and balance with my eyes closed. My eyesight, hearing and breathing were tested.

'Well, you seem okay to me, Ben. You can go next door now and get your chest and long bone X-rays. As long as they look okay, that will complete your dive medical and you'll be fine to dive. They'll do the X-rays again in five years to see how your bones are holding up,' he said.

I spent the next few days at Kimberley TAFE completing the Pearl Producers Association (PPA) diving course. The original Pearler Association was established in 1901 by a group of pearling masters who wished to govern the industry and its needs. This covered both economic and political aspects.

At TAFE I learnt about the physiological laws of diving, including the effects of prolonged exposure to pressure and breathing compressed air. The course also covered pearl diving specific concerns, such as decompressing on oxygen, bail-out procedures and the industry standard of ascending no faster than three metres a minute. This was achieved by coming up a line slowly hand over hand. I completed a 200-metre swim in under four minutes and finished the course with a short theory test.

I started work in the rope sheds on Port Drive. I met the head dumper, Jezza, who introduced me to my fellow dumpers and dump-offsiders: Deb, Steve, Buddha and Tristan.

'You'll be working with Deb, Ben,' Jezza said. 'And don't think that just because she's a girl she ain't tough. She can beat most of the guys around here… at the pub too.' Jezza laughed at his joke. 'But seriously, Deb's the only girl that's ever been allowed to dive for pearl shell around here, and she was the first female in Australia to ever do pearl diving.'

Deb eyed me like I was a high school freshman. She was the staunchest chick I'd ever met. I thought she could probably survive on a cattle station.

Deb showed me our dump boat, *Augustus*, where the two of us would spend a lot of time working over the coming months. Our job was to dump the catch the divers of *Marilynne* and *Paspaley Pearl* brought up onto the holding grounds.

The dump boats were large aluminium centre console speedboats with twin outboards and lots of deck space for carrying their loads of shell. They derived their names from prominent features within Paspaley pearling grounds: *Patterson* was named after Patterson Shoal off Eighty Mile Beach; *Knocker* got its name from Knocker Bay on the Coburg Peninsula, north-east of Darwin and one of Paspaley's first pearl farms; *Augustus* was named after Augustus Island by Kuri Bay.

Deb explained how the dumping system worked. Each dump boat was teamed up with two fishing vessels: one large vessel that carried eight divers and one smaller six-diver boat. The dumpers worked from, and on, the larger of the two vessels—the mother ship. Jezza and Buddha would be working on *Patterson*, collecting shell from *Clare 2* and *Odin 2*. Steve and Tristan would be working on *Knocker*, collecting shell from *Paspaley 2* and *Delumba*.

Days were easy-going in the rope sheds. We started at 6:00 am and finished at 2:00 pm. Work involved preparing hundreds of lines and buoys that would eventually hold and mark the lines of wild shell caught off Eighty Mile Beach and the Lacepede Islands. Old lines were repaired, new lines were cut and spliced, and buoys were branded with different numbers and brushed with different colours of paint for the different neaps.

Each fishing trip was conducted during a neap tide due to the smaller tidal variation and clarity of the water. Neap tides fall during the first and last quarter moon cycles, and generally allowed the fleet seven to 10 days at sea. During spring tides, over the full and new moon cycles, when the tidal range was more extreme, the fleet would head back to town for three to five days of much-needed rest.

We also constructed radar markers to mark out the shell holding grounds so that other vessels knew to stay clear of the area. The radar markers were simply a long stick of bamboo stuck through a float with a roll of lead at one end to keep it upright in the water. A radar reflector was placed at the other end to reflect radar waves.

I thought often of the crews on the pearl farms, chipping away in the exhausting humidity up the coast, battered with fireweed while they sweated with the cleaning machines under the steaming canopy of the ABs, struggling to clean their allotted lines for the day; the ocean a great mirror reflecting the sun's rays with intolerable brightness. The inevitable madness that quietly set in behind everyone's eyes on those stinking hot monotonous days was something I would never forget. Patience wore thin and tempers were hot at this time of year. Sitting down in the rope sheds in the shade with two industrial fans whirring flat out while listening to the radio, was far better work. It would take us through until the fishing season started.

I purchased all my dive gear later that week from Mick at Workline Dive and Tackle. Mick took care of all the pearl divers in Broome and knew them by name or face. He helped me with everything I needed to get the season started. I was nearly broke afterwards.

CHAPTER THRITY-SIX

THE FISHING SEASON BEGINS

'He who would search for pearls must dive below.'
— *John Dryden*

Marilynne steamed into Broome late in March. I met the crew. They were a hearty, macho, somewhat arrogant bunch of seasoned divers. It didn't take me long to work out what Fox had meant. Most of the men were a few years older than me. The other crew members included the skipper, cook, domestic, engineer and decky-spare.

It took the whole crew an entire day to prepare the boat for drift diving. Pallet loads of panels were craned aboard with lines, buoys and radar markers for the shell holding grounds. Large steel tanks as tall as a man and filled with oxygen were lashed down, dive gear and food stores came on while the divers rigged the booms with lines and dive hoses. The long, hectic, disorientating wharf day finally concluded with a wash down before anchoring *Marilynne* back out in Roebuck Bay.

Exhaustion and uncertainty lingered in the days ahead. I didn't know anyone on *Marilynne*, or anything about pearl fishing—I would be diving and getting to know new faces as well as new work routines and practices. It was like starting in the industry all over again.

The Paspaley fleet set sail for the Lacepede Islands fishing grounds, 75 nautical miles north of Broome, on the morning of March 21. Six white boats stretched out over the turquoise waters along the desolate coast, their sunset-orange booms like outstretched arms. Bright yellow dive hoses hung like golden threads with a multitude of lines and

The Fishing Season Begins

weights rigged fast for the commencement of the fishing season. White horses galloped from the warm ocean at their bows—a sight to behold in the eyes and in the imagination of a young adventurer. Long, white, desolate beaches, high sand dunes and red pindan cliffs struck out in blissful contrast.

On board *Marilynne*, I checked *Augustus*' tow line was secured. The divers hung their big-bags and smaller neck bags. They inspected their wetsuits, fins, masks, dive watches, gloves, socks, weight belts and stinger guards. Bail-out bottles were filled, regulators were tuned, and personal dive medical kits and spares rummaged through. The men's faces wore a mix of anxious, excited and determined expressions. I checked all our holding gear was ready to go for the morning.

Marilynne's decky-spare was a young Aboriginal named Paul. Paul was born and raised in Broome. He was only 19 years old, and he was a stand-up, down-to-earth bloke. It was also Paul's first year on the fishing grounds, so we found we had a great deal in common. While the divers sat in the mess relaxing, we got to know each other better as we splashed soap suds and water around the deck and superstructure.

One by one the fleet came to anchor at the Lacepedes as the brief tropical twilight swiftly faded into night. I rigged fenders with Paul and helped Deb tie *Augustus* alongside for the night. But for the hum of her generator, *Marilynne* sat like a swan in the smooth ocean. I glanced out over the Lacepede Channel before retiring for the night. The lights of the five other vessels at anchor reached across the dark horizon like a small, floating village. Fishing would begin in the morning.

Night still swam in the inky waters of the channel while the divers got ready for their first dive. I observed the men preparing themselves with routine confidence and anxious anticipation. They rubbed handfuls of paw paw ointment and lanolin onto the backs of their elbows and knees, under their arm pits and around their necks to prevent chaffing from their wetsuits during the long days ahead.

As *Marilynne* rolled lazily on the chop and churn of the warm ocean, my mind dived into those dark waters and swam with the lurking creatures below. I wasn't yet used to the idea of jumping off the side of a boat in the open ocean—it's just not what people do. The idea of swimming with the fish all day was a stretch for my imagination.

Deb gave me the order to drop *Augustus'* bowline and we headed off to mark out a holding site. *Marilynne's* anchor chain clunked and clanged as it climbed through the hawse pipe and the ship got underway to line up a shell patch for the first drift. From a distance, I watched the men let out their work lines, lower the down-weights and pay out their dive hoses. The drogue—a large black rectangular piece of heavy-duty canvas eight metres by six metres in size—was shoved overboard in a heave of strong arms. The drogue ballooned out in the water, catching the propeller wash and slowing the boat so the divers weren't pulled along too quickly while allowing adequate steerage of the vessel. The divers donned the last of their gear. Cobby, *Marilynne's* head diver—the industry's first Aboriginal head diver—instructed Paul on deck procedures.

The sun rose from the ocean in a coppery-brass glow like an old diver's helmet rising from the depths. *Marilynne's* horn peeled across the peach horizon. A second short blast informed the divers it was time to get in and start the drift. One by one, I watched them step down their ladders, plunge into the water and swim out to their lines with the help of the swim line—a rope running from the side of the boat to the outside line which aided the divers in getting to their lines without being left behind. They disappeared into the darkness below.

Deb turned on the GPS to mark out our first holding site. We chained trios of concrete blocks and heaved them overboard with long coils of line and buoyed radar markers to mark out a quarter mile square.

'How you getting on out there, Deb? Over.' It was Crido, our stout, long-haired, vertically challenged captain, on the radio.

'Yeah, good Crido, we have our holding site. Can we come alongside now? Over.'

'Yeah, come in when you're ready, Deb. Out.'

I noticed trails of bubbles bursting at the surface, marking the divers progress through the water. *Marilynne* ploughed slowly ahead with the control of the drogue like a white Clydesdale drawing a cart.

Several different horn signals sounded on deck. Cobby, who was in charge of the vessel's movements from below, communicated with Crido and Paul with different horn signals: if he wanted the boat to alter course, speed up or slow down, and whether he wanted the divers' down-weights adjusted on his side of the vessel (the starboard side). It was vital that the down-weights were adjusted to the correct height off the seabed to enable the divers to drift at just the right height to find shell. A slightly higher pitched horn sounded from the port side from time to time to let Paul know when the divers' weights needed adjusting on that side. Four divers fished from each side of *Marilynne*. The diver who had the signal hose dived on the inside line.

Cobby, as the head diver, always had the inside line on starboard side. The horn signals were either a short or long blast and were posted on a plaque where Paul and I could easily reference them. A dot represented one short blast and a dash one long blast. This information read as follows:

.	SLOW
. .	SPEED UP
. . .	DIVERS UP
. . . .	TURN AROUND
. . . . .	BUOY
_ .	WEIGHTS UP
. _ .	WEIGHTS DOWN
_ .	5 TO STARBOARD
. _ .	5 TO PORT
_ _	90 TO PORT
_ _ _	90 TO STARBOARD
_____	CHANGE DRIFT
. . . .	(SAND) DOUBLE SPEED UP
. . . .	O2

I had just got back to *Marilynne* with Deb when I heard one short blast of the horn—*slow*. Paul let the drogue out to slow the boat. Three short blasts followed—*divers up*. It was the end of the drift.

Paul picked up a steel bar and struck the stern samson posts on the port and starboard sides, three strikes on the head of each post, three times, to signal all the divers that the drift was over. Then he checked the valves for the oxygen supplies which the divers would use to decompress. A few minutes passed and the signal for *weights up* sounded. Paul and I started winching up the divers big-bags of shell. We hauled the dripping bounty aboard and began emptying their contents, bag by bag, onto the sorting tables set up in the centre of the aft deck in a large T-shape.

Crido deftly sifted, sorted and graded the shell using an aluminium stick with acceptable shell sizes notched into it—one notch represented the smallest allowable size to take, and one the largest. Anything of good quality in between was acceptable.

While Crido graded, I started hacking off unwanted marine growth with a meat cleaver. Deb, our engineer and domestic crew member assisted with this process. We then panelled the cleaned shells, tagged the panels, and placed them under a saltwater sprinkler system beneath a large tarpaulin to keep them hydrated.

As we worked, the hiss and blow of air through regulators climbed the ladders and the clap of fins on deck alerted us to divers back on board. The men joined us at the cleaning tables in a frenzy of excitable comments about the world below: a close shave, the one that got away, did you see the size of that? Turtles, sea snakes, leopard sharks, tiger sharks, hammerheads, sawfish, barracuda, eagle rays, bull rays, shovelnose rays. The divers jabbered enthusiastically. I envied their stories. I was hooked. Being a pearl diver looked like a hell of a job.

Paul finished hosing down the deck and prepared for the next dive while the divers shovelled down breakfast. Twenty minutes after surfacing, Crido sounded the horn again. 'All right you guys, time to get back in,' he called the order through an intercom from the wheelhouse. Five minutes later the divers donned the last of their gear and scrambled for their positions. As soon as the signal was given, they disappeared back over the side in a stream of bubbles. This rate of activity would continue all day.

After panelling the second dive's catch, Deb and I loaded the shell onto *Augustus*, covered it with a tarpaulin, and headed for *Paspaley Pearl*.

As we pulled alongside the *Pearl* to collect their catch, I saw Sam getting ready for his next dive.

'Sam!' I called out, unsure if he remembered me from our short introduction at the Osborn Islands last year.

Sam turned and stared for a moment. 'Benny, how's it going, bro? Look what I just found.'

Sam held up a small, maroon-coloured cowrie shell with milky yellow spots on it and gave me a big smile. I didn't know what the fuss was about, but Sam looked stoked with himself.

'Common Sam, put ya shell away and get ready to dive, you've got two minutes.' I couldn't see who was speaking but I guessed it was the head diver giving the order.

'See you later, bro.' Sam gave me a nod.

'That's a cribraria shell that he was holding,' Deb said, 'they're hard to find and quite valuable. All the divers get excited when they find one.'

Once the *Pearl's* divers were down, we pulled alongside and loaded their catch. Then we made for the holding grounds to get the panels of shell back in the water as soon as possible to reduce stress on the oysters.

Out on the holding grounds, Deb taught me how to tie the panels to the main line and the buoy line to the concrete block, which acted as an anchor at the start and end of each line. After tying the panels to the line, Deb started manoeuvring *Augustus* astern. As the boat tugged and pulled astern, I threw the buoy line over the side, followed by the concrete block and then the main line with its panels of shells in pairs. We tied another buoy to the remaining coil of line then left the site. *Marilynne* was already landing her third catch for the day when we pulled alongside.

This process continued right through the day, every second dive, Deb and I took the catch from *Marilynne* and the *Pearl* to the holding site and sent it back down to the seabed to await seeding. From breakfast time onwards, a meal was served up every second dive to keep the divers energy levels up.

By the ninth dive of the day the sun was low on the horizon. Fatigued divers exited the water after a lengthy decompression, or *hang-off* as they called it. They'd scoured miles of ocean bed through the course of the day and, from some of the incredible and surreal stories I heard on deck, had seen all manner of marine life. While they began bringing the dive gear in and rigging it fast for the night, I loaded the last of the day's catch onto *Augustus* with Deb and Paul. My new friend looked knackered. He'd had a grilling by Cobby about keeping the divers down-weights at the correct height and the stress of it seemed to have got to him.

We loaded the *Pearl's* final haul and got the day's tally off Hoffy, the *Pearl's* skipper. I realised I'd met Hoffy briefly once at the Osborn Islands when he came out to relieve the skipper there. I'd spoken to him about diving, and he recognised my face.

'Hey Benny!' I looked aft and saw Sam grinning at me from the stern of the *Pearl* while he pulled in his dive hose and coiled it on deck. He seemed pleased with his first day diving for shell. I gave him a quick wave and a nod as we departed, leaving the men to finish clearing away their dive gear for the night.

Out on the holding site I attached the end buoy line to the line of shell in the fading light and sent it to the bottom with its concrete blocks. In the morning I would be diving the line, my first real dive ever.

CHAPTER THIRTY-SEVEN

A DIVE TO REMEMBER

'You never enjoy the world aright, till the sea itself floweth in your veins, till you are clothed with the heavens and crowned with the stars.'

—*Thomas Traherne*

The sky was full of stars as we made our way to the holding site. Deb pulled up at the buoy that marked the start of the line. I donned my dive gear. A crack of light split the horizon in two and the distant coast materialised—remote beaches backed into high sand dunes and flat scrub-covered desert country. It looked wild, remote and dangerous. I thought of the sharks, jellyfish and crocodiles that inhabited the treacherous waters off the coast. I'd never dived in the open ocean, and now 15 metres of water lay between the panels of shell on the seabed and me. It wasn't a great deal, not by a long shot, but I'd never dived that deep in my life. My heart thumped, and I fumbled with my gear. I wasn't even sure I could make it to the bottom.

'You okay?' Deb asked, as I checked and rechecked my gear. 'Yep,' I said it quickly to hide the nervous stutter in my voice. I plugged the bright yellow air hose that connected me to *Augustus* into my regulator whip and pulled my mask on while Deb studied my disposition with hard eyes.

The moment the sun breached the horizon, I swung my legs over the side of the boat and splashed into the warm water. I looked at my dive watch, the temperature was 30°C. It was like a bath. I swam over to the buoy, eager to get to the bottom and ease my imagination of what might be lurking below.

'Are ya right?' Deb frowned through her staunch voice.

I tried to talk through the regulator, which exhibited an odd, muffled vibration of sounds like a gurgling sink. Deb's frown scrunched into a perplexed lack of confidence, and she raised her arms in question. I gave her the thumbs up and went down, realising that I should have given her an okay signal and a thumbs down.

I could feel my legs waving ridiculously in the air while I tried to descend. Finally, my fins found the water, gained traction and thrust me slowly down the buoy line.

The water morphed through shades of aquamarine, buccaneer-blue and deep purple as the pressure increased. A few drops of a green coloured liquid sprayed onto the inside of my mask. Was it really green? I paused my decent and thought for a second. It must have been blood. Red was the first colour in the light spectrum to be absorbed underwater. I had burst a blood vessel in my nose, but there was no pain. I continued down and finally saw the bottom looming up—a purple hued seabed of finely broken shells with colourful sponges and giant coral cups protruded from its surface. Large fan corals waved in dancing gyrations on the tide stream. Peculiar looking fish eyed me with caution. A scratching, rattling, static sound, I guessed from sand, shells and bits of coral being scrapped over the seabed on the tide, percolated through the water.

I stopped and peered around—no more than five metres of visibility as my eyes accustomed themselves to this new world. The hiss of air through the demand valve of my regulator as I inhaled, followed by the sound of it squeezing out of the exhaust vents and rising from the depths as I exhaled, made me acutely aware of the barrier that now separated me from the surface. I watched the bubbles expand and divide as they raced up, as if gasping for air themselves. I took one more look around, convinced myself I wasn't being stalked, then began making my way slowly along the line. As I swam the line, I turned the panels of shell so that they were all facing the same side up. One half of a pearl shell is rounded and the other flat. I sat them perpendicular to the line.

Up top, Deb followed my bubble-path progress. Half an hour later I arrived at the other end of the line. I slowly ascended and stopped to decompress.

While I floated in that primordial soup off the Lacepede Islands, swords of sunlight penetrated the water's surface. A myriad of marine life floating around me came into focus: jellyfish looked like tiny spaceships, colourful lights oscillating through their clear bodies. Other curious, bizarre and extraordinary organisms wriggled, waved, flicked and flashed as they floated by. All around me, a primal civilisation floated by.

I climbed back on to *Augustus*. As I took off my mask a long, stringy clot of blood clung to it from my nose. I quickly wiped it away with my wetsuit sleeve. Deb was watching me.

'Have you done much diving before?' Her frowning face was concerned, evaluating and experienced.

'Not much,' I said, knowing I'd just completed my first open water dive. I was already feeling more relaxed and looking forward to tomorrow's dive.

'That can happen the first few dives you make.' She was referring to my nose bleed. 'You're okay, though, aren't you?'

'I feel great.'

Diving would become my favourite part of the day.

Three days after my first dive, *Marilynne* punched her way through building seas as we steamed north to Talbot Bay, home of the Horizontal Waterfall. Talbot Bay was a 15-hour steam from the Lacepedes and there, in its sheltered confines, our cyclone mooring awaited.

The last two days had tested the pearling fleet as the weather freshened with a low pressure system in the north-east that threatened to develop into a cyclone.

We took such things seriously; in 1935 a cyclone hit the Lacepedes, devastating the pearling fleet and killing 141 people.

The *Pearl* was steaming further north, to a safe haven called Samson Inlet, near Kuri Bay. The rest of the fleet had already left the Lacepedes for fishing off Eighty Mile Beach and were now on their way back to Broome and the cyclone moorings there.

We arrived in Talbot Bay the following morning. *Marilynne's* bow sent a crowd wave rippling over the mirror-like surface of the ocean that rolled to the surrounding islands and headlands. It was oddly calm. After dropping anchor, all hands were called on deck. We stowed, lashed and secured diving apparatus and pearling paraphernalia.

That afternoon a Mallard flew in and carried out as many of the divers and farm crew members as it could take. Only a skeleton crew remained aboard.

Talbot Bay fell under the heavy, humid air of the building storm. Clouds mushroomed to the north in building towers of moisture and a tense calm enveloped the region. The sky settled in lurid interest over the bay.

We were trapped in Talbot Bay while the low pressure system developed rapidly into Severe Tropical Cyclone Glenda as it moved off the north-west Kimberley coast. Glenda reached category 5 intensity west of Broome as it tracked south, later hitting the town of Onslow as a category 3 cyclone before returning to a low pressure system further inland. Severe flooding was recorded in the Kimberley.

Four days passed before Crido was confident the sea-state had settled enough for us to depart from Talbot Bay. We weighed anchor and got underway with Glenda well south-west of us.

Other than a stiff breeze, I was disappointed with the lack of storm evidence until we approached the outskirts of the bay. The swell quickly increased in size and intensity until spindrift blew from the crests. Waves crashed over the bow of *Marilynne* and washed over her decks. I clung to the railing on the aft main deck as waves rolled past metres above the gunnels. They dwarfed *Augustus* as the boat snapped at its towline like a like a wild beast. *Marilynne* pitched, rolled and shook violently as she was shoved by the foaming breakers and punched her 500 tonnes through the heaving confused seas. Some of the crew members, seasick and salty, bounced, rolled and braced uncomfortably in their bunks below as we steamed back to Broome.

Plates, pots and pans clanged, rattled and jingled in the galley. Every wave sent a shuddering vibration of acoustics from stem to stern. The internal structures creaked and groaned in grumbling complaint. The noise and the motion kept me from sleeping. I volunteered my time to the bridge and helped with the watch while chatting with Crido about pearling.

We made Broome early the following morning. After wharf day, I headed off to Cable Beach for a surf.

Huge arching waves sparkled in the sun as they rolled in on a spring tide and a Cyclone Glenda swell, punishing the shoreline of Cable Beach and eating away at the bases of the towering dunes that rose above the beach. I struggled to paddle the longboard I'd borrowed from Cable Beach Backpackers through the waves. I recalled my days surfing on the Sunshine Coast as I ducked beneath another wave and got sucked back towards the shore. How was Joseph going, I wondered? It seemed like so long ago now, like another life, when I met him. Now I understood what he meant about opportunities and finding other places I would be just as happy. Broome was one of those places; pearling the opportunity.

CHAPTER THRITY-EIGHT

EIGHTY MILE BEACH

*'But where, after all, would be the poetry of
the sea were there no wild waves?'*

— Joshua Slocum

Eighty Mile Beach was originally known as Ninety Mile Beach but had presumably been re-measured in the 1930s when it was renamed. A major cyclone hit Ninety Mile Beach on April 22, 1887, destroying 18 pearling luggers, four schooners and killing 140 people. Off that remote and isolated coast, lie the richest pearling grounds in the world.

My day started in a world of darkness, pulling panels of shell off the seabed that were buried under sand and silt from the heavy swell Glenda had produced. I could hardly see my hands as I pulled myself along the line. I held the panels centimetres from my mask as I struggled to see what side up the shells were. Even with the bright yellow tags that secured the pockets which held the shells, it was nearly impossible. There was some concern that last neap's catch would die if it was buried. My only consolation was that the water temperature was a very mild 32°C.

The weather worsened before it improved. The ocean heaved a four-metre swell in from the west like small, undulating hills being pushed underwater. Strong winds from a category 2 Cyclone Hubert, which was a few hundred kilometres off the coast, was producing the heavy swell and poor visibility. I was glad Deb was a skilled tender driver. I didn't relish the thought of being dragged along the bottom by my dive hose like some of the stories I'd heard, or having it entangled in the propeller or, worse still, cut by it. I watched *Marilynne* dip her booms in the water as she rolled and thought of the divers being wrenched up and down on the bottom. Finding pearl shell in these conditions must have been gruelling, frustrating, tiring work. The catch was understandably low. The fleet moved often in search of better visibility. While the divers complained about the conditions, I tried to imagine what life was like for the old hard hat divers living on the cramped, damp and rickety wooden pearling luggers for months at a time.

After steaming back up to the Lacepedes for a day and struggling to make a good catch, we returned to Eighty Mile Beach to find conditions had improved markedly. During the last three days of the trip, the divers on board *Marilynne* caught nearly 10,000 shell. We suffered one accident where a diver was stung by an Irukandji. After climbing back on deck in throes of agony, he was given a shot of morphine, a dose of oxygen, and sent to bed to wait out the venom's course.

Irukandji were a potentially deadly threat to us divers. Common in the waters of north-west Australia, these jellyfish are tiny, about the size of the top of your thumb, but pack a punch with venom a hundred times more potent than a cobra. Their clear, bell-shaped bodies have four cotton-thin tentacles, one hanging from each corner of the bell, which are up to 50cm in length. Unlike most jellyfish, the whole body of this little predator is capable of stinging. Divers got stung either through carelessness or bad luck. Stings most commonly happened in the water when an area of exposed skin came into contact with the jellyfish. Occasionally, divers were stung out of the water when a part of the jellyfish had detached and stuck to the diver's suit or gloves and, unbeknown to the diver, was then touched. Hell follows. Symptoms, known as Irukandji Syndrome, include severe backache, headache, excruciating muscle cramps, shooting pains in chest and abdomen, nausea and vomiting, anxiety, restlessness, sweating and burning sensations on the skin. In severe cases, a victim may suffer pulmonary edema (fluid on the lungs), which can be fatal if untreated. Psychological phenomena, such as the feeling of impending death, severe hypertension causing brain haemorrhage, or heart failure, can also occur.

Box jellyfish, while not as common, were also a threat. These nasty stingers carry with them the deadliest venom known in the animal kingdom and are responsible for a large number of human fatalities.

'That's called the *Eighty Mile stare*,' commented diver Nick, as he waved his hand in front of diver Mark's face. 'That's what happens when you spend too much time underwater down here. You start to lose your mind.' Mark had been pearl diving for ten years.

It was our third neap.

'You want to have a drift?' Cobby asked.

'Now?'

'Next dive, make sure you're ready to go.'

I had been working as the decky-spare for most of the neap. Paul had been put in the water to replace a diver with a bad ear. Bad ears were one of the most common ailments of the divers, so they paid a lot of attention to keeping them in good health to prevent infection or injury from hard use.

Between adjusting dive weights and the drogue, I pulled on my dive gear in anxious spurts and nervous jerks. The divers emerged from the water and climbed back on deck. While *Marilynne* steamed back to the beginning of the shell patch, Cobby educated and instructed me on the rules and procedures to follow during the drift. 'Don't let go of your work line, or you'll get dragged to the surface by your hose. Keep an eye on me, swim out to your right, and when the drift is over, make sure you're ready to swim your big-bag across to my line so they can be winched up. If you get into trouble and you need to surface, use your bailout bottle.'

Marilynne turned to line up the drift. Crido sounded the horn, and the divers jumped back into the water. I glanced at Cobby. 'Just remember what I told you and you'll be fine.' He pointed to the ladder. I climbed down, jumped in and swam over to my line. I clipped on my big-bag and followed it to the bottom. Cobby gave me an *okay* hand signal when he saw me, then slid back along his work line as he gathered shell. To my right, diver Brad waved as he ducked and weaved in and out of view while he scoured the seabed.

I glanced around: hoses, lines, bags and weights hung, dragged and drifted in a diver's web of drifting gear. The first thought to race through my head was what to do if I needed to get to the surface in a hurry. With my right arm, I reached behind my back for my bailout bottle and checked the valve. My work line tugged in my left hand, and I allowed *Marilynne* to tow me through the water. I looked up and dodged a large green-back turtle. A huge sawfish, longer than me, swam beneath Brad's line.

I started searching for shell in distracted bursts. With so much going on around me I struggled to gauge the size of good shells, so I just started picking up everything I saw. Three metallic strikes resounded three times from above. The drift was over.

I felt ashamed of my catch as Crido threw the odd, ugly and old shells back. He held up a larger, older specimen and made a spectacle of it. 'Look at this one!' The men roared with laughter. Eleven shells were kept from my catch after grading—about half of what the lower scoring divers caught. The divers were paid per shell.

The fleet continued to fish different grounds off Eighty Mile Beach. Diving, eating, sleeping, diving; possessed by the ghosts of pearlers past and the lust for pearl shells and pearls, the fleet toiled day in and day out, neap after neap.

The water temperature dropped rapidly through May and June as cold easterly winds began to blow off the desert. The divers donned undergarments and thicker wetsuits. Even so, one by one, the men succumbed to the cold water and surfaced shivering, stiff, sore and chaffed from the long days underwater. Some of the men detested the decompression stops they had to make. Decompression stops were made at nine metres and lasted anywhere from five minutes after the first dive, up to half an hour on the last three dives. It was a long spell with nothing to do but hang in the depths. I watched their hunched, clenched figures huddle in the shelter of the aft deck out of the piercing winds, psyching each other into the next dive. Some of the men just sat, staring into the distance—the Eighty Mile glaze spread across their blank faces. I wondered if I could endure the long days underwater. That and the nasty chafing, rashes and ulcerated mouths they suffered from. These guys would be drying out for months to come.

As the neaps passed, I slowly got to know the crew of the *Pearl*. They were a colourful, friendly bunch of divers hunkered down on the oldest boat in the fleet. I wanted to be part of her crew.

Every evening Deb and I pulled alongside the *Pearl* to collect their last catch for the day, the divers wanted to know if they'd beaten *Marilynne*.

Doing so meant they'd done exceedingly well, given they had two divers fewer on board.

'What are you going to do when the fishing season ends?' Deb asked, as we made our way to *Odin 2* to drop off some dive gear.

'Not sure yet,' I said, realising I'd been too busy to think about it.

'You should speak to Rosco about turning. He's one of the divers on *Odin 2*, and he's usually one of the captains on there during the turning program.'

Turning would begin almost immediately after the fishing season, when *Paspaley 4* would come down to the Eighty Mile and begin operations. The *Pearl* and her crew would also be turning.

'Most likely be a spot for you, Ben,' Rosco said, when we dropped off the supplies to *Odin 2*. 'I don't know who my crew will be yet, but I'll put your name down and let you know when I need you.'

Marilynne caught her quota and steamed for Broome on June 8, having successfully fished over 80,000 shell. The entire fleet of 42 divers had caught over 420,000 shell. I was ready to spend a couple of weeks on land drying out.

CHAPTER THRITY-NINE

TURNING

'A friend is the hope of the heart.'
—Ralph Waldo Emerson

'I need you to start on *Odin* in two weeks, Ben, is that okay?' Rosco was straight to the point when he phoned. Turning would begin at the end of June.

I spent my days off in town working at the rope sheds and running or walking down Cable Beach at sunset. Tamarillo reds and tangerine oranges splashed with dashes of mango yellow set behind the old masts and rigging of restored pearling luggers as they operated their sunset cruises. Chains of camels ambled along the beach with their riders, delighting in Broome's remoteness. I was starting to understand why many people preferred Broome over Darwin.

Some of my most valuable time was spent walking on the beach and thinking about why things are as they are, and how they got to be that way. I often wondered about the intervention in my life that had taken me on such a journey.

The morning before I was due to set sail on *Odin 2*, I received a call from Hoffy. He needed an extra diver on the *Pearl* for their next turning trip and wanted to know if I could work for him. I said yes. I was now locked in to spend the next three weeks at sea diving.

The time at sea passed in the ebb and flow of neaps and springs. I got to know the turning operations routine and the crews of *Odin 2* and the *Pearl*.

As a turning diver my job was to swim along a line of shell as fast as I could while turning the panels of shell as I went. This process was repeated for several lines. Each diver had to turn a set number of lines each day. Depending on the number of lines we had to turn, and the amount of bottom time we had due to tide, the routine was conducted once or twice daily. Each line was a few hundred metres long and held 200 to 300 panels of shell. Five minutes per line was a good time. Bottom time was limited to avoid going into decompression times. Air was also a factor. During spring tides, the enormous movement of water pushed us along the bottom at a few knots, making it easy to conserve air. Neap tides, and especially neap days, were hard work and thirsty on the air.

The number of lines we had to turn increased as the shell technicians progressively made their way through the season's catch of virgin shell. Additional divers joined the turning crews to manage the extra workload.

For the first few weeks, I fought to keep up with the other men. They were all experienced divers, and I'd never had to work so fast underwater. As time progressed, I got up to speed and earned myself a firm foothold in the permanent turning crew.

Other than spending half the day employed in turning, the men kept themselves entertained with anything they could: reading, listening to music, playing games, watching movies, fishing, eating and sleeping. Life as a turning diver was a welcome contrast to the 14-hour days working as a dump-offsider. And it paid better.

By August, the prevailing winds had shifted to the west, bringing with them the most uncomfortable weeks on the Eighty Mile—sleepless nights and wretched days in the water where wind and tide rallied against each other. Tendering for another diver in these conditions challenged all the men. Some days we were forced to tackle choppy two-metre seas in the three-metre Zodiacs. Trying to spot a diver's trail of bubbles on the surface, in order to follow his progress along the bottom, was nearly impossible in the foaming, breaking wave crests. Getting the dive hose entangled in the propeller was a constant concern. Pumping water from the drowning Zodiac with the help of the Whale Gusher was an almost futile exercise as the boat inevitably filled with water on the next wave that crashed aboard.

Conditions on the bottom were always in stark contrast to the miserable experience above. Other than occasional ground swell, and perhaps poor visibility, it was generally calm, slightly warmer, and less strenuous. Occasionally, I'd get one hell of a tug on my dive hose and I knew that my dive buddy had lost sight of my bubbles. To prevent myself from being ripped to the surface, I'd grab hold of the long line, sometimes yanking it several metres off the bottom with me while my tender located me. The punishment our dive hoses took was nothing short of astonishing.

Then there were days when the ocean was so glassy it merged with the sky and the horizon couldn't be defined in any direction. It became an immense desert, an embodiment of the supernatural and wonderful; of love and emotion. During a spring tide on such calm days, I could stop the tender motor and drift with the tide in perfect tranquillity with the diver below. A silence, little known by most human beings, existed in timeless moments of serenity out there that made me consider that perhaps I had found the best job in the world.

As the months passed, and the seasons changed, humpback whales migrated down the coast from their breeding grounds around the equator to their summer feeding grounds in Antarctica. Often, I could hear their songs while I was diving: a concerto of zips, squeaks, moans, cries, grunts and booms that reverberated, buzzed and pierced the depths in a hauntingly beautiful voice of the ocean. As the pods moved south, we were privileged to sights of fluke waves and pectoral fin slaps, water spouts and Olympian breaches made with outrageous displays of power. The explosion of water when a whale crashed back into the ocean was spectacular. Occasionally, the whales were inquisitive enough to pay us a visit where we sat at anchor.

Life aboard the *Pearl* was different from the other pearling boats I had worked on. The *Pearl* was old-fashioned, slipping into a bygone era, a stone's throw from the time of luggers and hard hat divers. Her living space was miniscule, intimate and personal, like the old wooden pealing luggers would have been.

Paspaley Pearl was launched in 1973 as Paspaley's first modern purpose-built dive vessel. She was years ahead of her time when she joined the fleet. A fiberglass boat, the *Pearl* was the first dual-purpose fishing, shell carrying and farm supply vessel. She was also the first vessel to experiment with operations on board, rather than the usual practice on a raft or jetty, which later resulted in the development of operating systems on the pearling grounds and harvesting at farms. Her pearling heritage was rich.

Other than the galley, the only other living spaces on the *Pearl* were the wheelhouse, where Hoffy slept, and a large single U-shaped cabin where all the rest of the crew slept. Mealtimes were spent out on deck or around a small table in the main cabin sitting on the floor.

The crew of the *Pearl* were an interesting bunch of characters. Hoffy had been in the pearling industry for 17 years. He had watched the industry progress in innovative leaps and bounds. Mick, the *Pearl's* head diver, had been pearl diving for six years. He'd made his way over from Queensland, where he'd been working on fishing boats. The work seemed like a safer bet at the time. He'd just escaped with his life after the fishing vessel he was working on off the New South Wales coast had grounded on a reef. The vessel's hull was split open, and the boat foundered. After spending a night rocking back and forth in the boat on top of the reef while water washed around him, he and the rest of his crew were finally rescued by helicopter from HMAS Newcastle. Tim, who was also a Queenslander, had been diving for a couple of years. He was a boisterous lad who took the liberty of mooning Deb and me from the bow of the *Pearl*, was regularly chased off by Hoffy for doing so, and happily offered us evening snacks when we collected the last catch of the day. He was generally the life of the boat. Leos was a west Australian, Zen-like, and one of the older divers in the fleet. Then there was Brad, a real Broome lad. Brad had been involved with the pearling industry in one way or another for several years and, like Sam, had just seen his first season as a drift diver. One of Brad's favourite saying was: 'Let's get fucked up and do fucked up shit!' He lived up to the saying, often returning to work from a week off in Broome with a black eye, a fat lip, or a missing tooth. Some of us were never quite sure how he kept diving. Last, but not least, there was Sam. He loved his fishing and spearfishing. All of us did. Sam had been working in Broome for three years but every summer, he'd make his annual migration back to New Zealand to spend time with family and friends. Over the months on the Eighty Mile and back in Broome, he and I established a solid friendship.

The water temperature gradually rose. From 18°C through July and August, it climbed by nearly as much as a degree a week.

Between turning trips, I holed up at Cable Beach Backpackers, just up the road from Cable Beach and Divers Tavern. Many a pearl diver learnt to drink at Divers Tavern and the bar's history went back generations of divers. I covered my accommodation with odd jobs around the backpackers, clearing the overgrown tropical gardens and driving backpackers into town in the courtesy bus. Sometimes I got a little extra cash out of it, and I got to meet folk from all over the world.

'Is that you, Ben?' a voice asked one day while I was tearing some vines out of a tree.

'Deon, how are you?' I grinned back at my tall, blonde-haired, blue-eyed South African acquaintance.

Deon beamed a smile back at me that made me feel like I was the most important person in the world. 'Geez man, I was wondering where you'd got to. I was getting worried about you. Thought you'd up and left Broome without saying goodbye.'

'I wouldn't do that to you, Deon.'

'How's the diving going then?'

'Good, are you still on the farm?' I hadn't seen Deon since Kuri Bay.

'Yah yah, but I think I will finish up soon. I'm going to head back down to Fremantle. Why don't you come over to the old Healing Centre sometime and we have a braai, I'll cook some boerewors and you can bring the beer. It's really nice out there. You'll like it.'

Deon gave me the address and told me where to go. 'Just up the road from the backpacker's here. Let me know when you're coming, I'll see you later.'

I drove past mango orchards, a camel farm, several large properties with vibrant tropical gardens, and houses on stilts with large open balconies before I found the Healing Centre on Lullfitz Drive. Hidden Valley was the name of the suburb, and I could see why. It was tucked away behind half a kilometre of sand dunes that led to Cable Beach.

'Welcome.' Deon looked me squarely in the eyes, smiled and warmly shook my hand. 'I've been expecting you. So, I've been staying out here for a few weeks now, just in my tent, but I have everything I need here.'

Deon showed me an outdoor area where an open building had a barbeque, shower and toilet. Under a covered area was a couch and kitchenette. 'Let me show you around the rest of the property, it's really nice, and you can meet Lisa and Kamalii.'

I followed Deon's easy gait around the property. Three acres of sprawling tropical native bush tumbled over a maze of meandering paths. 'This place used to be an old healing centre. People used to come out here for days or weeks at a time and meditate, eat healthy and do yoga.'

'There's a very peaceful and relaxed energy here,' I said.

'Yah, you can really feel it.'

We approached a bungalow tucked away in the lush vegetation; a huge vine grew through the trees surrounding it. The bungalow was pentagonal in shape and sat on thick round posts a metre above the ground. Wooden steps curled their way up to a small triangular deck which led to double-fly-screened doors and the bungalow's interior. More fly screens encircled the entire building. Above, the roof rose steeply several metres to a centre point. 'Lisa lives here. She's from Victoria, and this is her second year out here.'

Just then an attractive young girl dressed in verdant green pantaloons and a laced cream shirt with flowing sleeves, appeared on the bungalow balcony. Her hair was dreadlocked, and she had blue eyes. 'Hi there Deon.' She flashed us a relaxed smile.

'Hi Lisa, I'd like you to meet my friend, Ben. I'm just showing him around.'

'Hi Ben.' Lisa smiled graciously. 'Maybe see you guys later then.' She went back to reading a book on her balcony.

As we wove our way down the maze of paths we came to another bungalow, the same as Lisa's but in a more open setting of coconut palms and flowering shrubs. 'Lehani lives here but she's at work at the moment.' Beyond this bungalow, a large building dominated the block. It appeared to be the main accommodation. It was made of huge orange coloured mud-brick slabs with many window openings to keep the interior cool. 'Jocko lives here, he's quite old, in his early 70s now. He came over from Scotland during the war and decided to stay. He also worked in the pearling industry, on the old pearl luggers as a shell opener. He even tried hard hat diving.'

Deon guided me down the maze of paths to another large building which he called the pavilion. The octagonal building sat roughly in the centre of the property, was made up of the same orange mud-brick slabs as the main house, and appeared to be some kind of a gathering space. Beside it was a small amenities block, similar to the one near where Deon was camped, made in the same style and material as the pavilion and the main house. Behind the pavilion, huge bush-covered sand dunes erupted sharply like small hills. 'If you climb to the top of those sand dunes you can see the ocean and watch the sunset.'

Deon pointed through the gardens towards a smaller white building made of tin. 'One of Jocko's sons, Dave, lives there with his partner Rosie. Dave was a pearl diver for a number of years. He and Rosie have a stall at the local markets on weekends. They also take care of injured wildlife, mostly wallabies, they find out here.'

We turned down another path. 'There's one more person I'd like you to meet.'

On our way I heard the enchanting piping sound of a flute rising and falling like a fairy dancing in the wilderness on a spring morning. 'Kamalii is from New Zealand too. He's travelled quite a lot. Now he lives in his truck and makes clay flutes to sell at the markets. He spends half the year up here and the other half down in the south-west.'

An old truck, painted in an abstract outback scene of reddish-brown, yellow, green and blue, was parked in the driveway.

'Pleased to meet you, Ben,' Kamalii said. He was tall, wiry and dreadlocked. 'And what are you up to, Deon?'

'Ben's just come over, and we're going to have a braai later if you want to join us?'

'I'll see how I go. I have to finish making these flutes for the markets tomorrow, but thanks for the offer.'

I handed Deon a stubby while he prepared dinner.

'So, what's your story then?' Deon asked.

I settled in and told him about my travels through Australia up until the present moment. 'Now I'm going to become a pearl diver.'

'And you haven't been home in all this time?'

'No.'

'Okay, well I've been in Australia for about five years myself now. I arrived when I was a little older than you.'

'Do you meditate?' he asked.

'No, never tried it, but I relish walking in nature. It's where I'm most happy.'

'Yah, nature is good, that's why I like it out here. Well, I can teach you some things if you like. Have you ever done yoga?'

'No.'

'Well, why don't we start with that sometime? You bring the beer, and I'll teach you something. I might cook as well.' Deon laughed at his generous double offer.

'Sounds like we have a deal,' I said, joining his contagious laughter.

Over the following months, whenever I was in town, I caught up with Deon out at the Healing Centre. I soon found his mind and heart were open to the very things I had discovered about life over the past few years. Between teaching me different yoga postures, breathing techniques and meditations, we spent hours sitting under the stars by the large outdoor fireplace, conversing about the powers we have as humans to create what we want in our lives: will and visualisation, commitment, dedication and devotion, our lives as children on this planet school, in our Earth paradise, learning and living, applying knowledge and wisdom in decision making, paying attention to our thoughts and energy. How it wasn't possible to throw a stone into the pond of life without creating ripples. How every new beginning came from some other beginnings end. Chance and coincidence, serendipity and karma. I welcomed the discourse and break from the months at sea on the pearling boats and with the pearlers. Love, compassion and friendship freely flowed from his being. Deon told me how he had been a professional golfer and a successful businessman; married and divorced, he told me how one day he had woken up and realised none of it was for him. Then he started on a different sort of journey to discover himself. He gave everything away, went travelling, and eventually ended up in Broome.

'Just remember, Ben, life isn't about finding yourself. Life is about creating yourself,' he said one day.

'What other clever quotes do you know?' I asked him.

Deon laughed, 'Well, there's a few actually. How about this: *He who speaks, does not know. He who knows, does not speak.* Or this is one of my favourites: *Live the life you love, and love the life you live.*'

Deon's little wisdoms reminded me of my own truth. He lent me a selection of inspiring spiritual books to read that helped me understand and piece together my journey in a way that made a lot of sense. They helped me to better understand why things had happened the way they had and for what reasons. Life was full of lessons. That understanding helped me to answer some of the questions, and doubts, I had about my journey, about life, and about love and acceptance from others and from myself.

It was during those days that I felt the arms of a new home envelop me in the warmth and radiance of a colourful cast of nomadic characters. I felt a sense of belonging that I hadn't felt in years.

The dry season drew to an end in the celebrations of the Shinju Matsuri Festival—Festival of the Pearl—which is held over several days around the full moon at the end of the traditional pearling harvest. The festival, which began in 1970, is one of Broome's largest and most important festivals celebrating the town's rich cultural history, arts, music and industry. It includes a Mardi Gras, float parade, food markets and fun fair. A small fireworks display closes the festival.

After the celebrations, town grew quiet and empty. It was finally returned to the locals in a string of backpacker and grey nomad departures for the southern summer.

I caught up with Deon one last time before he left for Fremantle.

'So, I'll see you down in Fremantle later in the year?' Deon asked, while we watched the sunset from Cable Beach, a ritual I never tired of.

'Sure, it would be nice to have a friend to show me around down there.'

CHAPTER FORTY

LOOSE ENDS AND NEW BEGINNINGS

'To see a world in a grain of sand and heaven in a wild flower, hold infinity in the palm of your hand and eternity in an hour.'
—William Blake

It was the last week of September when pickup began. Pickup involved hauling up all the lines of shell we had been turning for the past three months, then loading the panels of shell aboard the transport vessels where they were cleaned, consolidated and put into shell holding tanks. The transport vessels: *Paspaley 3*, *Paspaley 4*, *Clare 2* and *Marilynne*, delivered the shell to the pearl farms along the Kimberley coast and the Top End. All the lines and buoys were cleaned and taken back to Broome and stored in the rope sheds for next season. Soon, only memories of the hectic season would be left on the Eighty Mile.

It was the end of October when we hauled the last line of shell off the holding grounds. I gratefully turned my back on that remote coast, having spent 91 days over four months on the *Pearl* and *Odin 2*.

On the morning of October 31, the *Pearl* weighed anchor and steamed out of Roebuck Bay, heading north for her final trip for the year. Aboard were Hoffy, Sam, Brad, his girlfriend Megan, Mick and me.

Over the next three days we rotated on two-hour watches, stopping once to unload fuel at Kuri Bay.

About halfway through the trip, Hoffy called me up to the wheelhouse.

'So, Ben, I've decided to give you a line,' he said.

'Great, thank you,' I said. The reality of being a real pearl diver still felt like a long way off.

'Yeah,' continued Hoffy, 'I think you'll do well. You've got the drive. That's what you need.' He was a man of few words.

I left the wheelhouse, elated, and went back down to the main deck. For a long moment I lent on the bulwark and gazed over the distant islands of the Kimberley, glowing in the late afternoon light. I'd made it.

The *Pearl* arrived in Darwin on the morning of November 3. After navigating our way through the lock and into the Duck Pond, we docked her in her pen for the wet season. We unloaded all the dive gear and crew bedding, packed up the galley and stored everything in a sea container.

That night we all went out for an end-of-season crew dinner.

'So, everyone, I've decided to give Ben a line. He's going to be drift diving with us next year.' Hoffy officially welcomed me aboard. The men cheered their congratulations and welcomes. Conversation about where each of us was headed from Darwin filled the evening.

I flew back to Broome with Mick and Sam. Two days later, I cleared the last of my gear out of storage and hit the road.

I took the highway south from Broome, down the west coast, camping under the stars and reconnecting with myself and nature. It was exhilarating being on the road again, covering new country. I'd missed it. I explored places like the massive gorges of Karijini and its freshwater streams and pools, the tremendous array of corals and marine life on the Ningaloo Reef, and beautiful Kalbarri with its red cliffs by the sea. I was as young and free as I would ever be.

After nearly two weeks on the road, the scenery changed, slowly at first, then more dramatically. The desert country morphed into rolling farmland, green pastures and extensive areas of open woodlands and forests. Small towns became large towns, and finally I crossed the Darling Range to discover the most remote large city in the world, Perth. I navigated my way over to Fremantle.

Deon met me with the smile of an old long-lost friend. He embraced me in a bear hug. We went out to see the festivities I had so fortuitously timed—The Fremantle Festival. A showcase of local arts, music and fashion moved in fusion and profusion through the streets of Fremantle. In the bustling crowds, I met Michelle, a down-to-earth blonde-haired Fremantle girl. She was young, lovely and blue-eyed.

Michelle joined Deon, his girlfriend and me on a camping trip in the south-west. We spent three days surrounded by giant karri forests and explored the wild coastline. Unfortunately, Michelle was halfway through a work visa in the United Kingdom and was only back home for a short stay. As much as we would have liked to make a go of things, the timing just wasn't right. Meeting Michelle made it clear to me I was ready to finish up with life on the road.

From Fremantle I drove back down to the south-west and began the long journey along the south coast of Australia. The winding coastal highway unravelled between ancient towering karri trees, rolling green pastures and wineries. The Stirling Ranges and the Wheatbelt gave way to the spectacular beaches of Esperance. The Nullarbor Plain slid into a thousand kilometres of emptiness. I finally made Port Augusta, familiar country, and took a glance up the Stuart Highway into the empty void of the interior. It was hard to believe two years had passed since I took that road. I watched Aboriginal kids jumping off a jetty on the other side of an inlet as I drove over a bridge and through town.

As I made my way across South Australia and Victoria, I found myself recollecting my travels with Cloudy and Sunny, the friendly pair from South Africa and Germany whom I'd met in Grampians National Park. I visited Soapy in Adelaide, and we talked about the *old days* on the station. I thought of the many weeks I had spent on my own in the wilderness of Tasmania, the Climate Change Project I had worked on at Mt Rufus, and the catharsis that had taken place in that latitude.

After nearly two weeks on the road, I made Melbourne.

I hadn't seen my father in over four years when I knocked on his door. Work had recently taken him to Melbourne with his wife and my younger brother. I took a few deep breaths. I felt like a son, returned from his long journey a man.

An older man than I remembered answered the door. He flashed a smile, said hello and shook my hand. I wanted him to hug me. As great as it was to see him, it felt awkward. Time had created a distance between us. There was so much we didn't know about each other. He probably felt the same way.

Eleven years had passed since I spent a Christmas with my father. My sister had come over from New Zealand to celebrate with us. I hadn't seen her in years either. I became better acquainted with my father's partner and their son. He was no longer a toddler but a young boy full of fascination and admiration for his older brother.

Finally, we had an evening out together, just me and my father. Together we climbed the mountain of separation and the ocean of estrangement that had grown between us. It began with the conversation I had rehearsed so many times on the road. I painted a picture of my travels and experiences in Australia over the past four and half years, infused with the personal and spiritual obstacles I had faced—how my struggle was more than just physical—that it was the breaking of the shell that enclosed my understanding and awareness of life. Yet, as much as I tried, I couldn't find the words to describe the seconds, minutes, and hours that made up the days, weeks, months and years I'd spent journeying through the continent. The achingly beautiful moments of joy, and the moments of despair and loneliness that had, at times, haunted me. 'It changed me. The world I perceive now is not the world I knew before. Now it is all windows and doors waiting to be opened. Light shines through all of them.'

I shared with him how close he came to losing me; the ways in which I had planned out my demise, how I had so nearly given up on life in Christchurch.

'I'm sorry for the way things ended up, I really am. I'm sorry I wasn't there. All you kids went through a lot, and to be honest I'm very grateful you're all still here. I really thought your mother would have chosen better too. She had so much to offer, and she was a good-looking woman. I'll never know why she chose that guy.'

Then he opened up. He told me of his envy and his admiration of what I had achieved. He told me about his own childhood and family circumstances; about how the loss of both of his parents to suicide and the death of his two younger sisters by the time he was eight years old had affected him. How he and his brother were separated and fostered as extended family came to their aid. He told me about his life as a young man, and how hard it had been growing up without a father. He told me how his perception of life was always changing, always evolving. When I considered my father's life, I thought I was lucky to have him. I could see he was doing his best and getting through life with a positive attitude. Despite his childhood, he'd achieved a great deal. I could see his drive for life living on through me.

I had wanted to say more. I'd had so much time alone in the wilderness, and on the road, to think about our next meeting and all the things I wanted to say, but most of that dialogue had left me when the time came. It seemed then that little more actually needed to be said. Something had changed between us, and I'd come to understand many things better over my years on the road.

He hugged me before I left, and I saw a tear well in his eye. 'I'm upset to see you go. Take care out there, won't you? I'm looking forward to hearing how you get on with pearl diving.'

I'd never seen the emotion I saw in his eyes that day. 'I'll let you know,' I said, touched by the realisation that he was proud of who I had become.

A week later I made Queensland. I stayed with my brother in Springbrook National Park, on the McPherson Range in the Gold Coast's hinterland. There, tucked away from the summer heat and chaos of Surfers Paradise, high in the rainforest-clad mountains, he lived in a small cottage with his fiancée, Krystina. I relaxed, explored the ranges and prepared for the trip north.

Deon embraced me when we met at Brisbane International Airport. His girlfriend had just departed for Canada. 'I'm so happy to see you,' he gushed. 'I wasn't sure if you were coming to get me or not.'

Together we began tracking north, for Cairns and tropical north Queensland. We passed floods, sandbagged towns and abandoned cars until we couldn't go on. We spent two days and nights holed up in Ingham while the rain hammered the tin roof of the old Station Hotel. Two low pressure systems were expected to intensify, develop into cyclones, and possibly merge. One local newspaper's front page headline read: 'Superstorm'. Shortages of milk, bread, fresh fruit and vegetables threatened our stay.

Fortunately, the superstorm didn't eventuate. The weather cleared, and we pushed off to Mission Beach. There, at a market, I stumbled upon an old copy of the R.M Williams *OUTBACK* magazine with the article on Colonial that I had featured in all those years before. As I flipped through the pages, a younger version of myself stared back at me. He was a boy in search of meaning and adventure, full of wonder, questions and curious about life. He was also confused, lost and broken inside. I thought of everything that had happened since the photo was taken. Things I never would have imagined, but everything I ever could have dreamed of. The article was nearly four years old now.

We stopped in Port Douglas. Between spells of torrential rain and sweltering humidity, we explored the rainforests around Mossman Gorge in the Daintree National Park and drove up to Cape Tribulation.

I left Deon at Cairns International Airport. I was disappointed he wasn't joining me for the journey across to Broome. He was cash-strapped, homesick, and uncertain where his future was headed.

'Good luck, hopefully see you back in Broome if Fremantle doesn't work out?' I didn't know what to say when we hugged.

'Yah, thanks Ben, it's been nice to see Queensland and spend some time with you. Travel safe and good luck in Broome.'

I drove over the Atherton Tableland and into the desert. On the second day, I made Camooweal. After stopping for fuel, I made my way across to the local pub for a meal. Kris stood behind the bar.

'Kris, when did you move to Camooweal?' I asked.

'Bout-a-year-ago. It was a bit lonely out at Barkly Homestead, so I thought I'd move to town.' By town he meant an outpost with a population of 160 people. 'My partner likes it better. So, what brings you back out to these parts? Going back to the station?'

I couldn't have thought of a less appealing idea. 'On my way back to Broome. Pearl diving this year.'

'Pearl diving?' Kris exclaimed. The way he said it made me uncertain he'd ever seen the ocean.

'I decided to work at sea,' I explained, 'it's not as hot out there as in the outback.'

'Oh, okay, good luck with that.' Kris paused for a moment. The cogs in his brain were turning slowly but surely. 'Funny thing, life, isn't it? You just never know where you'll end up.'

'Not if you chose to explore it,' I replied.

After four solid days of driving, I watched the sunset from an empty Cable Beach. It was time to focus on finding that pearl.

CHAPTER FORTY-ONE

THE PEARL

'The deeper the blue becomes, the more strongly it calls man towards the infinite, awakening in him a desire for the pure and, finally, for the supernatural... The brighter it becomes, the more it loses its sound, until it turns into silent stillness and becomes white.'

—*Wassily Kandinsky*

At dusk, I lay in my hammock at the Healing Centre under arching coconut palms, surrounded by the tumbling tropical gardens of my new home. I rubbed the mother of pearl hook pendant hanging on the leather cord around my neck, and my thoughts drifted over the past few years. Now here I was, living in a small bungalow at the back of Cable Beach, where I could hear the Indian Ocean beyond the dunes, in a remote and half-forgotten corner of the world diving for pearl shell. I was truly grateful I had taken that step into the unknown.

The *Pearl* arrived in Broome during the last week of March. After wharf day, I stayed aboard in Roebuck Bay, on watch, while the rest of the crew made last-minute dive gear purchases and acquired their pearl diving licenses. We would set sail in the morning for the Eighty Mile fishing grounds.

Hoffy phoned me in the morning. 'G'day, Ben, there's a low pressure system that's threatening to develop into a cyclone, so we're staying in Broome until further notice. Someone'll be out in a few days to relieve you.'

Hoffy phoned again the following day. 'Hi Ben, we don't need to worry about the low pressure, we'll be out to the boat in an hour.'

Soon after the crew joined me on board, booms swung out over the water across the fleet. Divers yelled to each other, stays were tightened, weights secured, and dive hoses rigged. One by one the pearling fleet got underway, destined for the rich shell grounds off Eighty Mile Beach.

I laid out my dive gear, methodically and meticulously checking each item. Hoffy inspected all systems and ensured we were ready to go for the morning. Tomorrow, the pearling adventure would begin.

I'd hardly got a wink of sleep all night when I watched the other men get ready, the thrill of the catch resonated in their voices and animated their faces. They joked and talked excitedly about the day ahead. Could I actually spend nine hours a day underwater? Would my body hold up physically?

I plastered handfuls of paw paw ointment behind my knees, the back of my elbows, under my arms and around my neck, then I slipped into my first suit of the season. It was a light suit, only a millimetre thick. The strenuous workload of swimming for shell would keep me warm.

We weighed anchor and got underway, letting the work lines out, lowering the down-weights a few metres into the water, and paying out the long yellow dive hoses to their full length in large sweeping loops from boom to stern where they were secured. I connected my regulator.

As the new diver on board, I was placed beside Mick on the starboard middle line. From there, Mick could keep an eye on me underwater and give me instructions on deck.

Just before the sun broke the horizon, Hoffy sounded the horn informing us we had five minutes to get ready for the first drift. I donned my mask, stinger guard and fins. I clipped my dive hose to my belt and put my neck bag over my head and my big-bag over my shoulder. Lloydy, our decky-spare and Cobby's younger brother, eased out the drogue at Hoffy's direction to slow the boat to the appropriate speed. We shoved our regulators in our mouths. Hoffy sounded another short blast on the horn. It was time to get in.

'Righto, in ya get!' Mick shouted.

Dive hoses were unhooked, and the first divers climbed down the ladders and swam for the outside lines. Next came my turn. 'Have a good dive, Benny,' Sam called out as I climbed down the ladder and plunged into the warm water. I grabbed hold of the swim line, made my way to the middle line, clipped my big-bag on and dived below. Mick was already halfway down his line and Sean was already on the bottom searching for shell. I let go of the down-weight line and swam for my work line. As I grabbed hold of it, the slack pulled out and I felt the steady pull of the *Pearl*.

Visibility was poor. The low pressure had left a storm surge in its wake that had stirred the bottom into a dark cloud of silt. Light struggled to pierce the depths. As I peered through the murky water, searching the seabed, I spotted several pearl oysters and deftly shoved them into my neck bag. The water was 29°C.

Fifty minutes passed almost too quickly. My shell count looked low but there was still all day to make up the catch. Mick signalled to slow the boat and end the drift. Three hard strikes reverberated through the water three times from each side of the vessel, the sharp metallic sound informing us divers that the drift was up.

I hauled my way hand over hand up my work line and emptied my neck bag into my big-bag, then unclipped it from the down-weight line. I caught a glimpse of Mick reaching out, waving in the gloom for me to see him. I swam towards him and grabbed hold of the inside line. Sean soon joined us. Another line with two dive weights attached to it, and clipped to Mick's down-weight line, descended to us. We each hooked on our big-bags then Mick signalled *weights up* to inform Lloydy and Hoffy that our bags were ready to be winched up. The slack took up and, as it took the weight of the big-bags, Mick unclipped the line sending our catch aloft and out of sight.

Mick turned to Sean and me, and flicked his hand over the top of his neck bag enquiring about how many pearl shells we caught. I held up two fingers to let him know I got about twenty oysters. Sean held up three fingers. Mick nodded, then pretended to wipe his forehead. The water was so warm I was having to clear the sweat from my mask.

After a short decompression stop we ascended and joined Lloydy in cleaning and panelling the catch. Remarks about the conditions washed across the deck: 'poor visibility', 'not much shell', 'try moving'. I was relieved it hadn't been a prolific dive for anyone, and the scores soon showed.

Ange, our trusty cook, plonked trays of fruit and cereal, toast, bacon and eggs, tea and coffee on the shell tanks. Breakfast was inhaled in a matter of minutes. The five-minute horn sounded, and we got ready for the second dive of the day. Indigestion was a common complaint.

Drift after drift, we scoured the ocean floor. Days soon turned into weeks, and weeks into months. In that time, I learnt to discern with great detail the myriad wonders of the depths and identify the prolific numbers of pearl shells that lay on the seabed.

Being dragged over such vast areas of ocean floor for days on end revealed relics of the past: huge old admiralty anchors and smaller anchors, which I concluded were lost by some of the early pearl luggers and schooners wrecked by cyclones. Other relics were brought to the surface that season: an old wooden pulley and a hard hat diver's boot. Those endless nautical miles underwater also revealed how reliant we were on our diving apparatus, and just how far out of our element we were as the marine life of the Eighty Mile swam around us: massive rays, huge sharks, turtles, sea snakes and schools of fish; the weary and the inquisitive, the hunters and prey. Every day we spent in that aquarium of life, searching for treasure, was a day spent drifting through the dreams of the ocean.

After the last dive of the day we often hung in the dark depths, decompressing while the moon and the stars emerged above. Floating in that blackness was perhaps the closest thing to being in a womb; the umbilical cord yellow air hose feeding us vital oxygen through our regulators; our lifeline connecting us to the mother vessel. Bioluminescent sparks raced off our glowing figures like we were human meteorites flying through the blackness of space. I'd close my eyes, think of Broome, and slip into the pearler's dream. We never knew if we were being followed by anything down there, but I'm sure we were. We'd been stalked plenty of times during daylight hours. Waking from that floating slumber, we slowly ascended hand over hand, into the luminescent glow of the *Pearl's* lights; into a two-way mirror where the two worlds collided at the water's surface. Finally, we left the cold black void below for the night.

It was on my first pay day that I realised how far I had come. In a single day of diving for pearl shell, I could earn as much as I did in an entire month slogging it out under the hot sun in the outback.

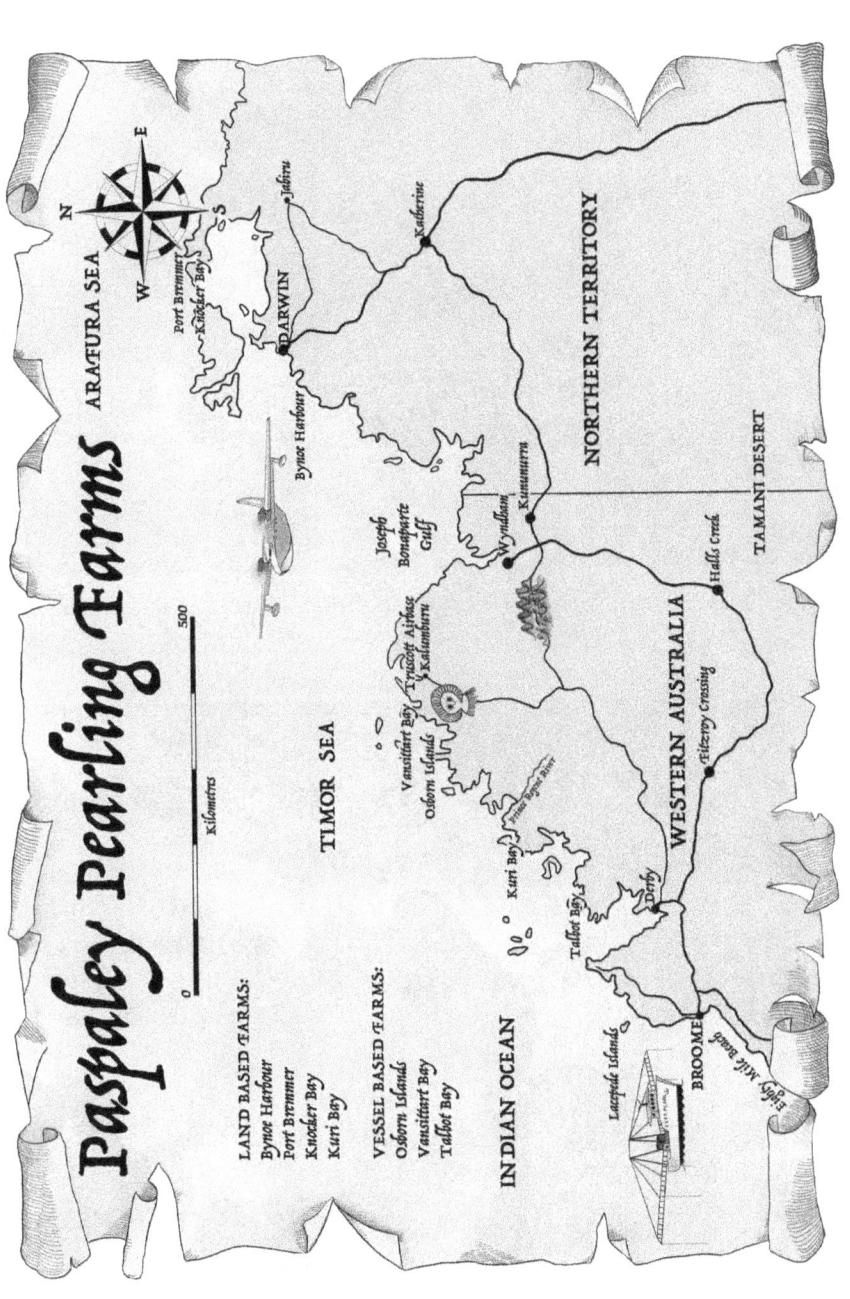

Vivienne, mother ship at Osborn Islands.

Bringing panels of shells on board for cleaning.

Removing growth off shells (chipping).

Danny at Middle Osborn Island.

Anchor work with Danny.

Collecting shell from *Paspaley 4*.

In charge of an AB, eastern flank of Middle Osborne Island in the background.

Flying into Kuri Bay, taken from the Mallard.

Perched above Kuri Bay after exploring the creek and gully below, having just received word I had a job as a dump-offsider.

Marilynne with her booms out, divers down, fishing 2006.

Waves well above the gunnels and washing across the aft main deck of *Marilynne*, steaming out of Talbot Bay after Severe Tropical Cyclone Glenda.

Dumping panels of shell off the dump boat *Augustus* onto the holding grounds.

About to dive a line of shell.

Paspaley Pearl with her booms out, divers down, fishing 2006.

Refuelling *Augustus* from *Marilynne*.

Plotting our course down the coast on *Odin 2* during turning.

Preparing the turning dinghy.

Sam waving a hang loose, turning off Eighty Mile Beach.

My bungalow at the Healing Centre.

Getting into the water on a rough morning, fishing 2007.

Mick sending up the big-bags.

Cleaning and paneling shell on deck after it has been graded.

Swimming my big-bag over at the end of a drift.

A clear day underwater to see the divers on port side
(Mick in foreground, starboard side).

Searching for shell.

From left to right: Sam, Ryan, Mick, Myself, Brad, Sean.

CHAPTER FORTY-TWO

THE JOURNEY BACK

'If one advances confidently in the direction of his dreams, and endeavours to live the life which he has imagined, he will meet with a success unexpected in common hours.'

—*Henry David Thoreau*

I folded the cloth back over the pearl and gazed around the bungalow. I recalled what Danny had said about finding a pearl and I knew I had found the knowledge and understanding I had been searching for all these years. It wasn't the pearl itself, that was merely the jewel that encompassed an idea that I could take home and show to others. It was the revelation that I could achieve anything I could imagine.

I propped open the shutters that covered the fly screens and the sweet, tropical native garden-smell flew into the bungalow on the wings of singing birds. I quietly thanked my friend Deon for introducing me to the Healing Centre. I was in want of nothing more. My own healing was complete.

Later that afternoon, I followed the camel track that twisted and wound its way through the sand dunes, rising and falling through native scrub and patches of remnant rainforest from Lullfitz Drive to Cable Beach. Somehow, things felt right, like they were always meant to be this way.

Five months later, when the pearling season finished up, I began my long-awaited journey back to New Zealand. It was time to reconnect with a place and time where I had left part of my heart.

Back in Queensland, I took a trip up to the Sunshine Coast and dived unexpectedly into the memories of my days there; surfing, my old friend Joseph, and that feeling of being so alive after returning from the outback reflected in the bays and waves of the Coral Sea. I shared with Biruta the tale of my life as a pearl diver in the remote north-west, and I stole a look into my old beach shack, where everything had begun; that first home in a new land and Biruta's unwavering support like a loving surrogate grandmother.

My mother visited from England. The awkwardness of the years that had passed subsided in her tear-filled smile and embrace. We spoke at length, to the point each of us could bare, about the things that had torn us all apart so early on. She apologised for the mess that had come of her second marriage, and for letting it take so much from her before she had the strength to do anything about it. I knew then that my mother's spirit had been broken, and that wound had changed her irrevocably. Her personality was splintered, indeed shattered, during those years. Her selflessness and trust had been abused. I considered that some of our best qualities might also be some of our greatest weaknesses, if exploited by other people.

My mother and father had married very young, aged 17 and 19. In a way, I understood that both my parents had moved into an unfamiliar world when their marriage ended. She had lost her way, and maybe my father had too. Before they married, my mother had been exposed to a variety of experiences around the world. Her father had been a merchant seaman and captain. She'd lived intermittently on ships and on shore, in boarding houses, or with her mother and brother. Her father was often away at sea for months at a time. She'd been married eight years and had two children by the time she was the age I was now.

In some ways, I saw my life as a mixture of what each of my parents had wanted for themselves; a position between their truths. I knew now, more than ever, that without the events that came after their breakup, I may never have been privileged to find my own truth, or able to share what I had learnt with anybody else.

I hugged my mother at the airport, unsure when I would see her again. On Wednesday evening, 13 February 2008, I watched from my window seat, the West Coast of the South Island of New Zealand erupt from the Tasman Sea. It was a clear, sunny day. Nostalgia plucked every fibre in my body like a mandolin as the mountains appeared in rows of sharp teeth. I saw Mt Cook's snow-capped peak out of the right side of the plane through rows of people who I knew by their accents to be Kiwis. I realised a part of me was home; that this was the place I was from.

Having crossed the broad, lush green patchwork quilt agricultural plains of Canterbury, the aircraft turned to line up the runway at Christchurch International Airport. Touch down. My two worlds collided: exhilaration exhaled and a mixture of anxiety and excitement, blended with the paradox of familiar sights that had become unfamiliar, inhaled. Memories and emotions churned, tumbled and turned in my mind.

I collected my bag, passed through customs, and waved down a taxi. 'Hackthorne Road, Cashmere, please,' I instructed the driver. As I got closer to the hills, I recalled the first road trip Stephanie and I ever took together, in the spring of 1999.

* * *

I pulled off the road so we could take in the view. She climbed out of the car and began collecting wildflowers, her golden blonde hair dancing about her serene face in a light breeze. She looked up, caught me with her blazing blue eyes and beamed a broad, loving smile at me. My heart flew away with welcome swallows as I forgot my cares. My stomach tingled in a moment of joy. I flashed a smile back at her and chuckled to myself. I was head over heels in love with her.

We were on holiday in Akaroa, a tiny French settlement on Banks Peninsula, in the South Island of New Zealand. Rolling green hills tumbled springtime colours into a mosaic of vibrant waves that anyone could get lost in for a moment. Sunlight sparkled upon the cool blue ocean that broke the sleepy coastline into scattered bays below; its air of adventure settling with the fragrant warm breeze of hope that was blossoming from the landscape.

We were young. Too young, perhaps, to really know what we were getting into. Two 16-year-olds with not a care for much else. I would marry her someday, I thought to myself.

* * *

I thought of the words she had spoken before I left: 'I don't think you should go, Ben.' Over the years I had often wondered what would have happened if I hadn't left, or if I could have persuaded her to join me when she finished university.

Stephanie answered the door. I gazed into her blue eyes and my restlessness faded. She smiled softly. 'Hello, Ben.'

Strangers as we were after the years that had passed, I could feel my love for her as fresh as a spring morning. 'Hi, Stephanie.' I reached out to hug her—uneasy, awkward almost, with the years between us.

'Come in, Hamish and Katie are home, so you can say hello to them. Dad is just at work, but he will be home soon.' We walked into her family's newly renovated home.

Years of history launched an attack on my senses and my psyche from all angles as we waded through school formals, parties, summer holidays, long winter nights and all that young love. I was nervous as all hell in that old, familiar setting. Despite my years on the road, nothing could have prepared me for this moment. We joined Stephanie's brother and sister, and their father soon returned from work. I didn't realise until that moment just how long I had been gone—five and a half years—an awkward distance sat between us all.

After dinner with Stephanie and her father, I showed them photos of Broome and spun stories about that life, and the life that had taken me there. In the uncomprehending folds of disbelief, and what I perceived as a flash of envy that my life had grown beyond what they thought I was capable of, I concluded with my return visit to New Zealand. Stephanie's father left us, and we continued the night with a wine and light conversation. The shock of landing back in my old life still lingered, like a passing dream. I suggested we take a walk.

Stephanie took me to a lookout not far from her house. I enjoyed the stroll and the fresh air, and I began to relax. I'd either never been to the lookout with her when we were dating, or I just didn't remember it, but when we sat down and I gazed over the city lights of Christchurch, sparkling and twinkling below us, I fell into a shimmering ocean of memories. Suddenly, I was back in that past life. I breathed deeply. I wanted to tell her I still loved her, had always loved her.

I reached into my pocket and grasped the piece of cloth wrapped around the pearl. Our conversation shifted through the low gears of casual and superficial subjects to her recent arrival from England, and her pending return.

It suddenly dawned on me. 'How have you been able to stay in England for so long?' I asked her.

There was a moment's hesitation. 'De facto visa,' she answered, gazing out over the city. Her thoughts were somewhere on the other side of the world with the man she loved.

As my heart sank, I felt a weight lift from me. An overwhelming peace descended like a wave washing over me. Something in me was set free. Something I had, for so many years, subconsciously held on to—the idea that one day I would return and somehow pick up where things left off.

I pulled my hand out of my pocket. 'It's for you, something I found on my travels. But don't open it until you get on the plane, when you leave. I'm sorry for taking so long to come back. I never meant for so much time to go by. Thank you for being there for me when we were together. I'll always cherish that time. I hope you have found and will always find everything you need in this life.' I placed the folded piece of cloth in the palm of her hand, wrapped her delicate fingers over it and looked at her. 'I loved you, you know. I really did love you.'

Like a building wave, nostalgia peeled across her face and shone from the night-blue ocean of her eyes. 'Thank you, Ben. You don't have to apologise. I know what you went through. I've also done a lot of growing these last few years, and I'm happy. I'll never forget the time we shared.'

Hours passed in easy conversation until we left the lookout and walked back down to her house.

The following day, I strode down Colombo Street in search of the Tattoo Company. Eventually, I found an empty shop front. I walked up and down the block again to make sure I had the right place. The building was abandoned. I paused for a moment to remember, wondering what might have become of my old friend and mentor; the man that had started me on my journey.

Before I left New Zealand and flew back to Australia, I found myself sitting on a quiet beach in Auckland, gazing out to sea. It was a hot, steamy, cloudy afternoon on the waterfront. Boats cruised by in the harbour, cars raced back and forth over Auckland Harbour Bridge, and a gull flew by. Life was moving about me, quickly. How many of those frenetic people stopped to really think about what else was out there waiting for them?

The scene seemed almost surreal, like an illusion, like I could bend it at will with my mind and change my reality with my perception. Then the image flickered, and I knew I could manipulate any of it because I now had an understanding beyond the physical realms. I had witnessed the real world behind the corporeal mask. I suddenly felt like I was from somewhere else, just here for a moment, on this planet, in this life; a parcel of energy travelling through space and time, a warrior of light. Everything around me seemed to hum to a new vibration. I had found that place that was as pure, uncritical, and joyful as love. I understood that I was whole and complete; that everything I ever needed and would ever need was inside of me. I was filled with enthusiasm, purpose and meaning. My life felt rich and full. I held no thoughts of bitterness. Wounds, ragged edges, hollow places were all gone, all healed. My heart lay at the centre of creation. I experienced the intelligence, radiance and love of the Universe. I gave myself up to a peaceful belonging so overwhelming that tears of relief poured from my eyes. I knew then, more than ever, that I had to take responsibility for the way my life was and would play out in the future. I was in charge. I had won my freedom; a freedom I would never lose. Now it was time to live for something bigger than myself.

I understood then that the real pearls are the people in our lives—the people we meet, who selflessly help us along the way, without whom we never would have been able to achieve what we have or become who we are. The people who care for us when we are ill, who look out for us when we are down. The people whom we never see or know or meet but without whom our lives wouldn't be possible. The people that play a bigger, more vital role in our lives than they know. We are, in the end, all in this journey together. The young need the old, the old the young, the weak the strong and the strong the meek. Sometimes we need to be shown the way, and sometimes it is up to us to reveal the path and be the teacher. The more we learn to love, understand, and respect each other, the more we will learn to love, understand, and respect our planet, a pearl in the cosmos.

I continued to gaze over the ocean and distant islands, and asked myself: What now? My perception and awareness increased for a moment, the sound of the waves lapping the shore echoed through eternity, the light flickered and brightened. I felt the tides of truth ebb and flow in my heart, and I knew the real journey was just beginning.

'What are you so happy about there, mate?' a passer-by asked.

I looked up, squinted in the light to catch their face and said, 'What if I were to tell you that anything you can imagine is possible?'

In memory of Michael O'Sullivan, my unexpected friend and mentor who pointed me down the road that changed my life.

1966–2017

ACKNOWLEDGEMENTS

Biruta Rubulis and her family for their loving support and continued friendship through all the years of my new life in Australia. Cameron and Felicity at Walhallow for helping me with research information and supporting the story. Wayne Lawler, who passed away in 2021, for reviewing and advising me on my manuscript, and for spending so many hours teaching me about the wonders of Carnarvon Gorge. Fred Conway for introducing me to the magic of Aboriginal culture and for allowing me to include photos of himself. Paspaley Pearls for allowing me to include photos of their pearling operations. Everyone who made a friend of themselves while I was on the road. All the friends, family, editors and anyone I may have failed to thank for their contributions, and those who read the manuscript and assisted in its journey.

BIBLIOGRAPHY

Bailey, John. *The White Divers of Broome. The true story of a fatal experiment.* Pan Macmillan, Sydney, 2002.

Ballantyne, R.M. *The Coral Island.* Better Books Co, United Kingdom, 1986.

Blake, William. *A letter to the Reverend John Trusler*, 1799.

Blake, William. *Auguries of Innocence.* Grossman Publishers, New York, 1968.

Blake, William. *The Selected Poems of William Blake.* Wordsworth Editions, United Kingdom, 2000.

Burdett, F.D. and King, Percy J. *The Odyssey of a Pearl Hunter.* Herbert Jenkins, London, 1931.

Bureau of Meteorology. *Cyclones, Queensland, Western Australia.* 2012.

Byron, George Gordon (Lord Byron). *Childe Harold's Pilgrimage.* Echo Library, United Kingdom, 2006.

Campbell, Joseph. *The Hero with a Thousand Faces.* New World Library, United States, 2008.

Chaffey, Will. *Swimming with Crocodiles: An Australian Adventure.* Pan Macmillan, Sydney, 2008.

Chatwin, Bruce. *The Songlines.* Penguin Books, New York, 1988.

Darwin, Charles. *The Life and Letters of Charles Darwin.* Basic Books, United States, 1959.

Dryden, John. *The Wild Gallant.* Forgotten Books, London, 2018.

Edwards, Hugh. *Crocodile Attack in Australia.* Gecko Books, Australia, 2007.

Edwards, Hugh. *Port of Pearls: Broome's First 100 Years.* Tangee Publishing, Western Australia, 2005.

Ehrlich, Gretel. *Islands, the Universe, Home.* Penguin Books, United

States, 1992.

Emerson, Ralph Waldo. *Compensation: An Excerpt from Collected Essays, First Series*. ARC Manor, United States, 2007.

Emerson, Ralph Waldo. *The Complete Works. Vol. III. Essays: Second Series*. Harvard University Press, United States, 1984.

Emerson, Ralph Waldo. *The Complete Works. Vol. VIII. Letters and Social Aims*. Houghton Mifflin, Boston, 1904.

Gautama, Siddhartha (Buddha). *The Teaching of Buddha (The Buddhist Bible): A Compendium of Many Scriptures Translated from the Japanese*. The Federation of All Young Buddhist Associations of Japan, 1934.

Gibran, Kahlil. *The Prophet*. Pan Macmillan, London, 1980.

Gill, Rob. "*Kuri Bay, Celebrating 50 Years*". Paspaley Magazine, Issue 13, 2005, pp. 6–17.

Howard, Robert E. *Swords of Shahrazar*. Futura Publications, London, 1975.

Jonson, Ben. *Timber: or Discoveries Made Upon Men and Matter*. Ginn & Co, Boston, 1892.

Keen, Sam. *Fire in the Belly: On Being a Man*. Bantam Book, United States, 1991.

Kerouac, John. *On the Road*. Penguin Books, United Kingdom, 2000.

Markham, Edwin. *The Man with the Hoe, and other Poems*. Wentworth Press, United States, 2016.

Marsden, John. *The Journey*. Pan Macmillan, Sydney, 2002.

Marshall, Don (ed). *Exploring Queensland's Parks and Forests: Your Guide to National Parks, State Forests, Forest Reserves, Conservation Parks, Recreation Areas and Resources Reserves*. Queensland Government, 2003.

Matthiessen, Peter. *The Snow Leopard*. The Viking Press, New York, 1978.

Millman, Dan. *Sacred Journey of the Peaceful Warrior*. New World Library, United States, 2004.

Millman, Dan. *Way of the Peaceful Warrior: A Book that Changes Lives.* New World Library, United States, 2000.

Muir, John. *"Mormon Lilies". Steep Trails.* Sierra Club Books, 1994.

Muir, John. *The Mountains of California.* Sierra Club Books, 1989.

Poe, Edgar Allan. *The Raven.* Simply Read Books, 2014.

Orwell, George. *Nineteen Eighty-Four.* Penguin Books, United Kingdom, 2000.

Remington, Frederic. *Men With the Bark On.* Harper & Brothers, United States, 1900.

Roberts, Gregory David. *Shantaram.* Scribe Publications, Australia, 2003.

Shakespeare, William. *Hamlet.* Wordsworth Editions, United Kingdom, 1997.

Shedd, John A. *Salt from My Attic.* Mosher Press, United States, 1928.

Sickert, Susan. *Beyond the Lattice: Broome's Early Years.* Fremantle Arts Centre Press, 2003.

Slater, Peter. *Slater Field Guide to Australian Birds: Second Edition.* Lansdowne Publishing, Australia, 2009.

Slocum, Joshua. *Sailing Alone Around the World.* Sheridan House, New York, 1999.

Slocum, Joshua. *Voyage of the Liberdade.* Dover Publications, United States, 1998.

Sue Neales. *"Those Wily Colonial Boys".* RM Williams OUTBACK Magazine, Issue 29, June/July 2003, pp. 46–50.

Thoreau, Henry. *A Week on the Concord and Merrimack Rivers.* Princeton University Press, United States, 2004.

Thoreau, Henry David. *Walden, and On the Duty Civil Disobedience.* Harper & Row, New York, 1965.

Thoreau, Henry David. *Where I Lived, and What I Lived For.* Penguin Books, United States, 2006.

Tolle, Eckhart. *The Power of Now: A Guide to Spiritual Enlightenment*. New World Library, United States, 1999.

Tolstoy, Leo. *Anna Karenina*. Penguin Books, United Kingdom, 2003.

Tolstoy, Leo. *War and Peace*. Wordsworth Editions, United Kingdom, 1997.

Traherne, Thomas. *Centuries of Meditations*. Kessinger Publishing, United States, 2007.

Van Gogh, Vincent. *The Letters of Vincent Van Gogh*. Penguin Books, United Kingdom, 1997.

Verne, Jules. *Twenty Thousand Leagues Under the Sea*. Pan Macmillan, Australia, 2017.

Vivekananda, Swami. *Talk given by Swami Vivekananda*, United States, 1895.

Vogler, Christopher. *The Writer's Journey: Mythic Structure for Writers. Third Edition*. Michael Wiese Productions, United States, 2007.

Walsh, Grahame. *Carnarvon and Beyond*. Takarakka Nowan Kas Publications, Queensland, 1999.

Wallace, Alfred. *A letter from Wallace to his brother-in-law Thomas Sims*, 1861.

Warner, Charles. *Exploring Queensland's Central Highlands: an introduction to the National Parks of the sandstone belt for experienced bushwalkers*. Yanderra, New South Wales, 1987.

Whelan, Howard. "*Touching the Spirit*". Australian Geographic, Issue 41, January/March 1996, pp. 34–57.

Yeats, William Butler. *The Land of Heart's Desire*. Jennings Press, United Kingdom, 2008.

www.ingramcontent.com/pod-product-compliance
Lightning Source LLC
Chambersburg PA
CBHW021140160426
43194CB00007B/643